DOGMATIC THEOLOGY
XI

THE SACRAMENTS

A DOGMATIC TREATISE

BY

THE RT. REV. MSGR. JOSEPH POHLE, Ph.D.,D.D.

ADAPTED AND EDITED

BY

ARTHUR PREUSS

VOLUME IV

Extreme Unction—Holy Orders
Matrimony

acc # 943

B. HERDER BOOK CO.,
15 & 17 SOUTH BROADWAY, ST. LOUIS, MO.,
AND
33 QUEEN SQUARE, LONDON, W. C.

NIHIL OBSTAT

Sti. Ludovici, die 9. Feb., 1929,

H. Hussmann,

Censor Deputatus

IMPRIMATUR

Sti. Ludovici, die 11. Feb., 1929,

✠ *Joannes J. Glennon,*

Archiepiscopus

Copyright 1917

BY B. Herder Book Co.

Thirteenth Printing, 1955

Library of Congress Catalog Card Number: 15-26945

Vail-Ballou Press, Inc., Binghamton and New York

TABLE OF CONTENTS

PAGE

INTRODUCTION I

PART I. EXTREME UNCTION I

Introduction I

CH. I. Extreme Unction a True Sacrament 4
§ 1. Divine Institution 5
§ 2. Matter and Form 16
§ 3. Sacramental Effects 24

CH. II. Necessity of Extreme Unction 35

CH. III. The Minister 38

CH. IV. The Recipient 44

PART II. HOLY ORDERS 52

Introduction 52

CH. I. Holy Orders a True Sacrament 54
§ 1. Divine Institution 54
§ 2. Matter and Form 62
§ 3. Sacramental Effects 72

CH. II. Division of Orders 78
§ 1. The Episcopate 80
§ 2. The Priesthood 94
§ 3. The Diaconate 99
§ 4. The Subdiaconate and the Four Minor Orders . 106

CH. III. The Minister 116

CH. IV. The Recipient 125
§ 1. Conditions of Valid Reception 125
§ 2. Clerical Celibacy 130

PART III. MATRIMONY 140

Introduction 140

CH. I. Marriage Between Christians a True Sacrament . 147
§ 1. Nature of the Sacrament and its Divine Institution 147
§ 2. Matter and Form 164
§ 3. Sacramental Effects 168

                                                        PAGE
Ch. II. The Properties of Christian Marriage 172
    § 1. Unity 172
    § 2. Indissolubility 183
    § 3. Extrinsic Dissolubility in Exceptional Cases . . 201
Ch. III. The Minister 214
Ch. IV. The Recipient 217
Ch. V. The Church's Control over Christian Marriage —
                Impediments 221
    § 1. The Church Has Control over the Sacrament of
                Marriage 221
    § 2. The Church's Control over Christian Marriage is of
                Divine Right and Independent of the State . . 229
    § 3. The Church Has the Right to Establish Diriment
                Impediments 234
Appendix I. The "Decretum pro Armenis" 243
Appendix II. All Three Impositions not Essential to the
                Sacrament of Orders 244
Appendix III. The Blessing of Deaconesses 245
Index 247

PART I

EXTREME UNCTION

INTRODUCTION

Extreme Unction, says the Tridentine Council, was regarded by the Fathers as the completion of Penance and of the whole Christian life.[1]

Outwardly the intimate relation existing between the two Sacraments of Extreme Unction and Penance is evidenced by the fact that the same Council deals with Extreme Unction in connection with Penance, as it deals with Confirmation in connection with Baptism.[2]

Aside from the decrees of Trent, the dogmatic teaching of the Church on Extreme Unction is stated most fully in the famous *Decretum pro Armenis,* issued by Pope Eugene IV, in 1439.

The name *Extrema Unctio* became a technical term in the West towards the end of the twelfth century. The adjective "Extreme" does not mean that the anointment given in this Sacrament

---

[1] *Conc. Trid.,* Sess. XIV, *De Extr. Unct.:* "*Sacramentum extremae unctionis non modo poenitentiae, sed et totius christianae vitae consummativum existimatum est a Patribus.*"

[2] *Conc. Trid.,* Sess. VII.

is the last, or that the subject must die after its reception. This is a superstitious belief which has often led to neglect and procrastination. How unfounded it is appears from the fact that theologians count the restoration of bodily health among the effects of Extreme Unction, though, of course, this is a secondary effect, conditioned upon the state of the patient's soul.

Extreme Unction is called the *last* anointment in a purely liturgical sense, because it is preceded by the anointments conferred in Baptism, Confirmation, and Holy Orders.

Extreme Unction can be administered only to persons who are dangerously ill, and hence is also called "the Sacrament of the departing" (*sacramentum exeuntium*).[3] Dr. Toner thinks that, "having regard to the conditions prevailing at the time when the name was introduced, it is much more probable that it was intended originally to mean 'the unction of those *in extremis*,' *i. e.* the dying."[4] This theory derives probability from the fact that the corresponding name, *sacramentum exeuntium*, became current during the same period.

In the East the technical term for Extreme Unction is τὸ ἅγιον ἔλαιον, *i. e.* "the holy oil," or τὸ

---

[3] Cfr. *Conc. Trid.,* Sess. XIV: " Redemptor noster . . . extremae unctionis sacramento finem vitae tamquam firmissimo quodam praesidio munivit."

[4] P. J. Toner in the *Catholic Encyclopedia,* Vol. V, p. 716.

εὐχέλαιον, *i. e.* prayer-oil, from εὐχή, *prayer,* and ἔλαιον, *oil.* The latter name is very appropriate, as prayer and oil constitute the external sign of the Sacrament.[5] In Milan, at the time of St. Ambrose,[6] it was known as "the imposition of hands upon the infirm." [7]

Extreme Unction is a Sacrament of the New Law instituted by Jesus Christ, in which the sick, who are seriously ill, by the anointing with holy oil and by the prayer of the priest, receive the grace of God for the good of their souls, and often also of their bodies.

The correctness of this definition will be shown in the process of our treatise, which we shall divide according to the scheme we have adopted for Baptism and Confirmation.

5 James V, 14.

6 Cfr. St. Ambrose, *De Poenit.,* I, c. 8.

7 See the *Manuale Ambrosianum,* published by Magistretti, A. D. 1905, from a codex of the eleventh century, Vol. I, pp. 79 sqq., 94 sqq., 147 sqq.

CHAPTER I

EXTREME UNCTION A TRUE SACRAMENT

To prove the sacramental character of Extreme Unction we must show that it is a visible sign communicating invisible grace, instituted by Jesus Christ for the salvation of souls. The argument rests mainly on the Epistle of St. James and on ecclesiastical Tradition.

SECTION 1

DIVINE INSTITUTION

1. Protestant Vagaries vs. the Teaching of the Church.—It is doubtful whether the Cathari, the Waldenses, the Wiclifites, and the Hussites merely rejected the Sacrament of Extreme Unction or formally denied it. Luther and the rest of the so-called Protestant Reformers openly denied the sacramental character of the rite.

a) Luther could not consistently uphold Extreme Unction after repudiating the Epistle of St. James, upon which the Church bases her teaching with regard to this Sacrament, and which he contemptuously called "a letter of straw," "unworthy of the Apostolic spirit." Calvin went so far as to denounce Extreme Unction as "fictitious" and a piece of "histrionic hypocrisy." [1] The symbols of the Lutheran and Calvinistic sects affirm that while Extreme Unction may have been a Sacrament in the early Church, it was a merely temporary institution, which lost its efficacy when the charismatic gift of healing ceased. Present-day Protestants generally adhere to this theory and regard the Jacobean rite either as identical with the ancient *gratia curationum,* now extinct, or as a sort

[1] *Instit.,* IV, 19, 18.

5

of natural remedy. Among the Anglicans, however, there has recently been a revival of Catholic teaching and practice.[2]

b) The Council of Trent defines the sacramental character of Extreme Unction against the Protestant "Reformers" as follows: "If anyone saith that Extreme Unction is not truly and properly a Sacrament, instituted by Christ our Lord, and promulgated by the blessed Apostle James, but is only a rite received from the Fathers, or a human figment, let him be anathema."[3]

The Council explains its meaning more fully in Chapter I, *De Extrema Unctione,* of its XIVth Session:

"This sacred unction of the sick was instituted by Christ our Lord as truly and properly a Sacrament of the New Law, insinuated indeed in Mark [vi, 13], but recommended and promulgated to the faithful by James the Apostle and cousin of our Lord. 'Is any man,' he saith, 'sick among you? Let him bring in the priests of the Church, and let them pray over him, anointing him with oil in the name of the Lord: and the prayer of faith

2 Cfr. Toner in the *Catholic Encyclopedia,* Vol. V, p. 717.

3 Sess. XIV, *De Extr. Unct.,* can. 1: "*Si quis dixerit, extremam unctionem non esse vere et proprie sacramentum a Christo Domino nostro institutum et a beato Iacobo Apostolo promulgatum, sed ritum tantum acceptum a Patribus aut figmentum humanum, anathema sit.*" (Denzinger-Bannwart, *Enchiridion Symbolorum, Definitionum et Declarationum de Rebus Fidei et Morum,* 12th ed., Freiburg 1910, n. 926. This useful work is quoted throughout the present treatise as "Denzinger-Bannwart.")

shall save the sick man; and the Lord shall raise him up; and if he be in sins, they shall be forgiven him.' [Jas. V, 14 sq.] In which words, as the Church has learned from Apostolic tradition, received from hand to hand, he teaches the matter, the form, the proper minister, and the effect of this salutary Sacrament."[4]

Some of the older Scholastics, notably Peter Lombard, St. Bonaventure, and Hugh of St. Victor, held, in opposition to the more common view, that the Sacrament of Extreme Unction was instituted by the Apostles after the descent of the Holy Ghost and by His inspiration. This thesis can now no longer be maintained in the face of the Tridentine declaration that the Sacrament was " instituted " by Christ Himself and " recommended and promulgated to the faithful " by St. James.

2. PROOF FROM REVELATION.—We have already quoted the Scriptural *locus classicus* for our dogma as reproduced in the Tridentine definition. It runs as follows in the original Greek: Ἀσθενεῖ τις ἐν ὑμῖν; προσκαλεσάσθω τοὺς πρεσβυτέρους τῆς ἐκκλησίας, καὶ προσευξάσθωσαν ἐπ' αὐτόν, ἀλείψαντες αὐτὸν ἐλαίῳ ἐν τῷ ὀνόματι τοῦ κυρίου. Καὶ ἡ εὐχὴ τῆς πίστεως σώσει τὸν κάμνοντα, καὶ ἐγερεῖ αὐτὸν ὁ κύριος· κἂν ἁμαρτίας ᾖ πεποιηκώς, ἀφεθήσεται αὐτῷ.

---

[4] *Ibid.*, cap. 1: " *Instituta est autem sacra haec unctio infirmorum tamquam vere et proprie sacramentum Novi Testamenti a Christo Domino nostro apud Marcum quidem insinuatum, per Iacobum autem Apostolum ac Domini fratrem fidelibus commendatum ac promulgatum: ' Infirmatur,' inquit, ' quis in vobis,' etc. Quibus verbis, ut ex apostolica traditione per manus accepta Ecclesia didicit, docet ma-*

"Is any man sick among you? Let him bring in the priests of the Church, and let them pray over him, anointing him with oil in the name of the Lord: and the prayer of faith shall save the sick man; and the Lord shall raise him up; and if he be in sins, they shall be forgiven him."

Here we have all the essential characteristics of a Sacrament.

a) There is, first, an external sign or rite, consisting of matter and form. The "anointment with oil"[5] is a visible act, like the ablution performed in the administration of Baptism. The prayer pronounced by the priest *over* the sick man (*super eum*, ἐπ' αὐτὸν, not *pro eo*, ὑπὲρ αὐτοῦ), and which St. James calls "prayer of faith,"[6] manifestly constitutes the form.

To this external sign or rite the Apostle ascribes internal grace: "salvation" (*salvabit*, σώσει), "upraising" (*alleviabit*, ἐγερεῖ), and especially "forgiveness of sins" (*si in peccatis sit, remittentur ei*, κἂν ἁμαρτίας ᾖ πεποιηκώς, ἀφεθήσεται αὐτῷ). This effect, which is produced *ex opere operato* in the properly disposed recipient, cannot possibly be confounded with the charismatic, nor yet with the natural cures reported elsewhere in the New Testament.[7]

Finally, the divine institution of this prayer-unction is at least intimated by St. James. For in the first

---

teriam, formam, proprium ministrum et effectum huius salutaris sacramenti." (Denzinger-Bannwart, n. 908).

5 *Ungentes eum oleo,* ἀλείψαντες αὐτὸν ἐλαίῳ.

6 *Oratio fidei,* ἡ εὐχὴ τῆς πίστεως.

7 Cfr. 1 Cor. XII, 28: "*gratia curationum,* χάρισμα ἰαμάτων. Cfr. Mark VI, 13. On the distinction mentioned in the text above see Oswald, *Die Lehre von den hl. Sakramenten,* Vol. II, 5th ed., pp. 261 sqq.

place he mentions it along with a number of positive precepts. Secondly, he says that the act is performed " in the name of the Lord " (*in nomine Domini*, ἐν ὀνόματι τοῦ κυρίου), that is to say, by command or through the power of the Lord. If Extreme Unction is administered by command of the Lord, it must be directly instituted by Him; if by His power, the same conclusion is inevitable, for no one but God can cause a visible sign to effect forgiveness of sins.[8]

b) The Tridentine Fathers observe that the Sacrament of Extreme Unction is " insinuated " in the Gospel of St. Mark; which raises the question whether St. Mark really knew this Sacrament. The passage (Mark VI, 13): " [The Apostles] anointed with oil many that were sick, and healed them," is understood of the Sacrament of Extreme Unction by St. Thomas, St. Bonaventure, Duns Scotus, Ambrosius Catharinus, Maldonatus, Berti, Sainte-Beuve, and other illustrious theologians. Bellarmine[9] and Suarez,[10] however, and with them the great majority of Catholic divines, are opposed to this interpretation for the following reasons:

(1) The anointment of which St. Mark speaks, affected only the body. The sick who were anointed were restored to health. The rite described by St. James, on the other hand, results in forgiveness of sins,— a distinctly spiritual effect.

(2) The anointment recorded by St. Mark was administered not only to the sick, but to the lame and blind, not only to Christians, but to unbelieving Jews and gentiles; whereas the " sacred unction " of St. James was strictly limited to the sick among the faithful.

---

8 Cfr. Trenkle, *Der Brief des hl. Jakobus*, pp. 384 sqq., Freiburg 1894.

9 *De Extrema Unctione*, c. 1.

10 *Comment. in Summam Theol.*, III, disp. 39, sect. 1, n. 4.

(3) The power of healing described by St. Mark was clearly a charismatic gift, for our Divine Saviour had shortly before commanded His Apostles to " heal the sick, raise the dead, cleanse the lepers, cast out devils," adding: " Freely have you received, freely give." [11]   Now since the charismata are not a permanent institution, but may cease temporarily or altogether, the anointing of the sick according to St. James belongs to an altogether different category, for it postulates " the priesthood " as its dispenser and consequently must last as long as the priesthood lasts, namely, to the end of time.[12]

But how, in view of these facts, could the Council of Trent say that the Sacrament of Extreme Unction is " insinuated " by St. Mark?   Because the anointment which St. Mark describes was a type of the sacred unction promulgated by St. James.   "*Insinuatum*," in the context of the Tridentine decree, as Berti notes, does not mean "*introductum*," but "*praefiguratum*." [13]

3. Proof from Tradition.—Even if there were no express Patristic testimony available to show the existence of Extreme Unction during the first five centuries of the Church, the fact could be established by an argument from prescription.

a) The Sacrament of Extreme Unction is to-day known and administered throughout the world, in the Greek [14]

---

[11] Matth. X, 8.

[12] For other differences between the two anointments see Bellarmine, *De Extr. Unct.*, c. 3; Alb. a Bulsano, *Instit. Theol. Dogmat.*, ed. Gottfr. a Graun, Vol. III, p. 197, Innsbruck 1896.

[13] On the N. T. evidence for the Sacrament see A. Quinn, *Some Aspects of the Dogma of Extreme Unction*, Dublin 1923, Ch. I.

[14] The Greek schismatic Council of Jerusalem, of 1672, confesses: " *Septimum est unctio, quam vocamus* εὐχέλαιον, *cuius duplex effectus*

schismatic as well as in the Latin Church. It was known to the Council of Constantinople of 1672 and to the Greek Emperor Michael Palæologus in 1274.[15] It was recommended to the faithful by the councils of Worms (868), Mayence (847), Aix-la-Chapelle (836), and Châlons (813).[16] This brings us to the schism of Photius (869). The liturgical books take us still farther back. Thus the Sacramentary of Pope St. Gregory the Great[17] and the newly discovered Euchologium of Serapion of Thmuis (+ about 362)[18] contain the rite of administering and blessing the holy oils. The Nestorians and Armenians, who no longer have the Sacrament of Extreme Unction, knew it in former times, as their ancient rituals testify.[19] Since these sects cut loose from the Roman Church as early as the fifth century, the Sacrament of Extreme Unction must have formed part and parcel of the Apostolic Tradition. All the facts that have so far come to light point towards the time when the Sacrament was "promulgated" by St. James.

b) But how are we to explain the relative scarcity of Patristic testimonies in favor of Extreme Unction?

est, animae nimirum corporisque sanatio." (Hardouin, Concil., XI, 275).

15 " Aliud [sacramentum] extrema unctio, quae secundum doctrinam b. Iacobi infirmantibus adhibetur." (Denzinger-Bannwart, n. 465). On the present-day practice of the Greek schismatic Church see C. Rhallis, Περὶ τῶν μυστηρίων τῆς μετανοίας καὶ τοῦ εὐχελαίου, Athens 1905.

16 Cfr. Conc. Cabilon. II (813), can. 48: " Secundum b. Apostoli Iacobi documentum, cui etiam documenta Patrum consonant, infirmi

oleo, quod ab episcopo benedicitur, a presbyteris ungi debent. Sic enim ait: Infirmatur quis, etc. Non est itaque parvipendenda huiusmodi medicina, quae animae corporisque medetur languoribus." (Hardouin, Concil., IV, 1040).

17 Apud Migne, P. L., LXXVIII, 233 sq.

18 Edited by Wobbermin in Altchristliche Stücke aus der Kirche Ägyptens, Leipzig 1898.

19 Cfr. Denzinger, Ritus Orientalium, Vol. II, pp. 483 sqq., Würzburg 1864.

Partly, no doubt, by the Discipline of the Secret, but mainly by the fact that this Sacrament, regarded merely as a complement of Penance, did not become conspicuous and, furthermore, was not in frequent demand at a time when many of the faithful died as martyrs, while others subjected themselves to public penance or postponed Baptism until they were on their death-bed.

Such Patristic evidence as we possess on the subject has reference to the Epistle of St. James, which may be said to be the pivot around which the whole Tradition revolves.

The earliest extant witness is Origen. After enumerating the different ways of obtaining remission of sins, this writer (+ 254) comes seventhly to "the hard and laborious" way of penance. He quotes the Psalmist in support of confession and adds: "In this is fulfilled also what St. James the Apostle says: 'If anyone is sick,' etc." [20] Let it not be objected that several of the means of grace mentioned by Origen (martyrdom, almsgiving, etc.) are not Sacraments, for he puts the anointment of the sick on a par with Baptism and Penance, which he undoubtedly regarded as true Sacraments.

St. Chrysostom says the dignity of the priesthood springs from the power of forgiving sins, which is exercised in administering the sacred unction to the sick. "Not only in our regeneration," he writes, "but likewise after regeneration, have they the power to forgive sins. For the Apostle says: 'Is any man sick among you?

[20] *Hom. in Lev.*, II, n. 4 (Migne, *P. G.*, XII, 418).

Let him bring in the priests of the Church,'"
etc.[21]

The most striking Patristic authority on the subject is
Pope Innocent I. " The words of St. James," he says,
" must without doubt be taken or understood of the
faithful who are sick, who may be [lawfully] anointed
with the holy oil of chrism, of which, having been prepared by the bishop, not only priests, but all Christians
may avail themselves for anointing in their own need, or in
that of their connections. We notice the superfluous addition of a doubt, whether a bishop may do what is
said to priests, for the reason that bishops, hindered
by other occupations, cannot go to all the sick. But
if the bishop is able to do so, or thinks anyone specially worthy of being visited, he, whose office it is to
consecrate the chrism, need not hesitate to bless and
anoint the sick person. For this unction may not be given
to penitents [i. e. to those undergoing canonical penance],
inasmuch as it is a kind of Sacrament. For to persons
to whom the other Sacraments are denied, how can it be
thought that one kind of Sacrament can be granted?" [22]

This remarkable, though in several respects obscure passage, is clear on at least four points:

(1) The anointing of the sick with the " holy oil of

21 *De Sacerdotio*, III, 6 (Migne,
P. G., XLVIII, 644). See Boyle's
translation (*On the Priesthood*, 2nd
ed., p. 41, Dublin 1910).

22 *Ep.* 25, c. 8: " *Quod [Iac.
V, 14] non est dubium de fidelibus
aegrotantibus accipi vel intellegi debere, qui sancto oleo chrismatis
perungi possunt, quo ab episcopo
confecto non solum sacerdotibus, sed
omnibus uti Christianis licet in sua
aut suorum necessitate ungendum.
Ceterum illud superfluum videmus
adiectum, ut de episcopo ambigatur*

*quod presbyteris dictum est, quia
episcopi occupationibus aliis impe-
diti ad omnes languidos ire non possunt. Ceterum si episcopus aut potest aut dignum ducit aliquem a se
visitandum, et benedicere et tangere
chrismate sine cunctatione potest,
cuius est ipsum chrisma conficere.
Nam poenitentibus [scil. publicis]
istud infundi non potest, quia genus
est sacramenti; nam quibus reliqua
sacramenta negantur, quomodo unum
genus putatur posse concedi?*"
(Denzinger-Bannwart, n. 99).

chrism" was regarded as a "*genus sacramenti*," from which public penitents were excluded;

(2) The Sacrament of the sick was administered by priests and bishops, but only the bishops had power to bless the oil;

(3) Extreme Unction was administered to "the faithful" when they were "sick";

(4) The term *chrisma* does not refer to Confirmation, because that Sacrament is mentioned earlier in Pope Innocent's letter,[23] but must be understood in the wider sense of "oil blessed for purposes of anointment."

Incidentally also it seems from Pope St. Innocent's letter that in his day laymen in case of urgent necessity were permitted to apply the holy oil to themselves or others near and dear to them. Needless to say, such lay anointment was not a Sacrament but merely a sacramental.

Another important testimony is that of John Mandukani (Montagouni), Catholicos of the Armenians from 480 to 487. This patriarch, who is called "the second Chrysostom," in one of his addresses inveighs against magic incantations in case of sickness as an abuse current even among the clergy. The faithful, he writes, "despise the gifts of grace; for the Apostle says: 'If anyone is sick,' etc. They [the shepherds] themselves have gone astray, they have relinquished the grace of God, prayer, and the oil of anointment, which is prescribed by law for the sick, seeking refuge [rather] in incantations and magic writings."[24]

In a homily ascribed to St. Caesarius of Arles (+ 542) we read: "As often as some sickness comes, let him

23 See Denzinger-Bannwart, n. 98.   *kani*, pp. 222 sqq. Cfr. Kern, *De*
24 *Hom.*, 26, cited by M. Schmid,   *Sacram. Extr. Unct.*, pp. 46 sq.
Heilige Reden des Johannes Mandu-

who is ill receive the Body and Blood of Christ, and then anoint his body, in order that the Scripture may be fulfilled which says: ' If anyone is sick,' etc. Behold, brethren, how whoever in his infirmity has recourse to the Church, deserves to obtain health of body and forgiveness of sins." [25] This coupling of the remission of sins with bodily healing recurs in another homily of St. Caesarius, in which he says that the person anointed with the sacred chrism " receives both health of body and remission of sins, for the Holy Ghost has given this promise through James." [26]

[25] *Serm.*, 265, n. 3: " *Quoties aliqua infirmitas supervenerit, corpus et sanguinem Christi ille, qui aegrotat, accipiat et inde corpusculum suum ungat, ut illud quod scriptum est impleatur in eo: Infirmatur aliquis, etc. Videte, fratres, quia qui in infirmitate ad Ecclesiam cucurrerit, et corporis sanitatem recipere et peccatorum indulgentiam merebitur obtinere.*" (Migne, *P. L.*, XXXIX, 2238 sq., Append.). Later testimonies and examples of the reception of Extreme Unction from the fourth to the ninth century are given by Kern, *De Sacram. Extr. Unct.*, pp. 6–50.

[26] *Serm.*, 279, n. 5. On the Patristic evidence for the Sacrament of Extreme Unction see A. Quinn, *Some Aspects of the Dogma of Extreme Unction*, Dublin 1920, Ch. II, for later testimonies, cfr. Ch. III, *ibid.*

SECTION 2

MATTER AND FORM

The *matter* of a Sacrament, generally speaking, is the natural act which has been raised by our Lord to the supernatural sphere. In certain of the Sacraments, however, which make use of material, tangible objects, these are sometimes called "the matter" of the Sacrament, in the sense of *remote matter,* while the application of them is the *proximate matter.*

The remote matter of Extreme Unction is pure olive oil blessed by a bishop. The proximate matter is the act of anointing the organs of sense. The sacramental form lies in the words: "By this holy unction," etc.

1. THE REMOTE MATTER OF THE SACRAMENT. —St. James, in saying, "Anointing him with oil," employs the word ἔλαιον, which literally means oil of olives. Consequently oil of olives is the remote matter of the Sacrament of Extreme Unction. This deduction is expressly confirmed by the *Decretum pro Armenis.*[1]

---

[1] "*Materia est oleum olivae per episcopum benedictum.*" (Denzinger-Bannwart, n. 700).

a) All other oils, such as that derived from nuts, sesame, etc., are not valid matter for Extreme Unction.[2] The olive oil used in the administration of this Sacrament must furthermore be pure, without admixture of any other substance, such as perfume, for the oil used in anointing the sick is simply called *oleum* (from *olea,* olive), or in Greek, ἔλαιον,— not *chrisma* (μύρον, *chrism*), like that employed in Confirmation. The Nestorians add a little water and a pinch of ashes or dust from the sepulchre of some saint. This mixture they call *hanana* or *taibutha,*[3] and the rite of applying it to the sick — a mere sacramental among these heretics — has gradually usurped the place of the Sacrament of Extreme Unction.[4] In Russia a little wine is added to the oil in memory of the good Samaritan, but this custom cannot be very ancient because the Archpriest Archangelsky, who has made a study of the subject, says that no such mixture is mentioned in the Russian rituals of the fifteenth and sixteenth centuries.[5] In the Greek Church, this custom is undoubtedly older, as it is mentioned in the " profession of faith " of Metrophanes Kritopulos, composed in the year 1625,[6] and by Simeon of Thessalonica, who died in 1429.

Olive oil is soothing, penetrating, and invigorating, and thus aptly symbolizes the healing and strengthening power of the Sacrament. " The unction," says the Tridentine Council, " very aptly represents the grace of the Holy Ghost, with which the soul of the sick person is invisibly anointed." [7]

---

[2] On the use, by dispensation, of cottonseed oil, see Herder's *Kirchenlexikon.* Vol. IX, 2nd ed., col. 712, Freiburg 1895.

[3] " *Gratia talis sancti.*"

[4] Cfr. Benedict XIV, *Opera Inedita,* published by Heiner, p. 359, Freiburg 1904.

[5] Archangelsky, *Inquisitio de Evolutione Historica Ritus Benedictionis Olei,* pp. 113 sqq., St. Petersburg 1895.

[6] Cfr. Kimmel, *Libri Symbolici Ecclesiae Orientalis,* Appendix, p. 154, Jena 1843.

[7] *Conc. Trid.,* Sess. XIV, *De*

b) That the oil must be blessed or consecrated before use is the unanimous testimony of all ages. The question arises whether such consecration is merely a matter of precept or whether it is an essential requisite for the validity of the Sacrament.

Tradition since Pope Innocent I insists on the oil being blessed by a bishop, which indicates that this blessing is a condition of validity. "The Church has understood the matter thereof [*i. e.* of Extreme Unction] to be oil blessed by a bishop," says the Council of Trent.[8] The S. C. S. Officii has decided (see *Acta S. Sedis* Vol. 29, p. 576) that it is forbidden to use oil other than that blessed by a bishop, because oil blessed by a priest is "*materia prorsus inepta Sacramento Extr. Unctionis conficiendo.*" A decree of Paul V (1611) proscribes as "rash and bordering on error" the proposition that Extreme Unction may be validly administered with oil not consecrated by a bishop.[9] In 1842, the Congregation of the Holy Office, reaffirming a previous decree, replied negatively to the query whether a parish priest, in case of necessity, could validly use oil blessed by himself.

Though theologians agree that the blessing of the oil used for Extreme Unction is an episcopal prerogative, most of them hold that priests can be empowered by the Pope to perform this function.[10] In the East they have

---

Extr. Unct., cap. 1: "*Nam unctio aptissime Spiritus Sancti gratiam, qua invisibiliter anima aegrotantis inungitur, repraesentat.*"—On the use of olive oil see Gihr, *Die hl. Sakramente,* pp. 245 sqq.; Kern, *De Sacr. Extr. Unct.,* pp. 115 sq.

8 Sess. XIV, *De Extr. Unct.,* cap. 1: "*Intellexit enim Ecclesia, materiam esse oleum ab episcopo benedictum.*" (Denzinger-Bannwart, n. 908).

9 (Denzinger-Bannwart, n. 1628).

10 Quinn (*Some Aspects of the Dogma of Extr. Unction*) is of the opinion that "priests both of the Eastern and Western Churches have the power of Orders requisite to bless the oil, just as they have the power of Orders to administer the Sacrament of Penance. In the latter case they, nevertheless, require jurisdiction in order to act validly; possibly, in the former case also, jurisdiction, or something akin to it, is likewise required. Jurisdiction, expressly or tacitly given by the Holy See, would thus be essential to enable priests to validly bless [*sic*] the oil."

done so for many years, and the custom among the Uniats has the express approval of the Holy See.[11]   In regard to the schismatics " one may say either that they have the tacit approbation of the Pope or that the reservation of episcopal power does not extend to them." [12]

2. THE PROXIMATE MATTER OF EXTREME UNCTION.—St. James says that the sick are "anointed with oil," but gives no hint how or to what parts of the body the oil is applied.   The ancient rituals show a great diversity of practice in this regard.[13]

In the Eastern Church,[14] the parts usually anointed are the forehead, chin, hands, and knees (sometimes the forehead, nostrils, knees, mouth, breast, and both sides of the hands; or the forehead, knees, lips, breast, and hands).[15]   The Roman Ritual says the oil should be applied to the organs of the five external senses (eyes, ears, nostrils, lips, hands), to the feet, and, in the case of male patients, where the custom exists and the condition of the subject permits of his being moved, to the loins or reins.[16]   As the unction of the loins is now always omitted (cfr. *Codex Iuris Canonici*, can. 947, § 2) it

11 See the Constitution of Clement VIII, of Aug. 30, 1595, which says: " *Non sunt cogendi presbyteri graeci, olea sancta praeter chrisma ab episcopis latinis dioecesanis accipere, quum huiusmodi olea ab eis in ipsa oleorum et sacramentorum exhibitione ex veteri ritu conficiantur seu benedicantur.*" (*Bullarium Romanum*, ed. Taur., Vol. X, p. 212). Cfr. Benedict XIV, *De Synodo Dioecesana*, VIII, 1, 4; Kern, *De Sacr. Extr. Unct.*, pp. 119 sqq.

12 Cfr. P. J. Toner in the *Catholic Encyclopedia*, Vol. V, p. 724.

13 Cfr. Martène, *De Antiquis Ecclesiae Ritibus*, I, 7, 3.

14 Cfr. Goar, *Euchol.*, p. 440.

15 Cfr. G. Jaquemier, " *L'Extrême Onction chez les Grecs*," in the *Echos d'Orient*, 1899, p. 194.

16 *Decr. pro Armenis* (1439): ". . . *qui* [*infirmus*] *in his locis ungendus est: in oculis propter visum, in auribus propter auditum, in naribus propter odoratum, in ore propter gustum vel locutionem, in mani-*

cannot belong to the essence of the Sacrament.   The same
holds true of the anointing of the feet which "may be
omitted for any reasonable cause " (*Codex Iuris Canonici,*
can. 947, § 3).[17]   Whether the remaining five unctions
are necessary for the validity of the Sacrament *iure
divino* or merely by ecclesiastical precept, is a controverted question.   The older Scholastics held with St.
Thomas [18] that all five are strictly essential.   Modern
theologians differ on this point.   The best of them have
long inclined to the view favored by Albertus Magnus,[19]
that a single unction is sufficient for the validity of the
Sacrament.   In taking this ground they were impelled
by a number of reasons, which Dr. Toner briefly sum-
marizes as follows: " No ancient testimony mentions
the five unctions at all, much less prescribes them as
necessary, but most of them speak simply of unction in
a way that suggests the sufficiency of a single unction;
the unction of the five senses has never been extensively
practiced in the East, and is not practiced at the present
time in the Orthodox Church, while those Uniats who
practice it have simply borrowed it in modern times from
Rome; and even in the Western Church down to the
eleventh century the practice was not very wide-
spread, and did not become universal till the seventeenth
century, as is proved by a number of sixteenth-century
rituals that have been preserved." [20]   The new Code of
Canon Law says (can. 947, § 1) that " in case of necessity

bus *propter tactum, in pedibus propter gressum, in renibus propter delectationem ibi vigentem."* (Denzinger-Bannwart, n. 700). Cfr. Toner, *Catholic Encyclopedia,* Vol. V,
p. 725.

17 Cfr. Suarez, *Comment. in S.
Theol.,* III, disp. 40, sect. 2, n. 6.

18 *Summa Theol., Supplementum,*
qu. 32, art. 6: " *Illa unctio ab
omnibus observatur, quae fit ad quin-*

*que sensus quasi de necessitate sa-
cramenti."*

19 *Comment. in Sent.,* IV, dist.
23, art. 16. Cfr. Kern, *De Sacram.
Extr. Unct.,* p. 138.

20 *Cath. Encyclopedia,* V, 724.—
Cfr. Kern, *De Sacram. Extr. Unct.,*
pp. 133 sq.; Ballerini-Palmieri, *Op.
Theol. Moral.,* Vol. V, 3rd ed., pp.
686 sqq., Prati 1900.

one unction is sufficient, [applied] on one of the sense
organs or, more correctly, on the forehead, with the
shorter formula prescribed; but the obligation remains to
supply the other unctions when the danger ceases."

3. THE FORM OF THE SACRAMENT.—In the
Latin Church, for the past five hundred years, the
form employed at each unction, with mention of
the corresponding sense or faculty, has been that
prescribed by Eugene IV in the *Decretum pro
Armenis*. It runs as follows: "Through this
holy unction and His own most tender mercy, may
the Lord pardon thee whatever faults thou
hast committed by sight (hearing, smell, taste,
touch, walking, carnal delectation)." [21]

a) This form was not always in use. Many others,
substantially different in both sense and wording, were
at various times employed in the West and in the
East; [22] whence it may be concluded that our Lord specifically determined the form of Extreme Unction only
in so far as it must be a prayer for the sick. This demand is complied with in the shorter formula permitted
in urgent cases by decree of the Holy Office of 1906:
" By this holy unction may the Lord pardon thee whatever faults thou hast committed." [23] Hence neither
mention of the senses, severally or *in globo,* nor any
express reference to the divine mercy is essential for

21 *Decretum pro Armenis:* "*Per
istam sanctam unctionem et suam
piissimam misericordiam indulgeat
tibi Dominus, quidquid per visum,
(auditum, odoratum, gustum et locutionem, tactum, gressum, lumbo-
rum delectationem) deliquisti.*"—
Cfr. *Conc. Trid.,* Sess. XIV, cap. 1.

22 Cfr. Martène, *De Antiquis Eccles. Ritibus,* I, 7, 4; a selection in
Kern, *De Sacram. Extr. Unct.,* pp.
146–152.

23 " *Per istam sanctam unctionem
indulgeat tibi Dominus, quidquid deliquisti.*" (*Acta S. Sedis,* Vol.
XXXIX, p. 273).

the validity of the Sacrament. Neither of these ideas, in fact, is expressed in the present Greek or in any of the ancient Latin formulas.

If the "prayer of faith" spoken of by St. James is the sole requisite of validity, it follows that a priest would probably administer the Sacrament validly (though not, of course, licitly) if he were to omit the words prescribed by the Roman Ritual for each separate unction and simply, after giving all the unctions, pronounce the first oration following them in the Ritual, which embodies the prayer that formerly constituted the essential form of Extreme Unction in the Church of Narbonne.

b) Another controverted question is whether a merely indicative form, such as "I anoint thee," etc., would be sufficient for the validity of the Sacrament.

Albertus Magnus, Paludanus, Durandus, and other eminent Scholastics, followed by a number of modern writers (Morinus, Becanus, Tournely, etc.), hold that the indicative form is sufficient. The Thomists and the Scotists maintain the opposite view, basing their contention chiefly on the Jacobean demand: "*Orent* (προσευξάσθωσαν) *super eum."* But the problem cannot be solved by *a priori* reasoning; it must be dealt with historically.

History tells us that the indicative form has been widely used in the East and still more widely in the West.[24] This form occurs in the most ancient ritual that has come down to us, that of the Celtic Church: "I anoint thee with sanctified oil in the name of the Trinity, that thou

---

24 See, *e. g.,* the so-called *Ambrosiana, apud* Martène, *De Antiquis Ecclesiae Ritibus,* I, 7, 4: "*Ungo te oleo sanctificato in nomine* *Domini, ut more militis unctus praeparatus ad luctam aereas possis superare catervas."*

mayest be saved for ever and ever." [25]   Pope Benedict
XIV insists on the validity of the indicative form, but at
the same time admonishes parish priests to employ the
form prescribed in the Roman Ritual, " which," he says,
" most assuredly cannot be altered by private authority
without committing a grave crime." [26]   The congruity of
the deprecative form is shown by the Roman Catechism,[27]
and its necessity is defended by De Augustinis.[28]   It
should be noted, however, that an indicative sentence may
be virtually deprecatory,[29] and that all the formulæ of
Extreme Unction which we know to have been used at
some time or other in the Church, have in fact virtually
embodied a petition.[30]   Hence Fr. Kern is fully justified in concluding that the validity of the form in itself,
i. e. necessitate sacramenti, does not require an explicit
mention of the act of anointing, or of any sacramental effect, or of the divine mercy, or of the organs anointed,
but that the sole essential requisite is a (formal, or at
least virtual) prayer for the recipient.[31]

25 " *Ungo te de oleo sanctificato
in nomine Trinitatis, ut salveris in
saecula saeculorum.*" (*Apud* War-
ren, *The Liturgy and Ritual of the
Celtic Church,* p. 168).

26 *De Synodo Dioecesana,* VIII,
2, 3.

27 P. II, c. 6, n. 7.

28 *De Re Sacramentaria,* Vol. II,
2nd ed., pp. 375 sqq.

29 Cfr. John XI, 3: "Lord, behold, he whom thou lovest is sick."

30 *E. g.,* the ancient formula of
the Church of Tours: " *Ungo te
oleo sancto in nomine Patris et Filii
et Spiritus Sancti, obsecrans misericordiam,*" etc.

31 See Kern, *De Sacram. Extr.
Unct.,* pp. 152–160.

SECTION 3

SACRAMENTAL EFFECTS

The fact that Extreme Unction produces internal grace is clearly stated in St. James' Epistle (*salvabit, alleviabit, remittentur peccata*). Nevertheless it is not easy to decide wherein the principal effect of the Sacrament (*effectus primarius*) consists. Our only safe guide in the matter are the decisions of various councils. The *Decretum pro Armenis* merely says: "The effect [of this Sacrament] is the healing of the mind and, so far as is expedient, of the body also." [1] This is more fully explained by the Council of Trent, which defines: "If anyone saith that the sacred unction of the sick does not confer grace, nor remit sin, nor comfort the sick, but that it has now ceased, as though it had been of old only the grace of working cures, let him be anathema." [2]

According to this authentic declaration the

[1] "*Effectus vero est mentis sanatio, et inquantum autem expedit, ipsius etiam corporis.*" (Denzinger-Bannwart, n. 700).

[2] Sess. XIV, *De Extr. Unct.*, cap. 2: "*Si quis dixerit, sacram infirmorum unctionem non conferre gratiam nec remittere peccata nec alleviare infirmos, sed iam cessasse, quasi olim tantum fuerit gratia curationum, anathema sit.*" (Denzinger-Bannwart, n. 927).

Sacrament of Extreme Unction produces three principal effects:

(1) It confers grace and forgives sin;
(2) It comforts the sick, and
(3) It conditionally restores health to the body.

1. THE FIRST AND PRINCIPAL EFFECT OF EX-TREME UNCTION: HEALING AND STRENGTHEN-ING THE SOUL.—According to the *Decretum pro Armenis* Extreme Unction "heals the mind." This effect must have reference to the impending death struggle, for the Sacrament was instituted for the dying.

a) How is this effect produced in the soul? Extreme Unction, be it remembered, belongs to the Sacraments of the living and therefore presupposes sanctifying grace. Hence, when the Tridentine Council says that this Sacra-ment " confers grace," it must mean an increase of sancti-fying grace and a claim to all those actual graces that flow from the nature of the Sacrament. Now it belongs to the nature of the Sacrament that it (1) alleviates or comforts the sick and (2) strengthens the soul. These two effects (*alleviatio — confirmatio*), according to the Tridentine definition, are produced simultaneously, since the Sacra-ment "excites a great confidence in the divine mercy," which in turn " supports " the recipient and enables him to " bear more easily the inconveniences and pains of his sickness " and to " resist more readily the tempta-tions of the devil." [3]

The reality of the first-mentioned effect can be shown

3 *Conc. Trid.*, Sess. XIV, *De Extr. Unct.*, cap. 2.

from the scriptural use of the terms *salvare* (σώζειν) and *alleviare* (ἐγείρειν). These words designate absolute effects of the Sacrament, and hence cannot have reference to the body alone, because the Sacraments are intended primarily for the soul. In so far as it strengthens the soul for the final conflict, Extreme Unction is related to Confirmation, which enables the recipient to sustain the battle of life. In so far as it alleviates, *i. e.* comforts the sick, it has a special relation to Penance. Both these features constitute Extreme Unction a consecratory as well as a medicinal rite. The fact that it cannot readily be repeated seems to indicate that this Sacrament imprints a sort of character (*quasi-character*).

b) Father Joseph Kern, S. J., in a remarkable treatise *De Sacramento Extremae Unctionis,* published at Innsbruck in 1907,[4] insists that the proper object of Extreme Unction is the perfect healing of the soul (*perfecta sanitas animae*) with a view to its immediate entry into glory, unless indeed it should happen that the restoration of bodily health were more expedient. He holds that this view may be traced to the Fathers, that it is expressed in the ancient rituals, clearly propounded by Bl. Albertus Magnus, St. Bonaventure, St. Thomas, Durandus, Innocent V, and practically all pre-Tridentine theologians up to Ruardus Tapper.[5] This teaching, says the learned Innsbruck Jesuit, far from being opposed to, is in full conformity with, that of Trent. It was only under the influence of the Protestant Reformation that it began to wane. The denial of purgatory with its corollary that the souls of the just enter immediately into glory, led

4 Pages 81–114. For an extended review, with a synopsis, of this book see the *Irish Theological Quarterly,* Vol. II (1907), No. 7, pp. 330–345.

5 Born 1488, died 1559. Tapper was one of the most eminent theologians who took part in the Council of Trent. See Buchberger, *Kirchliches Handlexikon, s. v.*

to an attenuation of the traditional teaching on the part of Catholic theologians. This tendency is particularly noticeable in the writings of Suarez. Jansenism with its rigoristic notions and its exaggerated views of divine justice and vengeance, did not improve the situation. As the older view gradually fell into desuetude, theologians forgot that Extreme Unction remits temporal punishments and preserves the soul from purgatory, which, according to the ancient Fathers, really was its main object;—"*ut anima eius aeque pura sit post obitum ac infantis, qui statim post baptisma moritur,*" as the so-called Penitential of St. Egbert of York has it.[6]

To gain all the fruits of Extreme Unction, the recipient must be rightly disposed. If he is rightly disposed, it follows from Father Kern's argument that the remission of all temporal punishments still due to his sins must be one, indeed the principal, effect of the Sacrament. Of course this full effect is gained only by those who receive the sacred unction with due preparation and great devotion at a time when they are still able to coöperate with the sacramental grace.

The objections raised against his view are effectively refuted by Father Kern.[7] Most important among them are these four:

(1) If Extreme Unction had for its main object the remission of temporal punishments, the Mass, prayer, and indulgences for the dead would lose their value and importance.

Answer: No one ever knows for certain whether a departed person has observed all the conditions necessary for gaining the full sacramental effect of Extreme Unction, and therefore it will still remain a duty of Christian

6 *Poenit. Egb.,* I, c. 15 (Migne, P L., LXXXIX, 416).

7 *De Sacram. Extr. Unct.,* pp. 190 sqq.

charity to offer up Masses, prayers, and indulgences for the departed.

(2) The plenary indulgence granted by the Church to the dying would be useless.

Answer: That the dying man gains this indulgence may be a secondary effect of Extreme Unction.

(3) Extreme Unction would be on a level with martyrdom.

Answer: By no means. It is the peculiar privilege of a martyr to go straight to Heaven, provided he has imperfect contrition for his sins, no matter how defective his disposition may otherwise be.[8] This privilege is not claimed for Extreme Unction.

(4) Extreme Unction, in Father Kern's hypothesis, is not sufficiently differentiated either in character or purpose from Baptism.

Answer: Extreme Unction, in order to obtain its complete effect, requires more of the recipient than Baptism, namely, faithful coöperation with the grace of the Sacrament. The two Sacraments differ essentially in the following points:

(a) That Extreme Unction demands more of the recipient than Baptism, follows from the fact that

(b) Baptism is

(a) the Sacrament of spiritual regeneration;

(β) the mystic representation of the death, burial, and resurrection of Christ; and

(γ) the efficient cause of our incorporation with the mystical body of Christ; whereas

Extreme Unction is none of these things.

It is consoling to have a truth so long forgotten restored to its proper place in dogmatic and moral theology.

---

[8] Hence the ancient ecclesiastical maxim: " *Iniuriam facit martyri, qui orat pro martyre.*"

Father Kern's thesis is apt to arouse interest and sharpen the sense of duty in the clergy as well as the faithful, thereby leading to a more frequent and devout reception of the Sacrament of the dying. At the same time it is calculated to increase the confidence of the living in the fate of their brethren who have departed this life fortified by a Sacrament which, if properly received, will spare them the sufferings of purgatory. Since, however, the counsels of Divine Providence are inscrutable and the ways of men obscure and tortuous, we must never cease to pray for the poor souls.

2. THE SECOND EFFECT OF EXTREME UNCTION: CURE OF THE SPIRITUAL DEBILITY CAUSED BY SIN, AND REMISSION OF SINS, VENIAL AS WELL AS MORTAL.—St. James expressly teaches: "If he [the sick man who is anointed with the sacred unction] be in sins, they shall be forgiven him." [9] The Tridentine Council says: "[Extreme Unction] blots out sins, if there be any still to be expiated, as also the remains of sins." [10] The question arises: What sins does Extreme Unction blot out—venial sins, mortal sins, or merely the debility and depression caused by the consciousness of having sinned? Theologians are not unanimous on this subject. A distinction must be drawn between "the remains of sin" (*reliquia peccati*) and sins (*peccata*). Both are remitted by the Sacrament.

[9] "*Et si in peccatis sit, remittentur ei*" (Jac. V, 15).
[10] "*Delicta, si quae sint adhuc expianda, ac peccati reliquias abstergit.*" (Sess. XIV, *De Extr. Unct.*, cap. 2).

a) That Extreme Unction cures the soul and strengthens it against the debility caused by sin,— it is this debility which the Tridentine Council calls "the remains of sin,"—is the unanimous teaching of all theologians.

"Another advantage of the sacred unction," says the Roman Catechism,[11] "is that it frees the soul from the languor and infirmity which it has contracted from sins, and from all the other remains of sin."

Sin, especially if it has grown to be a habit, leaves in the soul a certain debility or moral weakness, which makes the last battle with the powers of darkness more difficult. This weakness the Tridentine Council means by "the remains of sin," as can easily be shown by exclusion.

The remains of sin mentioned by the Council may mean one, or more, or all of the following:

(1) The eternal punishment of sin. But this cannot properly be called a relic of sin because it stands and falls with sin and is not forgiven unless the guilt has first been blotted out.

(2) The temporal punishments due to sin. These are a real remnant of sins forgiven, and are cancelled by Extreme Unction according to the disposition of the recipient, *ex opere operato*.[12] However, this is not the primary object for which Extreme Unction was instituted, but rather appertains to indulgences and works of satisfaction, and hence we are dealing with a merely secondary effect of the Sacrament, though if the recipient is properly disposed, this effect is infallible.

---

11 *Cat. Rom., De Extr. Unct.*, qu. 14: "*Altera est sacrae unctionis utilitas, quod animam a languore et infirmitate, quam ex peccatis con-traxit, et a ceteris omnibus peccati reliquiis liberat.*"

12 Cfr. St. Thomas, *Summa contra Gentiles*, IV, 73.

(3) Concupiscence. Concupiscence is a relic not of actual but of original sin, and hence can no more be removed by Extreme Unction than by Baptism.

(4) Former mortal sins omitted in confession, or new ones committed since the last confession. Mortal sins unconsciously omitted in confession are forgiven together with those actually confessed. Freshly committed mortal sins belong before the tribunal of Penance. Of course, this proves no more than that the remission of mortal sins is not a primary and proper effect of Extreme Unction.

b) Does Extreme Unction remit mortal sins, or only venial sins?

There can be no doubt that St. James has reference to personal or actual sins when he says that sins are forgiven in Extreme Unction. It is not so clear whether he means venial sins, or mortal sins, or both. The Scotists limit the efficacy of Extreme Unction to venial sins. Extreme Unction, they say, is essentially a Sacrament of the living, and mortal sins committed after Baptism can be forgiven only in the tribunal of Penance. While this interpretation is not directly opposed to the Tridentine decree, it leaves open the question whether the Council did not also have in mind mortal sins. The general term *peccata* or *delicta* seems to indicate that it did. A careful study of St. James' Epistle renders this interpretation certain. Mere sins of weakness are to the Apostle a matter of course. In speaking of them he says, " For in many things we all offend." [13] In speaking of the Sacrament of Extreme Unction, however, he employs the hypothetical

---

[13] Jas. III, 2: " *In multis enim offendimus omnes.*"

phrase: "If he [the sick man] be in sins," thereby evidently meaning mortal sins. Bellarmine, Tournely, Sainte-Beuve, Tepe, Kern, and other theologians probably go too far when they assert that Extreme Unction is intended *per se* and directly for the remission of mortal sins, even though only *ex secundaria institutione*. If this were true, Extreme Unction would not be a Sacrament of the living, but a Sacrament of the dead; Penance could not in justice be termed "a second plank after shipwreck," [14] and the power of the keys could be dispensed with. We can imagine only one case in which Extreme Unction could forgive mortal sins without trenching on the Sacrament of Penance, namely, if a dying man were unable to confess his sins and had at least imperfect contrition. In that case Extreme Unction, as a sacramental rite, would remit his sins *ex opere operato,* though only *per accidens.* The *necessitas medii* of Penance is safeguarded by the condition that if the patient recovers, he must submit himself to the power of the keys, *i. e.* go to confession and ask for the priestly absolution. With this limitation we may subscribe to Oswald's dictum: "Extreme Unction not only completes the Sacrament of Penance, but in certain cases takes its place." [15]

3. THIRD (CONDITIONAL) EFFECT: THE RESTORATION OF BODILY HEALTH.—The restoration of bodily health is a secondary and purely conditional effect of Extreme Unction. The condition upon which it depends is expressed thus by the *Decretum pro Armenis* and the Council of

14 Cfr. *Conc. Trid.,* Sess. XIV, *De Poenit.,* can. 2.

15 *Die Lehre von den hl. Sakra-menten,* II, 282; cfr. Kern, *De Sacram. Extr. Unct.,* pp. 169 sqq.

Trent: "When it is expedient for the soul's salvation." [16]

Does the Sacrament always restore health when it is expedient for salvation? *"Sanitatem corporis interdum, ubi saluti animae expedierit, consequitur,"* says the Tridentine Council. How are we to interpret *interdum?* St. Thomas holds that the patient will surely recover after receiving Extreme Unction if his recovery will redound to his spiritual benefit.[17] Dr. Oswald goes so far as to assert that the Sacrament of the dying has a charismatic effect similar to that produced by the *gratia curationum.* However, it is more reasonable to assume that the restoration of bodily health, if it lies in God's plan, is effected by the powers of nature, stimulated supernaturally by the Sacrament. We prefer the explanation given by the older Scholastics and approved by the Council of Trent, *viz.:* that the Sacrament of Extreme Unction, by relieving anxiety, banishing fear, giving comfort, and inspiring confidence in God's mercy and humble resignation to His will, reacts favorably on the physical condition of the patient. If this explanation is correct, the sacramental effect in question can be expected only when the priest is called in time and the body not too badly ravaged by disease.[18]

The reality of this effect is proved by theologians from the words of St. James: "And the prayer of faith shall save (σώσει) the sick man: and the Lord shall raise him up (ἐγερεῖ)." Though, as we have seen,[19] these expres-

---

16 *" Ubi saluti animae expedierit."* (Denzinger-Bannwart, n. 909).

17 Cfr. the Supplement to the *Summa Theologica,* which, while it was not written by the Angelic Doctor himself, but presumably by his favorite disciple Reginald of Piperno, undoubtedly reflects his opinions.

18 Cfr. Kern, *De Sacram. Extr. Unct.,* pp. 205 sqq., 194-205

19 *V. supra,* No. 1.

sions refer primarily to the soul, it is the constant belief of Tradition that they also include the body. The Apostle employs positive rather than hypothetic terms, because he regards the supposition that the recovery of bodily health must redound to the patient's spiritual benefit as a matter of course, and, secondly, because the spiritual " saving " and " raising up " of the sinner are absolute effects which, by reacting upon the body, may restore bodily health.[20]

20 Cfr. J. Schmitz, *De Effectibus Sacramenti Extremae Unctionis*, Freiburg 1893; Kern, *De Sacram. Extr. Unct.*, pp. 194–215.

CHAPTER II

NECESSITY OF EXTREME UNCTION

A Sacrament is necessary for salvation either as a means (*necessitate medii*) or by way of precept (*necessitate praecepti*).

1. EXTREME UNCTION IS NOT NECESSARY AS A MEANS OF SALVATION.—This is evident from the fact that the Sacraments of the living presuppose the state of sanctifying grace, and the graces bestowed by Extreme Unction can, in case of necessity, be supplied by extraordinary helps.[1]

It follows that one who is dangerously sick is not obliged to have a desire for Extreme Unction (*votum sacramenti*) if he cannot actually receive it. However, if his conscience is burdened with mortal sin, for which he has only imperfect contrition, and he finds himself unable to go to confession, Extreme Unction may be for him the only, and therefore a necessary, means of salvation.

2. WHETHER EXTREME UNCTION IS NECESSARY BY WAY OF PRECEPT.—Theologians are not agreed as to whether or not a person who is

[1] Cfr. *Codex Iuris Can.*, can. 944.

seriously ill is *per se* under a grave obligation
of seeking this Sacrament.

a) St. Thomas, Suarez, Gotti, Billuart, and the
majority of modern authors hold that no such
obligation exists. Billuart [2] points out that the
phrases *"inducat presbyteros"* and *"ungi debent"*
in the Epistle of St. James have been interpreted
by various synods as embodying merely a counsel,
not a command. The Council of Trent speaks of
Extreme Unction as a *"sacramentum fidelibus
commendatum,"* which it would be a crime to con-
temn. Now mere neglect or refusal to receive a
Sacrament is not contempt. Billuart adds that if
Extreme Unction were absolutely necessary for
salvation, the Church could not suspend the administration of this Sacrament, as she sometimes
does during an interdict, because a divine law is
always binding.

b) Peter Lombard, St. Bonaventure, Peter
Soto, and Tournely, on the other hand, interpret
the *"inducat presbyteros"* of the Jacobean Epistle
as a divine command and the *"ungi debent"* as an
ecclesiastical precept.

Billuart's appeal to the Tridentine Council is not convincing, for that Council interprets the words of St.
James as follows: "This unction must be applied to
the sick," [3] and rejects the assertion that Extreme Unction

---

2 *De Extr. Unct.*, art. 7.

3 ". . . *esse hanc unctionem in-* *firmis adhibendam."* (Sess. XIV,
cap. 3; Denzinger-Bannwart, n. 910).

" is a human figment or a rite received from the Fathers, which neither has a command from God, nor a promise of grace." [4]   Moreover, thoughtless neglect or obstinate refusal to receive the Sacrament undoubtedly verges on that " contempt " of which the Council says that it involves " a heinous crime and an injury to the Holy Ghost Himself." [5] The new Code of Canon Law says (can. 944) that " no one is permitted to neglect " Extreme Unction and that those who have charge of the sick (physicians, nurses, relatives, etc.) should exercise great care and diligence, in order that this Sacrament is administered while the patient still has command of his reason.   Christ would not have instituted a special Sacrament for the dying if it were merely useful.   Extreme Unction is necessary.   Only on this assumption is there any force in the well-known argument that congruity demands a Sacrament of the nature of Extreme Unction in the septenary number of the Sacraments.   Justly, therefore, does Dr. Schell observe: " The necessity and obligation of Extreme Unction is of divine right and follows from the simple fact that this Sacrament was instituted by Christ. . . . In sickness and danger of death the duty of properly providing for body and soul is self-evident; there is no need of an express law." [6]

4 " *Hanc unctionem vel figmentum esse humanum vel ritum a Patribus acceptum nec mandatum Dei nec promissionem gratiae habentem* " (*l. c.*).

5 " *Nec vero tanti sacramenti contemptus absque ingenti scelere et ipsius Spiritus Sancti iniuria esse potest* " (*l. c.*). Cfr. Sess. XIV, can. 3; Denzinger-Bannwart, n. 928.

6 *Kath. Dogmatik*, III, 2, 636 sq. Kern contends that those who are sick unto death are obliged *sub gravi* to receive Extreme Unction. (*De Sacram. Extr. Unct.*, pp. 364 sqq.)

CHAPTER III

THE MINISTER

The Sacrament of Extreme Unction can be validly administered only by "presbyters," *i. e.* bishops and priests. This is an article of faith, for the Tridentine Council says: "The proper ministers of this Sacrament are the presbyters of the Church; by which name are to be understood in that place [James V, 15] not the elders by age, or the foremost in dignity among the people, but either bishops, or priests rightly ordained by bishops. . . ." [1] And again: "If anyone saith that the presbyters of the Church, whom Blessed James exhorts to be brought to anoint the sick, are not the priests who have been ordained by a bishop, but the elders in each community, and that for this reason the priest alone is not the proper minister of Extreme Unction, let him be anathema." [2]

---

[1] Sess. XIV, *De Extr. Unct.*, cap. 3: "*. . . aut episcopi aut sacerdotes ab ipsis rite ordinati.*"

[2] Sess. XIV, *De Extr. Unct.*, can. 4: "*Si quis dixerit, presbyteros Ecclesiae, quos beatus Iacobus adducendos esse ad infirmum inungendum hortatur, non esse sacerdotes ab episcopo ordinatos, sed aetate seniores in quavis communitate, ob idque proprium extremae unctionis ministrum non esse solum sacerdotem, anathema sit.*" (Denzinger-Bannwart, n. 929).

It is not difficult to prove this dogma from Sacred Scripture and Tradition.

1. PROOF FROM SACRED SCRIPTURE.—St. James says by implication that the *presbyteri Ecclesiae* (πρεσβύτεροι τῆς ἐκκλησίας) alone can administer the Sacrament of Extreme Unction.

If the sacred unction were nothing but a natural or charismatic cure of the body, there is no reason why it should be administered by priests. The natural ministers in that case would be physicians, or deacons, or lay persons endowed with the *gratia curationum*. The Protestant contention that St. James meant the elders of each community was rejected by the Tridentine Council, which defines that πρεσβύτεροι τῆς ἐκκλησίας means members of the sacerdotal college, men ordained by the bishop and empowered to administer the Sacrament of Penance, of which Extreme Unction is the complement.

2. PROOF FROM TRADITION.—The Sacrament of Extreme Unction has never been administered in the Church by any other persons than validly ordained priests. Origen and St. Chrysostom regarded its administration as a sacerdotal privilege. Pope Innocent I (402–417) says in his famous letter to Bishop Decentius of Eugubium, already quoted by us on a previous page: "We notice the superfluous addition of a doubt whether a bishop may do what is said to priests, for the reason that bishops, hindered by other occupations, cannot go to all the sick. But if the bishop

is able to do so, or thinks anyone specially worthy
of being visited, he, whose office it is to consecrate
the chrism, need not hesitate to bless and anoint
the sick person." [3]   Church history furnishes no
instance of the administration of Extreme Unction by deacons or laymen.

But what does Pope Innocent mean when in the same
letter he says: " The holy oil of chrism . . . it is permitted not only to priests but to all Christians to use for
anointing in their own need or that of their families "? [4]
This passage led the famous Carmelite Thomas Netter, of Walden (+ 1430), Launoy,[5] and latterly Boudinhon,[6] to assume that at the time of Pope Innocent the First
lay persons of either sex were permitted to administer
Extreme Unction to themselves and their families in
case of necessity. But to interpret the Pope's letter
thus is to make him contradict himself. By vindicating
the right of administering this Sacrament to bishops as
well as simple priests, the Pontiff manifestly meant to
exclude deacons, and, *a fortiori,* laymen. What, then, is
the meaning of his rather obscure dictum? The words
of the Pontiff may be interpreted in three different ways.
The first and simplest explanation is that the anointment
administered by laymen was not a Sacrament but merely
a sacramental. This explanation gains weight from the
fact that at the time of Pope Innocent I, consecrated elements, like baptismal water and chrism, were often em-

---

3 *Ep.,* 25, c. 8 (Denzinger-Bannwart, n. 99). (Latin text quoted
supra, p. 13, note 22).

4 ". . . *non solum sacerdotibus,
sed omnibus uti Christianis licet in
sua aut suorum necessitate inungendo* [*al. ungendum*]."

5 *Opera Omnia,* Vol. I, pp. 569
sqq.

6 *Revue Catholique des Églises,*
1905, p. 400.

ployed for other than sacramental purposes, *e. g.* the restoration of health.[7] Another interpretation (Bellarmine, Estius) is that the Pontiff employs the gerund "*inungendo*" passively, thereby indicating that "all Christians may use the holy chrism to have themselves and their families anointed in their need." A third explanation is suggested by Dr. Schell: "The Pope's decision is probably to be understood as applying to a sort of unction by desire in case of necessity (an analogue of lay confession), showing the patient's good will to do what is in his power." [8] Launoy's [9] distinction between the ordinary and the extraordinary minister of Extreme Unction has no basis in Tradition.

Clericatus [10] asserts that in case of urgent necessity a priest may administer Extreme Unction to himself. This view is untenable because priests are not exempt from the general rule that no one can administer a Sacrament to himself.

3. Incidental Theological Problems.—Extreme Unction may be validly administered by one priest or by several priests.

a) One priest is sufficient for the validity of the Sacrament. This clearly appears from the constant teaching and practice of the Latin Church. The *Decretum Gratiani* expressly declares that one priest may anoint a sick person.[11]

It is true that St. James speaks of *presbyteri* in the plural. But this does not mean that several priests are

---

[7] Cfr. A. Franz, *Die Kirchl. Benediktionen im Mittelalter*, I, 258.

[8] *Kath. Dogmatik*, III, 2, 623.

[9] *Opera Omnia*, Vol. I, pp. 569 sqq.

[10] *Decis. de Extr. Unct.*, n. 75.

[11] *Decr. Grat.*, l. V, tit. 40, c. 14: "*Sacerdos uno praesente clerico et etiam solus potest infirmum ungere.*"

required to administer the Sacrament. It is simply a popular and familiar way of saying: "Let the sick call for priestly ministrations," just as one might say: "Let him call in the doctors," meaning, "Let him procure medical aid." In other words, the plural stands by a figure of speech (enallage) for the singular, as in Luke XVII, 14: "Go, show yourselves to the priests." Doubtless St. James did not wish to exclude the participation of a number of priests where they were available. This may have been the case in Jerusalem, Antioch, or Corinth; but there were many places where only one bishop or presbyter could be summoned. Surely in such places the faithful were not to be deprived of this important and necessary Sacrament. In the "Orthodox" (schismatic) Church of the East it has been customary for seven priests to take part in the administration of the Sacrament. Owing partly to the difficulty of obtaining the simultaneous presence of so many priests, and partly perhaps to a misunderstanding of the rite, the Nestorians abolished Extreme Unction altogether and substituted in its place a new rite (*cornu gratiae sancti*), which is performed by a single priest with oil mixed with dust from the grave of St. Thomas the Apostle.

b) The Oriental custom of the administration of Extreme Unction by seven (or sometimes three) priests,[12] to which we have just referred, seems at one time to have been known also in the West.[13] Some schismatic theologians [14] hold that one priest cannot administer the Sacrament validly.[15] We on our part have rather to consider the question whether and under what conditions

---

[12] V. Goar, *Euchol.*, p. 438.

[13] Cfr. Martène, *De Antiq. Ecclesiae Ritibus*, I, 7, 3.

[14] E. g., Simeon of Thessalonica.

[15] Cfr. C. Ralli, Περὶ τῶν μυστηρίων τῆς μετανοίας καὶ τοῦ εὐχελαίου, p. 114, Athens 1905.

Extreme Unction can be validly administered by a number of priests conjointly. There are three possibilities to be considered.

(1) If one of the priests performs the unctions while another pronounces the prayer, the rite is invalid, because matter and form of a Sacrament constitute an indivisible whole.[16]

(2) If the Sacrament is administered by several priests, each in turn performing the complete rite, both matter and form, in regard to one or more of the several senses, the ceremony is probably valid, because in that case the partial acts coalesce into one whole, as when one priest consecrates the bread and another the wine during the same Mass. The Gregorian Sacramentary seems to direct that while one priest performs the unction, another should pronounce the form. Kern is of opinion that the Sacrament could be validly administered by two because of the moral unity of the ministers present for the administration; but the form must not be in the first person, or a false sense is conveyed. Quinn comments that if the validity of the Sacrament so administered is secured by the moral unity of the ministers, then the use of the first person singular is justified by the same reason.

(3) If the whole rite is performed by several priests either simultaneously or successively, provided the unctions are properly performed and the prayers simultaneously recited by all, all coöperate in administering the Sacrament, just as at ordination all the priests ordained celebrate the same Mass with the bishop. If the whole series of unctions is performed by several priests successively, it is likely that the first alone administers the Sacrament, while the others merely confer a sacramental.[17]

16 Cfr. Suarez, *Comment. in S. Th.*, III, disp. 43, sect. 2, n. 3.

17 Cfr. *Summa Theologica, Suppl.*, qu. 29, art. 2, ad 3; Pesch, *Praelect. Dogmat.*, Vol. VII, 3rd ed., pp. 279 sqq.; Kern, *De Sacram. Extr. Unct.*, pp. 263 sqq.; A. Quinn, *Some Aspects of the Dogma of Extreme Unction*, Dublin 1920.

CHAPTER IV

THE RECIPIENT

The conditions of valid administration of Ex-treme Unction on the part of the recipient are three: (1) He must be baptized; (2) he must be sick of a disease which is judged dangerous, and (3) he must be morally responsible.

1. THE RECIPIENT MUST BE BAPTIZED.—Baptism is "the spiritual door" to all the Sacraments. Hence no unbaptized person, how pious soever or how well prepared, can validly receive Extreme Unction. This has been the invariable teaching and practice of the Catholic Church, based on St. James' Epistle: "Is any man sick among you (ἐν ὑμῖν, i. e. you who are baptized Christians)." [1]

2. THE RECIPIENT MUST BE SICK OF A DISEASE WHICH IS JUDGED DANGEROUS.—The *Decretum pro Armenis* defines: "This Sacrament must not be given except to one who is sick and judged likely to die." [2] Substantially identical with this declaration is that of the Tridentine

---

[1] Iac. V, 14.

[2] "Hoc sacramentum nisi in-firmo, de cuius morte timetur, dari non debet." (Denzinger-Bannwart. n. 700).

Council, that "This unction is to be applied to the sick, but to those especially who are in such danger as to seem to be about to depart this life." [3]

This teaching is also based on the Epistle of St. James. When the Apostle says: "If any man is sick [4] among you," he plainly means so sick that he can no longer betake himself to a priest.

a) In the Latin Church Extreme Unction has always been known as the Sacrament of the departing (*sacramentum exeuntium*). This explains how some Catholics got the mistaken notion that once a man had this Sacrament administered to himself, his account with the world was closed,— a belief which at times resulted in much delay and negligence. " In the Middle Ages," says Oswald, " the reception of Extreme Unction was often regarded as a complete break with the world, a formal exit from the various relations of denizens of this terrestrial globe. One who had been anointed in a dangerous illness and happened to recover, was treated as if he had come back from the other world. He was not allowed to continue his conjugal relations nor to take an oath; in fact he was held to all practical intents and purposes to be dead." [5]

In the Greek Church the faithful are regularly anointed with holy oil on Maundy Thursday as a preventive of disease. Provost Maltzew writes on this subject: " Though the sacerdotal *Ordo* prescribes that a priest should not administer this Sacrament to subjects who are in good

---

3 Sess. XIV, *De Extr. Unct.*, cap. 3: ". . . *esse hanc unctionem infirmis adhibendam, illis vero praesertim, qui in exitu vitae constituti videantur."* (Denzinger-Bannwart, n. 910).

4 *Infirmari*, ἀσθηνεῖν.

5 *Die hl. Sakramente der kath. Kirche*, II, 296.

health, it is an ancient custom in the Greek as well as in the Russian Church (at Moscow and Nowgorod) that the bishop applies the holy oil once a year, on Holy Thursday, to the healthy." [6]

The Greek theologian Arcudius inveighs against this custom as an abuse bred by ignorance and greed. Goar seeks to justify it by saying that the anointment administered in Holy Week is not regarded as a Sacrament, but merely as a ceremony or sacramental.

According to Sainte-Beuve [7] the example of the Greek Church proves that Extreme Unction can be validly administered to persons in good health. This assertion drew a sharp criticism from Benedict XIV. [8] Ralli [9] and Mesolaras [10] have shown that the sacramental anointment of persons not ill with any disease is widely practiced in the kingdom of Greece and the Patriarchate of Constantinople, whereas the Russian Church officially teaches that Extreme Unction can be validly administered only to those who are seriously sick.

The Catholic Church holds that no one who is not seriously ill can receive Extreme Unction, even though he be in danger of death from external causes, as a soldier going into battle or a condemned criminal ascending the scaffold. If a man is dangerously ill, however, it makes no difference, so far as the Sacrament is concerned, whether his sickness arises from an internal disease or an external lesion. Senile decay qualifies for Extreme Unction when it has advanced so far that death seems probable (*"senectus est morbus"*). Calvin's jibe that the

---

6 A. Maltzew, *Die Sakramente der orthodox-kath. Kirche des Morgenlandes*, p. 549, Berlin 1898.

7 *De Extr. Unct.*, disp. 7, art. 1.

8 *De Synodo Dioecesana*, VII, 5, 4.

9 Ralli, *op. cit.* (see page 42, *supra*, n. 15), p. 115.

10 *Enchiridion*, pp. 218 sq.

Catholic Church anoints " semi-putrid corpses " (*cadavera semi-mortua*), is meaningless, for it is the danger of death (*periculum mortis*), and not the death struggle (*articulus mortis*), which the Church regards as marking the proper time for the administration of the Sacrament. We advisedly say, the Church; because unfortunately it can not be denied that, beginning with the twelfth and thirteenth centuries, sacerdotal greed often caused the faithful, especially of the poorer class, to forego Extreme Unction altogether or to postpone it until it was too late.[11] Repeated protests on the part of bishops and councils failed to uproot this deplorable abuse,[12] which was furthered by the erroneous teaching of the Scotists that led people to conclude that Extreme Unction should be postponed until the patient was no longer able to commit even a venial sin. Our schismatic critics are justified in censuring this grievous abuse; but it would be unjust to blame the Church for it. The Tridentine Council is in accord with Tradition when it says that Extreme Unction " is to be applied to the sick, especially to those who are in such danger as to seem to be about to depart this life." [13]

b) It is forbidden to receive Extreme Unction more than once in the course of the same sickness. This brings us to the question of the *repetition* of the Sacrament.

The Tridentine Council says: " If the sick recover

11 V. Pelliccia, *De Christ. Ecclesiae Politia*, l. VI, sect. 2, c. 3, § 1.
12 Cfr. Kern, *De Sacram. Extr. Unct.*, pp. 282 sqq.
13 Cfr. *Cat. Rom.*, P. II, c. 6, § 9. The anointment of the dead mentioned in the writings of the Pseudo-Dionysius (*De Eccles. Hier.*, VII,

2), and which formed the subject of a discussion between the Latins and the Greeks at the Council of Florence (A. D. 1439), was not the Sacrament of Extreme Unction, but a mere ceremony. Cfr. the *Theol. Quartalschrift*, of Tübingen, 1904, p. 382.

after receiving this unction, they may again be aided by
the succor of this Sacrament, when they fall into another
like danger of death." [14]   Hence, though Extreme Unction is not, as regards repetition, in the same class with
Baptism, Confirmation, and Holy Orders, it differs essentially from Penance and Holy Communion, which can
be received often.   Only in Matrimony do we find something of the same quasi-character, as neither party to a
marriage can again receive this Sacrament validly while
the other lives.

There was an ancient Latin custom, also found among
the Copts, of administering Extreme Unction on seven
successive days, or repeating it seven times by as many
different priests.   Theologians do not know what to think
of this.   Fr. Schmid [15] and Gutberlet [16] hold that the seven
unctions coalesced into one sacrament.   The Scotists
maintain that, when Extreme Unction is administered according to the present Roman rite, there are seven different partial Sacraments.   Father Kern on the other hand
maintains [17] that each separate rite is fully sacramental
and concludes from the fact that this practice is still in
vogue in the Orient that, speculatively speaking at least,
Extreme Unction may be repeated during the same sickness.   However, this view is difficult to reconcile with
the teaching of Trent.

3. THE RECIPIENT MUST BE MORALLY RE-
SPONSIBLE.—As one of the effects of Extreme
Unction is the cure of the spiritual debility caused

[14] Sess. XIV, *De Extr. Unct.*,
cap. 3: " *Quodsi infirmi post sus-*
ceptam hanc unctionem convalue-
rint, iterum huius sacramenti subsi-
dio iuvari poterunt, quum in aliud
simile vitae discrimen inciderint."

[15] *Zeitschrift für kath. Theologie*,
Innsbruck, 1901, p. 261.

[16] Heinrich's *Dogmatische Theolo-*
gie, Vol. X, p. 231.

[17] *De Sacram. Extr. Unct.*, pp.
342 sqq.

by sin,[18] those only who are morally accountable and capable of committing sin (either mortal or venial), are fit to receive this Sacrament. Extreme Unction, being the complement and consummation of Penance, is evidently intended for penitents who have led a life not entirely free from sin.[19]

a) Upon this dogmatic basis rests the ecclesiastical practice of refusing Extreme Unction to infants who have not yet attained the use of reason and to adults who have always been insane or idiotic. Theoretically, those also who have led a stainless life are incapable of receiving the Sacrament of the dying. But such holiness is attainable only by virtue of a special grace like that granted to the Blessed Virgin Mary.[20] Children who have attained the use of reason can and should receive Extreme Unction when they are dangerously ill.[21]

b) Suarez,[22] Atzberger,[23] Kern,[24] and other theologians claim that one need not have committed a sin in order to be able to receive Extreme Unction, the real purpose of the Sacrament being to strengthen the soul for its last struggle. In order to square this theory with the present formula of administration the writers in question are compelled to interpret the latter as though it read: " *Indulgeat tibi Deus culpam, si adsit, et reliquias eius, si*

18 *V. supra*, pp. 29 sqq.

19 Cfr. the *Supplementum* to the *Summa Theologica* of St. Thomas, qu. 32, art. 4, ad 2.

20 See Pohle-Preuss, *Grace: Actual and Habitual,* 2nd ed., p. 116, St. Louis 1917.

21 Cfr. Sainte-Beuve, *De Extr. Unct.*, disp. 7, art. 3.

22 *Comment. in S. Th.*, III, disp. 42, sect. 2, n. 7 sqq.

23 In Scheeben's *Handbuch der kath. Dogmatik*, Vol. IV, 3, 749, Freiburg 1903.

24 *De Sacram. Extr. Unct.*, pp. 307 sqq.

necesse sit." This artificial construction does not inspire confidence. Theologians generally are convinced, and their conviction is borne out by experience, that even the most saintly men and women, and the best-behaved children do not escape ordinary venial sins (*peccata quotidiana*),[25] and hence no morally responsible person is likely to receive Extreme Unction without having those *peccata* and *reliquiae peccati* which the Sacrament is calculated to blot out.

Quite a different question is this, whether Extreme Unction, like Penance, presupposes personal sins committed after Baptism, or whether it may exercise its effects upon the debility contracted before Baptism. The S. Congregation of the Propaganda has decided [26] that one who is baptized during a serious sickness should be given Extreme Unction immediately afterward, and hence it is safe to say that spiritual debility of whatever kind, whether due to sins committed before or after Baptism, is cured by the Sacrament of the dying.[27]

READINGS: — Besides the general works on the Sacraments mentioned in Pohle-Preuss, *The Sacraments,* Vol. I, pp. 3 and 4, the student may consult the following:

St. Thomas, *Summa Theologica, Supplementum,* qu. 29 sq.; IDEM, *Contra Gentiles,* IV, 73, and the commentators, especially Suarez, *Comment. in S. Theol.,* III, disp. 39 sqq., and Billuart, *De Extrema Unctione.*

* Card. Bellarmine, *De Extrema Unctione.*— A. Victorelli, *De Extrema Unctione,* 1609.— N. Serarius, S.J., *De Sacramento Extremae Unctionis,* Mayence 1611.— J. Launoy, *De Sacramento Unctionis Infirmorum,* Paris 1673.— Rosignoli, *Tractatus de Sacramentis Poenitentiae et Extremae Unctionis,* Milan 1706.— De Gaëtanis, *De Suprema Unctione,* 1747.— Benedict XIV, *De Synodo*

25 *V. Conc. Trid.,* Sess. VI, cap. 11 (Denzinger-Bannwart, n. 804).

26 Sept. 21, 1821.

27 Cfr. Billuart, *De Extr. Unct.,* art. 6.

Dioecesana, l. VIII.—*Sainte-Beuve, *De Sacramento Unctionis Infirmorum Extremae,* in Migne, *Theol. Curs. Complet.,* Vol. XXIV. — M. Heimbucher, *Die hl. Oelung,* Ratisbon 1888.— Ign. Schmitz, *De Effectibus Sacramenti Extremae Unctionis,* Freiburg 1893.— Boudinhon in the *Revue Catholique des Églises,* 1905, pp. 385 sqq.—*J. Kern, S. J., *De Sacramento Extremae Unctionis,* Ratisbon 1907.— W. Humphrey, S.J., *The One Mediator, or Sacrifice and Sacraments,* pp. 188–201, London 1890.— A. Devine, C.P., *The Sacraments Explained according to the Teaching and Doctrine of the Catholic Church,* pp. 383–399, 3rd ed., London 1905. — P. J. Toner, art. "Extreme Unction," in the *Catholic Encyclopedia,* Vol. V, pp. 716–730.— W. McDonald, "The Sacrament of Extreme Unction," in the *Irish Theological Quarterly,* Vol. II (1907), No. 7, pp. 330–345.— P. J. Hanley, *Treatise on the Sacrament of Extreme Unction,* New York 1907.— Th. Slater, S.J., *Questions of Moral Theology,* "Repetition of Extreme Unction," pp. 368–387, New York, 1915.— B. J. Otten, S.J., *A Manual of the History of Dogmas,* Vol. I, St. Louis 1917, pp. 52, 168, 355, 474; Vol. II (1918), pp. 387 sqq.—J. B. Bord, *L'Extrême Onction,* Bruges 1923.—A. J. Kilker, *Extreme Unction,* St. Louis 1927.

Non-Catholic works: J. H. Blunt, *Sacraments and Sacramental Ordinances,* London 1867; Morgan Dix, *The Sacramental System,* New York 1893; F. Kattenbusch, in the *New Schaff-Herzog Encyclopedia of Religious Knowledge,* Vol. IV, pp. 251–253, New York 1909; Puller, *The Anointing of the Sick in Scripture and Tradition,* London 1904. (Puller's contentions are criticized and, so far as necessary, refuted by Dr. Toner in his article in the *Catholic Encyclopedia,* Vol. V, pp. 716–730, and by Austin Quinn in his Maynooth doctoral dissertation, *Some Aspects of the Dogma of Extreme Unction,* Dublin 1920.

---

* The asterisk before an author's name indicates that his treatment of the subject is especially clear and thorough. As St. Thomas is invariably the best guide, the omission of the asterisk before his name never means that we consider his work inferior to that of other writers. There are vast stretches of theology which he scarcely touched.

PART II

HOLY ORDERS

INTRODUCTION

Between the priesthood (*ordo in esse*) and ordination to the priesthood (*ordo in fieri*), there is a distinction similar to that between the married state and matrimony.

The election of a pope is not a Sacrament, and it is possible to conceive of a divinely instituted priesthood into which a man could enter without receiving a Sacrament. In order, therefore, to show that Holy Orders is a true Sacrament, it is not enough to prove that the priesthood has been divinely instituted; it must also be demonstrated that the act by which a man becomes a priest is a true Sacrament (*sacramentum ordinis,* or, more correctly, *ordinationis*). In other words, we must prove that the distinction between the clergy (from κλῆρος, a lot, or something assigned by lot, especially the portion of an inheritance, an allotment) and the laity (from λαός, the people),[1] is based upon a Sacrament.

---

[1] Cfr. *Conc. Trident.,* Sess. VII, can. 10.

A specific question to be answered is whether the three hierarchical orders existing in the Catholic Church,—the episcopate, the priesthood, and the diaconate,—are sacramental, and what is the nature of the subdiaconate and the four minor orders.

CHAPTER I

HOLY ORDERS A TRUE SACRAMENT

SECTION 1

DIVINE INSTITUTION

1. HERETICAL VAGARIES VS. THE TEACHING OF THE CHURCH.— Luther denied the existence of a Christian priesthood, and his example was followed by Flacius Illyricus, Martin Chemnitz, and other faithful disciples.

a) Calvin hesitated to deny the sacramentality of " the imposition of hands by which the Church introduces her ministers into office." [1] Melanchthon, after many tergiversations, in the later editions of his *Loci* admitted ordination to be a Sacrament. To-day nearly all Protestant sects reject the episcopal form of church government and with it all semblance of a Sacrament of Order.

b) The Catholic doctrine on the subject is thus authoritatively stated by the Council of Trent: "If anyone saith that Order, or sacred ordination, is not truly and properly a Sacrament instituted by Christ the Lord; or that it is a kind of human figment devised by men unskilled in ecclesiastical

---

[1] *Instit.*, IV, 14, 20: " *Impositionem manuum, quâ Ecclesiae ministri in suum munus initiantur, ut non invitus patior vocari sacramentum, ita inter ordinaria sacramenta non numero.*"

matters; or that it is only a sort of rite for choosing ministers of the word of God and of the Sacraments; let him be anathema." [2]

This canon does not decide the question whether and to what extent the different orders participate in the sacramentality of Holy Orders, but merely declares in general terms that the rite of ordination is a true Sacrament. This teaching can easily be demonstrated from Scripture and Tradition.

2. PROOF FROM SACRED SCRIPTURE.—Though it seems that Christ called His Apostles to the priesthood without any special ceremony,[3] He undoubtedly instituted a sacramental rite for the purpose of transmitting the power of orders (*potestas ordinis*), for Holy Scripture speaks of an external sign combined with internal grace, which can derive its efficacy only from being divinely instituted.

a) The external sign is the imposition of hands (*manuum impositio*, ἐπιθεσία τῶν χειρῶν, χειροτονία). The "prayer" mentioned in connection with this ceremony does not seem to be the sacramental form, but merely a worthy preparation for the reception of the Sacrament.

---

2 Sess. XXIII, can. 3: "*Si quis dixerit, ordinem sive sacram ordinationem non esse vere et proprie sacramentum a Christo Domino institutum, vel esse figmentum quoddam humanum excogitatum a viris rerum ecclesiasticarum imperitis, aut esse tantum ritum quendam eligendi ministros verbi Dei et sacramentorum, anathema sit.*" (Denzinger-Bannwart, n. 963).

3 Cfr. Card. Bellarmine, *De Sacramento Ordinis*, I, 2.

In the sixth chapter of the Acts we are told that the disciples, at the bidding of the Apostles, chose seven deacons. "These they set before the Apostles, and they praying, imposed hands upon them (καὶ προσευξάμενοι ἐπέθηκαν αὐτοῖς τὰς χεῖρας)." [4] The *matter* of the Sacrament is here plainly indicated. It is the *impositio manuum.* The prayer might be taken for the *form,* were it not that the aorist προσευξάμενοι seems to indicate a mere preparation for the imposition of hands, connected with this rite in a purely external way. This is still more clearly brought out in the biblical account of the ordination of Paul and Barnabas, where we read: "Then they, fasting and praying (νηστεύσαντες καὶ προσευξάμενοι) and imposing their hands upon them (καὶ ἐπιθέντες τὰς χεῖρας αὐτοῖς), sent them away." [5] Here prayer is put on a level with fasting as a preparation for the sacred rite.

It is important to note that Paul and Barnabas exercised the power which they had themselves received, by ordaining priests for the different churches. Acts XIV, 22: "And when they had ordained to them priests in every church (χειροτονήσαντες πρεσβυτέρους) and had prayed with fasting (προσευξάμενοι μετὰ νηστειῶν), they commended them to the Lord, in whom they believed." [6]

That the power of ordination was to be transmitted by means of an external rite appears from St. Paul's command to his disciple Timothy: "Impose not hands lightly upon any man (χεῖρας ταχέως μηδενὶ ἐπιτίθει)." [7]

b) The "imposition of hands" communicates

---

4 Act. VI, 6: "*Hos statuerunt ante conspectum Apostolorum et orantes imposuerunt eis manus.*"

5 Act. XIII, 3: "*Tunc ieiunantes et orantes imponentesque eis manus, dimiserunt illos.*"

6 Act. XIV, 22: "*Et quum constituissent illis per singulas ecclesias presbyteros et orassent cum ieiunationibus, commendaverunt eos Domino, in quem crediderunt.*"

7 1 Tim. V, 22: "*Manus cito nemini imposueris.*"

divine grace. This can be shown from St. Paul's Epistles to Timothy.

"I admonish thee," he says (2 Tim. I, 6), "that thou stir up the grace of God (τὸ χάρισμα τοῦ Θεοῦ), which is in thee by the imposition of my hands (διὰ τῆς ἐπιθέσεως τῶν χειρῶν μου)." A careful analysis of this text leads to the following conclusions:

(1) According to the context the grace conferred on Timothy by the imposition of hands was to qualify him for the worthy administration of the episcopal office, and consequently this particular χειροθεσία cannot be identical either with Confirmation or Extreme Unction.[8] St. Chrysostom paraphrases the Pauline passage as follows: "Excite anew the grace which thou hast received for the purpose of presiding in the Church." [9]

(2) Χάρισμα here cannot simply mean a charismatic gift (*gratia gratis data*), for St. Paul frequently employs the term as a synonym of χάρις (*caritas, gratia gratum faciens*),[10] and this meaning is clearly demanded by the context of the passage quoted, which enumerates the qualities that render men pleasing in the eyes of God. 2 Tim. I, 7: "For God hath not given us the spirit of fear, but of power, and of love, and of sobriety." [11] Moreover, a permanent grace which is capable of being "kindled anew" by the personal efforts of its possessor cannot be a charismatic gift, but must be identical with sanctifying grace.

A sort of parallel passage to the one just analyzed is 1 Tim. IV, 14: "Neglect not the grace that is in thee

8 Cfr. Mark XVI, 18.
9 *Hom. in 2 Tim.*, 1.
10 Cfr. Rom. V, 16; VI, 23; 1 Cor. XII, 31.

11 2 Tim. I, 7: "*Non enim dedit nobis Deus spiritum timoris, sed virtutis et dilectionis* (ἀγάπης) *et sobrietatis.*"

(τοῦ ἐν σοὶ χαρίσματος), which was given thee by prophecy, with imposition of the hands of the priesthood (μετὰ ἐπιθέσεως τῶν χειρῶν τοῦ πρεσβυτερίου)." [12] Here again the permanent grace communicated by Holy Orders is described as an effect of the imposition of hands, the only difference being that the Apostle does not speak of the rite as administered by his own hands, but by the *presbyterium*.[13] But what had "prophecy" to do with the ordination of Timothy? St. Paul probably means that he himself was prophetically inspired when he chose his favorite disciple for episcopal honors.[14]

c) That the rite of ordination was instituted by Christ follows from the scriptural teaching that this rite is a visible sign conferring invisible grace. No one but the God-man Himself could establish this connection. The institution of the Sacrament probably took place between the Resurrection of Christ and His Ascension.

3. PROOF FROM TRADITION.—An argument from Tradition may be construed (a) from the consentient teaching of the Catholic Church, the Greek schismatics, and heretical sects; [15] (b) from ancient ordination formularies that have come down to us, and (c) from the express testimony of the Fathers. We shall confine ourselves to the latter.

---

12 1 Tim. IV, 14: "*Noli negligere gratiam, quae in te est, quae data est tibi per prophetiam cum impositione manuum presbyterii.*"

13 On the meaning of this term cfr. Ch. II, Sect. 1, *infra*.

14 Cfr. 1 Tim. I, 18.

15 Cfr. Goar, *Euchol.*, pp. 194 sqq.; Denzinger, *Rit. Orient.*, I, 416 sqq.

St. Gregory of Nyssa says: "The same power of the word renders sublime and honorable the priest, who by the newness of ordination has been singled out from the multitude; he who was yesterday and previously one from among the people [*i. e.* a layman], suddenly becomes a commander, a presiding officer, a teacher of righteousness, the dispenser of hidden mysteries. . . . Though in his external appearance he is the same as he was before, yet in his invisible soul, by a certain unseen power and grace, he is transformed into a higher being." [16]

St. Chrysostom says in his famous treatise "On the Priesthood": "The office of the priesthood is exercised on earth, but it ranks amongst things that are heavenly, and with good reason. For it was neither a man nor an angel nor an archangel nor any other created power, but the Paraclete Himself that established this ministry. . . . If you consider what it is for a man clothed in flesh and blood to be able to approach that pure and blessed nature [of the angels], you will easily understand to what a dignity the grace of the Holy Ghost has raised priests." [17]

This sublime dignity is acquired by ordination. "If the pledge of the Holy Spirit no longer existed," says the same writer, "there would be no Baptism and no remission of sins, . . . nor should we consume the mysteries; for the mystic Flesh and Blood does not exist except by the grace of the Holy Ghost. Nor should we have priests, because without such a descent, [Holy] Orders would be impossible." [18]

St. Jerome deduces the validity of orders conferred by

16 *Orat. in Bapt. Christi* (Migne, P.G., XLVI, 582).

17 *De Sacerdot.*, III, n. 4 (*P. G.*, XLVIII, 642). Translation by P. Boyle, C.M., *On the Priesthood.*

A Treatise in Six Books by Saint John Chrysostom, 2nd ed., pp. 36, 37, Dublin 1910.

18 *Hom. de Resurrect. Mort.*, n. 8 (*P.G.*, L, 432).

heretics from the fact that Baptism administered by them is valid.[19] St. Augustine puts the two Sacraments on the same level: "Each is a Sacrament and is given by a certain consecration: the one when a man is baptized, the other when he is ordained, and therefore in the Catholic [Church] it is not permitted to repeat either." [20] He asks the Donatists to "explain why the Sacrament of the baptized cannot be lost, while the Sacrament of the ordained can be lost. If both are Sacraments, which no one doubts, how is the one not lost [by apostasy], while the other is? No injury should be done to either Sacrament." [21]

In a treatise on the dignity of the priesthood, often ascribed to St. Ambrose, but probably composed by Pope Sylvester II, we read: "Who gives the episcopal grace, O brother? God or man? You answer without hesitation: God. But God gives it through man. A man imposes his hands, God showers down His grace. The priest raises his right hand in supplication, and God blesses with His mighty right hand. The bishop confers the order, God bestows the dignity." [22]

The Sacrament of Holy Orders has always been ad-

19 *Adv. Lucif.*, n. 11: "*Si in fide sua baptizato baptizans nocere non potuit, et in fide sua sacerdotem constitutum non inquinavit.*"

20 *Contr. Ep. Parmen.*, II, c. 13, n. 28 (Migne, *P. L.*, XLIII, 70): "*Utrumque enim sacramentum est et quadam consecratione datur, illud quum baptizatur, istud quum ordinatur, ideoque in catholica [Ecclesia] utrumque non licet iterari.*"

21 *Op. cit.*, II, n. 30: "*Ipsi explicent, quomodo sacramentum baptizati non possit amitti et sacramentum ordinati possit amitti. Si enim utrumque sacramentum est, quod nemo dubitat, cur illud non amitti-*

tur? *Neutri sacramento iniuria facienda est.*"

22 *De Dignit. Sacerdot.*, c. 5: "*Quis dat, frater, episcopalem gratiam? Deus an homo? Respondes sine dubio: Deus. Sed tamen per hominem dat Deus. Homo imponit manus, Deus largitur gratiam. Sacerdos imponit supplicem dexteram, et Deus benedicit potenti dexterâ. Episcopus initiat ordinem, et Deus tribuit dignitatem.*" Other Patristic testimonies *apud* Albert a Bulsano, *Instit. Theol. Dogmat.*, ed. G. à Graun, Vol. III, pp. 249 sqq., Innsbruck 1896; Palmieri, *De Rom. Pontif.*, 2nd ed., pp. 76 sqq., Rome 1897.

ministered in the Church. The Fourth Ecumenical Council of Chalcedon (451) forbade bishops to ordain unworthy candidates to the episcopate, the priesthood, or the diaconate, under penalty of being deprived of their office and dignity.[23] Simonistic ordinations were strictly prohibited by the councils of Orleans (533), Braga (563), Toledo (653), and the Second Ecumenical Council of Nicaea (787).

The Patristic Tradition was continued by the Schoolmen [24] up to the threshhold of modern times.[25]

23 Canon 2, *apud* Hardouin, *Concil.*, II, 601.

24 Cfr. Petr. Lombard., *Sent.*, IV, dist. 24.

25 The befittingness of the sacramental character of Orders is well shown by Gihr, *Die hl. Sakramente der kath. Kirche,* Vol. II, 2nd ed., pp. 282 sq.

SECTION 2

MATTER AND FORM

1. THE MATTER.—In trying to ascertain what constitutes the matter of this Sacrament, we must make a distinction between the three major orders on the one hand, and the subdiaconate and minor orders on the other. We are here concerned only with the so-called major or sacred orders (the episcopate, the priesthood, and the diaconate), because the others, as we shall see presently, are not sacramental.

In the Orient the Sacrament of Holy Orders is conferred solely by the imposition of hands (*manuum impositio*), whereas in the Latin Church the delivery of the instruments (*traditio instrumentorum*) forms an important part of the ordination rite. The question arises: Which of these two ceremonies constitutes the matter of the Sacrament? There has been a celebrated controversy on this subject.

a) St. Bonaventure,[1] Peter Soto,[2] Morinus, Goar, Martène, Tournely, Perrone, Franzelin, Schwetz, Oswald, Pesch, Tepe, and the majority

[1] *Comment. in Sent.*, IV, dist. 24, p. 2, art. 1, qu. 4.   [2] *De Instit. Sacerd.*, lect. 5.

of present-day theologians hold that the imposition of hands is the sole matter of the Sacrament.

The arguments in favor of this view are very strong, not to say conclusive.

a) As we have seen,[3] Holy Scripture ascribes the conferring of grace exclusively to the imposition of hands. We cannot reasonably assume that the Bible omits to mention the rite which constitutes the essential matter of the Sacrament, insisting on something entirely non-essential.[4] Moreover, the rite of ordination is undoubtedly older than the Book of the Gospels, which plays so important a part in the "*traditio instrumentorum.*"

β) The Fathers and the Church councils held during the first nine centuries do not mention the "*traditio instrumentorum,*" but merely speak of the "*impositio manus*" (χειροτονία, χειροθεσία),[5] as does the Council of Trent.[6] This silence cannot be explained by the Discipline of the Secret.

γ) The delivery of the instruments is not mentioned in any ritual composed before A. D. 900.[7] The early Scholastics speak of it as a merely declarative and consequently non-essential ceremony.[8] Hence the rite cannot have been introduced earlier than the tenth century and must be of ecclesiastical institution.

May it not be possible that the Church received from

3 *V. supra*, Sect. 1.

4 Cfr. 2 Tim. I, 6.

5 See the testimonies collected by Pesch, *Praelect. Dogmat.*, Vol. VII, 3rd ed., pp. 310 sqq., Freiburg 1909.

6 Sess. XIV, *De Extr. Unct.*, cap. 3; Sess. XXIII, cap. 2 and 3.

7 Cfr. Morinus, *De Sacris Ecclesiae Ordinationibus*, Antwerp 1695.

8 Thus Hugh of St. Victor (+ about 1141) says of the rite of ordination to the priesthood: "*Accipiunt et calicem cum vino et patenam cum hostiis de manu episcopi, quatenus his instrumentis potestatem se accepisse cognoscant placabiles Deo hostias offerendo.*" (*De Sacram.*, II, 3, 12).

Christ the power to determine the specific matter of this Sacrament, but failed to exercise that power until the tenth century? We answer that this hypothesis is incompatible with the teaching of the Tridentine Council,[9] and, moreover, intrinsically improbable, because we can not reasonably assume that the Church degraded the original rite instituted by the Apostles to the rank of a non-essential ceremony and in its place adopted an entirely new one.[10]

δ) Our fourth and final argument is that the Greek Church has always employed the *impositio manuum* as the sole rite of ordination from the beginning to the present day. Nor was the Greek teaching or practice on this head ever denied or challenged in the course of the many debates held at Florence, 1274, and at Lyons, 1439, with a view to reunite the two churches.

De Lugo maintained [11] that both rites — the imposition of hands and the giving of the instruments — constitute the matter of the Sacrament, the one for the East, the other for the West. This view was approved by Cardinal Franzelin [12] and recommended by Msgr. Gutberlet.[13] But it seems to us incompatible with the Catholic doctrine of the unity and immutability of the Sacraments. The Church has never claimed the right to change either the matter or the form of any Sacrament.[14]

If the *impositio manuum* constitutes the sole matter of the Sacrament, it follows that the *traditio instrumentorum* is a non-essential ceremony added by the Church and that the subdiaconate and the four minor orders, in

9 Sess. VII, can. 1; cfr. Pohle-Preuss, *The Sacraments,* Vol. I, pp. 101 sqq.

10 Cfr. Benedict XIV, *De Synod. Dioeces.,* VIII, 10, 10.

11 *De Sacram. in Genere,* disp. 2, sect. 5, n. 85 sqq.

12 *De Sacram. in Genere,* 4th ed., pp. 47 sq., Rome 1888.

13 See the Innsbruck *Zeitschrift für kath. Theologie,* 1901, pp. 621 sqq.

14 Cfr. Pohle-Preuss, *The Sacraments,* Vol. I, pp. 107 sqq.

which there is no imposition of hands, are not sacramental rites.

b) The view held by Dominicus Soto, Capreolus, Gregory of Valentia,[15] Gonet, Estius, and many other Scholastic theologians, that the delivery of the instruments constitutes the matter of the Sacrament, whereas the imposition of hands is accidental and merely a matter of integrity (*materia integrans*), may now be considered obsolete.

The advocates of this theory derived their main argument from the *Decretum pro Armenis* of Pope Eugene IV, which says: "The sixth Sacrament is Order, of which the matter is that by the giving of which Order is conferred, as the priesthood by the giving of the chalice with the wine and the paten with the bread; the diaconate by handing [to the ordinand] the Book of the Gospels; the subdiaconate by the giving of the empty chalice with an empty paten resting upon it," etc.[16] But the *Decretum pro Armenis* (drawn almost literally from St. Thomas' *Opusculum de Fidei Articulis et Septem Sacramentis*), while it possesses very high authority, is not an *ex-cathedra* decision, but merely a papal instruction issued for the purpose of effecting conformity between the Armenian and the Roman rites. Hence its characteristic reference to the Roman Ritual,

15 *De Ord.*, disp. 9, qu. 1.

16 *Decr. pro Armen.* (Denzinger-Bannwart, n. 701): "*Sextum sacramentum est ordinis, cuius materia est illud, per cuius traditionem confertur ordo, sicut presbyteratus traditur per calicis cum vino et patenae cum pane porrectionem; diaconatus vero per libri evangeliorum dationem; subdiaconatus vero per calicis vacui cum patena vacua superposita traditionem; et similiter de aliis,*" etc.

which expressly prescribes the imposition of hands, a practice that had long been in use among the Armenians.[17] Benedict XIV correctly estimates the import of the *Decretum* for our purpose when he says: " It is therefore necessary to admit that Pope Eugene spoke of the integrating and accessory matter and form [of the Sacrament], which he desired the Armenians to add to the imposition of hands long employed by them, in order that they might conform themselves to the custom of the Latin Church." [18]

In the light of this interpretation it is easy to refute Döllinger's specious contention that the *Decretum pro Armenis,* because of its false teaching on the subject of Holy Orders, furnishes an argument against the infallibility of the Pope.[19]

c) Bellarmine, De Lugo, Hallier, Vasquez, Maldonatus, Ledesma, Billuart, Berti, Gotti, and others hold that the imposition of hands and the delivery of the instruments conjointly constitute the matter of the Sacrament. This view has found two eminent modern defenders in Cardinal Billot [20] and Msgr. Gutberlet.[21]

Assuming that Christ, in instituting the Sacrament of Holy Orders, determined its matter and form only in a generic way, leaving the specific determination to the

17 See Adhémar d'Alès in the *Constructive Review,* Vol. IX (1921), No. 2.

18 *De Synod. Dioeces.,* VIII, 10, 8: " *Necesse est igitur fateri Eugenium locutum esse de materia et forma integrante et accessoria, quam optavit ab Armenis superaddi manuum impositioni iam diu ab illis adhibitae, ut Ecclesiae latinae moribus se accommodarent."*

19 Döllinger, *Der Papst und das Concil,* new edition under the title, *Das Papsttum,* by J. Friedrich, Munich 1892. See appendix I, *infra,* p. 243.

20 *De Sacram.,* Vol. II, 4th ed., thes. 30.

21 In Heinrich-Gutberlet, *Dogmat. Theologie,* Vol. X, pp. 288 sqq.

Church, the writers of this group describe the *traditio instrumentorum* as a palpable sign of the grace conferred by the *impositio manuum,* and therefore as a co-essential factor forming a moral whole with the *impositio.* The author of the *Supplementum* to the *Summa Theologica* [22] says that when a man is ordained to the priesthood, the imposition of hands symbolizes and bestows the power of absolution, while the delivery of the instruments (chalice and paten) symbolizes and bestows the power of consecration.

If we examine this theory in the light of the arguments adduced above under a), we find that it is not well founded. The Bible, the Fathers, the councils, and the ancient liturgies all agree that the imposition of hands alone is essential to the Sacrament of Holy Orders. As, however, the *pars tutior* must always be followed in the administration of the Sacraments, the Church in her ordinations strictly carries out the ceremony of the delivery of instruments.

2. THE FORM.—The difference of opinion existing with regard to the matter of Holy Orders involves a similar difference in regard to its form. If the imposition of hands constitutes the sole matter of the Sacrament, the form must be sought in the prayer accompanying this rite.

The sacred anointment which the Church uses in ordaining bishops and priests is an ancient ceremony, described by Pope St. Leo the Great, but it does not form part of the essential matter of the Sacrament and there-

22 *Supplementum,* qu. 37, art. 5.

fore does not affect its form, though it is well to remember that the Tridentine Council pronounced anathema against those who despise this beautiful rite.[23]

a) In ordaining a priest to the episcopacy, the consecrating bishop and his two assistants place the Book of the Gospels upon his neck and shoulders, touch his head with their hands, and together pronounce the words: *"Accipe Spiritum sanctum."* Then the consecrator alone recites the following prayer: *"Propitiare, Domine, supplicationibus nostris et inclinato super hunc famulum tuum cornu gratiae sacerdotalis benedictionis tuae in eum infunde virtutem."* Here we have two separate and distinct prayers,— one imperative in form, the other precatory. Church historians tell us that the imperative form, *"Accipe Spiritum sanctum,"* which is likewise employed in the ordination of priests and deacons, is of comparatively recent origin and does not occur in the ancient rituals of the Latin or the euchologia of the Greek Church.[24] Hence it is reasonable to conclude that the second prayer, which is recited by the consecrating bishop alone, embodies the sacramental form of episcopal ordination. This does not derogate from the Tridentine canon which declares: "If anyone saith that, by sacred ordination, the Holy Ghost is not given, and that vainly therefore do the bishops say, 'Receive ye the Holy Ghost,' . . . let him be anathema." [25] For to say that the Holy Ghost is given in the rite of ordination is not tantamount to saying that He is imparted through this particular set of words. In the second prayer the phrase *"cornu gratiae sacerdotalis"* also signifies the power of the Holy Ghost.

23 Sess. XXIII, can. 5.

24 Martène, *De Antiquis Ecclesiae Ritibus*, Vol. II, pp. 21, 27.

25 Sess. XXIII, can. 4: *"Si quis dixerit, per sacram ordinationem non dari Spiritum Sanctum ac proinde frustra episcopos dicere: 'Accipe Spiritum Sanctum' . . .; anathema sit."* (Denzinger-Bannwart, n. 964.)

The same argument applies to the two other hierarchical orders,— the priesthood and the diaconate.

b) There is, however, some difficulty in regard to the former, since the rite of ordination to the priesthood seems to contain no less than three distinct impositions. First the bishop silently lays both hands on the head of the ordinand. The same is done by all the priests who are present. Then bishop and priests together extend their right hands, while the former prays: *" Oremus, fratres carissimi, Deum Patrem omnipotentem, ut super hunc famulum suum, quem ad presbyterii munus elegit, caelestia dona multiplicet et, quod eius dignatione suscipit, ipsius consequatur auxilio. Per Christum Dominum nostrum, Amen.— Exaudi nos, quaesumus, Domine Deus noster, et super hunc famulum tuum benedictionem sancti Spiritus et gratiae sacerdotalis infunde virtutem."* This part of the ceremony is known as *manuum extensio* or χειροτονία. After Communion, the bishop imposes his hands upon the candidate for the third time and says: *" Accipe Spiritum Sanctum, quorum remiseris peccata, remittuntur eis, et quorum retinueris, retenta sunt."* This is the *impositio manuum* proper, or χειροθεσία. The question arises: Which of these three rites, with its accompanying prayers, is sacramental? The first laying-on of hands cannot be essential, because it is accomplished silently. Van Rossum considers it as merely a part of the second imposition. The third and final *impositio* seems equally non-essential, because the candidate has already exercised the sacerdotal power by co-consecrating the bread and wine, and for the further reason that this rite is unknown to the Greek Church. Hence the prayer accompanying the last *impositio manuum,* or χειροθεσία, cannot be the form of the Sacrament, and the conclusion is inevitable that the matter of the Sacrament consists in the second imposition — the *manuum extensio,* or χειροτονία, conceived as a continuation of the physical contact embodied in the first.[26] If this rite constitutes the matter, then the accompanying words of the bishop must constitute the form of the Sacrament. We must reject as inconsistent the opinion of those who hold that all three of these ceremonies, because intrinsically connected with one another and together constituting one moral act, with their accompanying prayers (as partial forms) are essential to the validity of the Sacrament.[27]

c) The ordination rite for the diaconate contains only one imposition of hands, and consequently the sacramental form must be contained in the prayer *" Domine sancte Pater omnipotens,"* which accompanies this ceremony. It is not likely that the form is in the words *" Accipe Spiritum Sanctum ad robur et ad resistendum diabolo,"* etc., because this phrase, as Martène has shown, is " hardly four hundred years old." [28]

The ordination rite for the subdiaconate contains no *impositio manuum,* but merely a *traditio instrumentorum,* and consequently cannot claim to be sacramental.[29] This applies *a fortiori* to the four minor orders.

3. ANGLICAN ORDERS.—The question regarding the validity of Anglican Orders gave rise to a long controversy, which was definitively decided by Leo XIII in his dogmatic Bull *"Apostolicae curae"* of Sept. 13, 1896.

26 Cfr. *Greg IX Decret.,* l. I, tit. 16, cap. 3: *" Presbyter et diaconus quum ordinantur, manus impositionem tactu corporali recipiunt."*

27 Cfr. Ballerini, *Opus Theol. Moral.,* ed. Palmieri, Vol. V, 3rd ed., pp. 716 sq., Prati 1900. See Appendix II, p. 244, *infra.*

28 On the rite of ordination for deacons see Gihr, *Die hl. Sakramente der kath. Kirche,* Vol. II, 2nd ed., pp. 319 sqq.

29 Denzinger-Bannwart, n. 153: *" Subdiaconus quum ordinatur, quia manus impositionem non accipit, pa-*

The decision against the validity of these orders rests, not on the historic fact that William Barlow, who consecrated Dr. Matthew Parker, the first Anglican archbishop of Canterbury, at Lambeth on Dec. 7, 1559, was not a validly consecrated bishop, but on the dogmatic fact that the Edwardine rite of ordination, drawn up in 1549, had purposely altered the sacramental form of Holy Orders so as to exclude the intention of bestowing the power of consecration and absolution. This perversion, together with the manifest lack of a proper intention, deprives the rite of its sacramental effect.[30] " It is clear," says St. Thomas, " that if any substantial part of the sacramental form be suppressed, the essential sense of the words is destroyed, and consequently the Sacrament becomes invalid." [31] This principle explains the custom existing long before the Leonine decision (practically since 1554) of unconditionally reordaining converted Anglican clergymen. The orders conferred under the Edwardine Ordinal were declared null and void by Paul VI as early as 1555.[32]

tenam de episcopi manu accipiat vacuam et calicem vacuum."

30 Cfr. Pohle-Preuss, *The Sacraments*, Vol. I, pp. 110 sq.

31 *Summa Theol.*, III, qu. 60, art. 8: " *Manifestum est autem quod si diminuatur aliquid eorum quae sunt de substantia formae sacramentalis, tollitur debitus sensus verborum, et ideo non perficitur sacramentum.*"

32 On the question of Anglican Orders see A. Boudinhon, *Sur les Ordinations Anglicanes*, Paris 1894; S. F. Smith, S. J., *The Bull on Anglican Orders*, London 1897; Idem, in the *Catholic Encyclopedia*, Vol. I, pp. 491–498; S. Brandi, S. J., *Delle Ordinazioni Anglicane*, 4th ed., Rome 1908; (cfr. *Am. Eccl. Review*, XVI, 1897); Von Hackelberg-Landau, *Die anglikanischen Weihen und ihre neueste Apologie*, Graz 1897; J. Souben, *Nouvelle Théologie Dogmatique*, Vol. VIII, pp. 77 sqq., Paris 1905; H. C. Semple, S.J., *Anglican Ordinations: Theology of Rome and Canterbury in a Nutshell*, New York 1906; V. Hornyold, S.J., *Catholic Orders and Anglican Orders*, London 1917; A. S. Barnes, *Bishop Barlow and Anglican Orders*, London 1922.

SECTION 3

SACRAMENTAL EFFECTS

1. INCREASE OF SANCTIFYING GRACE.—Being a Sacrament of the living, Holy Orders must be received in the state of sanctifying grace (*gratia prima*), which it augments (*gratia secunda*). The *Decretum pro Armenis* says: "The effect [of this Sacrament is] an increase of grace, [given] in order that one may be a fit minister." [1] The phrase *"ut quis sit idoneus minister"* points to an additional grace pertaining to the sacerdotal office (*gratia sacramentalis*).

Wherein does this special grace consist? It is a claim, based on the possession of sanctifying grace and the sacramental character, to those actual graces which render the recipient fit to administer his office. The Tridentine Council [2] describes this grace as the reception of the Holy Ghost *per modum sacramenti*.

2. THE SACRAMENTAL CHARACTER.—Like Baptism and Confirmation, Holy Orders imprints an indelible mark on the soul of the recipient.

---

[1] " *Effectus* [*est*] *augmentum gratiae, ut quis sit idoneus minister."* (Denzinger-Bannwart, n. 701).

[2] Sess. XXIII, can. 4.— *V. infra,* No. 2.

This is the so-called sacramental character,[3] which renders repetition impossible and bars the subject from returning to the lay state. The Council of Trent expressly defines: "If anyone saith that, by sacred ordination, the Holy Ghost is not given, and that vainly therefore do the bishops say, 'Receive ye the Holy Ghost,' or that a character is not imprinted by that ordination, or that he who was once a priest can again become a layman; let him be anathema."[4]

a) The second of these effects is called by Suarez[5] the *effectus primarius* or primary object of the Sacrament, because the character is the foundation of ecclesiastical jurisdiction. That this is so can be demonstrated from St. Paul's exhortation to Timothy to revive (*resuscitare,* ἀναζωπυρεῖν) the grace given him by the imposition of hands. This exhortation presupposes two things:—first, the existence of a form which is permanent and cannot be lost, and, secondly, the possibility of forfeiting a grace connected therewith. The form is the sacramental character; the grace, sanctifying grace.

b) For the argument from Tradition see Pohle-Preuss, *The Sacraments,* Vol. I, pp. 79 sqq.

---

[3] *V.* Pohle-Preuss, *The Sacraments,* Vol. I, pp. 76 sqq.

[4] Sess. XXIII, can. 4: " *Si quis dixerit, per sacram ordinationem non dari Spiritum sanctum ac proinde frustra episcopos dicere: Accipe Spiritum sanctum, aut per eam non imprimi characterem vel eum qui sacerdos semel fuit, laicum rursus fieri posse, anathema sit.*" (Denzinger-Bannwart, n. 964).

[5] *Comment. in S. Theol.,* III, disp. 11, sect. 1.

Although the Fathers expressly admit the validity of ordination when given by heretics, the early history of the Church offers several examples which seem practically to deny what St. Augustine and other Patristic writers positively affirm. Peter Lombard [6] was so perplexed by the many reported cases of reordination that he declared the validity of heretical ordinations to be an " insoluble " question. St. Thomas,[7] on the other hand, gave cogent reasons for accepting the ordinations of heretics as valid, and his view has been adopted by nearly all later theologians. Up to the close of the Middle Ages this question was an open one and hard to decide " on account of the difficulty of determining the conditions of valid ordination and legitimate succession." [8] To-day we are better able to solve the difficulty. There can be no doubt that in ancient times priests ordained by heretical ministers were frequently reordained on the ground that their orders were null and void. It should be noted, however, that these reordinations were often the work of ignorant, vindictive or jealous bishops. The Roman pontiffs, in condemning heretical ordinations as " *irritae,*" " *vanae,*" " *inanes,*" or " *nullae,*" in most instances probably meant that they were illicit because given or received in the state of mortal sin and by men lacking ecclesiastical jurisdiction, who could not authorize the recipient lawfully to exercise his sacerdotal powers. Not infrequently when a bishop imposed hands on a priest who had returned to the true fold from some heretical sect, he did not mean to reordain, but simply to receive him back into the fold and grant him permission to exercise the powers received in ordination.[9]

6 *Sent.,* IV, dist. 20.

7 *Summa Theol., Supplement.,* qu. 38, art. 2.

8 P. Schanz, *Die Lehre von den hl. Sakramenten,* p. 694, Freiburg 1893.

9 Cfr. Fulbert, *Ep.,* 13 (Migne, *P. L.,* CXLI, 207); L. Saltet, *Les Réordinations,* Paris 1907.

c) How is the sacramental character of Holy
Orders related to that of Baptism and Confirmation? The answer to this (purely speculative)
question may be gathered from what we have said
in a previous volume of this treatise,[10] when dealing with the sacramental character in general.
The character imprinted by Holy Orders is not
merely an extension or a development of the
other two; it is a new quality communicated to
the soul, by virtue of which the subject receives
certain special faculties, the priesthood is established in the Church, and the clergy set apart from
the laity.

Needless to say, the character of Holy Orders presupposes the baptismal character as its necessary foundation.
As for the character peculiar to Confirmation, it is required as a condition for Holy Orders merely by ecclesiastical precept.

It is somewhat more difficult to determine the mutual
relations existing between the characters of the episcopate,
the priesthood, and the diaconate, because these three
are really but one, imprinted by one and the same Sacrament.

Speaking of the episcopal and the sacerdotal characters,
Vasquez [11] expresses the opinion that the two are substantially identical, and that the only difference between
them is that the former bestows greater power than the latter. This hardly solves the problem at issue, for the reception of episcopal power must be based on some intrinsic

quality of the soul and consequently postulates a character distinct from that imprinted by the priesthood. Such is, indeed, the common teaching of theologians. A few (Paludanus, Coninck, Sylvester Maurus) hold that the episcopal character consists in a purely modal extension of the sacerdotal character. But this is improbable for the reason that the power of conferring ordination is so great and so clearly distinct from the ordinary powers of the priesthood that it demands a separate character.[12]

Whether the episcopal character can be imprinted on a soul that has not yet received the sacerdotal character is open to debate. Bosco, Thomassin, Martène, Schell, and other writers maintain that one need not be a priest to be capable of receiving episcopal consecration. The more common opinion, however, is that one must have received ordination to the priesthood before he can be consecrated. This last-mentioned opinion must be followed in practice. The historical arguments that have been drawn against it from certain utterances of Popes Zosimus and Celestine the First are unconvincing.[13]

3. THE BESTOWAL OF HIGHER POWERS.—Although the character imprinted by Holy Orders of itself includes certain higher powers, the latter are more correctly regarded as *effects* of the Sacrament, because character and power, while reciprocal, are by no means synonymous terms.

That is to say: — while the sacramental character and spiritual power as a rule go hand in hand, they may

---

12 For a more complete treatment of this topic the student is referred to Tepe, *Inst. Theol.,* Vol. IV, pp. 573 sqq., Paris 1896.

13 Cfr. De Augustinis, *De Re Sacrament.,* Vol. II, 2nd ed., pp. 541 sqq.

exist separately. Our Lord Jesus Christ undoubtedly exercised the plenitude of spiritual power, though he had not received the sacramental character. On the other hand, bishops and priests retain the character in Heaven, though they no longer have power to consecrate, absolve, or ordain there.

The faculties attached to the sacramental character of Holy Orders vary according to the rank of the bearer. A bishop has greater powers than a priest, the priest's powers exceed those of the deacon, and so on to the lowest degree. In a similar manner the powers attaching to the lower orders decrease by degrees. Note, however, that in the case of the subdiaconate and minor orders the power conferred by the ordination rite does not flow from the sacramental character because these orders are not Sacraments.

CHAPTER II

DIVISION OF ORDERS

There are eight different orders: bishop, priest, deacon, subdeacon, acolyte, exorcist, lector, and porter or door-keeper (*ostiarius*). All these are expressly mentioned by the Fourth Council of Carthage (398). The five lowest are of ecclesiastical institution and therefore not Sacraments.

The higher three, called hierarchical orders, were instituted by our Lord Himself, and therefore at least one of them must be a true Sacrament because ordination is a true Sacrament. Which one, is a question that remains to be examined.

The dogmatic teaching of the Tridentine Council on Holy Orders is as follows:

(1) "Besides the priesthood, there are in the Catholic Church other orders, both greater and smaller, by which, as by certain steps, entry is made into the priesthood." [1]

(2) "In the Catholic Church there is a hierarchy, instituted by divine ordination, consisting of bishops, priests, and ministers." [2]

(3) "Order, or sacred ordination, is truly and properly a Sacrament instituted by Christ." [3]

[1] Sess. XXIII, can. 2.
[2] Sess. XXIII, can. 6.
[3] Sess. XXIII, can. 3.

(4) Bishops are superior to, and have greater power than, priests.[4]

We shall, therefore, treat first of the Episcopate (Sect. 1), second, of the Priesthood (Sect. 2), third, of the Diaconate (Sect. 3), and fourth, of the Subdiaconate and the Four Minor Orders (Sect. 4).

4 Sess. XXIII, can. 7.

SECTION 1

THE EPISCOPATE

The Tridentine Council defines (1) that "bish-ops are superior to priests," and (2) that "they have the power of confirming and ordaining." That episcopal consecration is a true Sacrament follows as a theological conclusion.

Thesis I: The episcopate is, by divine institution, an order distinct from, and superior to, the priesthood.

This proposition embodies an article of faith.

Proof. The divine institution of the episcopate and its superiority to the priesthood were denied by Aërius in the fourth century, by Marsilius of Padua in the fourteenth,[1] and by the followers of Wiclif and Hus in the fifteenth.[2] Against these later heretics the Council of Trent defined: "If anyone saith that in the Catholic Church there is not a hierarchy instituted by divine ordination, consisting of bishops, priests, and ministers, let him be anathema."[3] And: "If anyone saith

---

1 Cfr. Denzinger-Bannwart, n. 498.
2 *Ibid.*, n. 675.
3 Sess. XXIII, can. 6: " *Si quis dixerit, in Ecclesia catholica non esse hierarchiam divinâ ordina-* *tione institutam, quae constat ex episcopis, presbyteris et ministris, anathema sit."* (Denzinger-Bann-wart, n. 966).

that bishops are not superior to priests, . . . let him be anathema." [4]

The Council does not expressly say that the superiority of the episcopate over the priesthood is divinely instituted, but this proposition is deducible from the nature of the episcopal faculties, especially that of giving confirmation and ordination.[5]

a) The hierarchic distinction of the episcopate and its superiority as compared to the priesthood cannot be proved from the name *episcopus* (ἐπίσκοπος), because the terms ἐπίσκοπος, πρεσβύτερος, and διάκονος are used loosely and oftentimes synonymously in the New Testament.[6] A convincing argument for the dogmatic teaching of the Church can, however, be drawn from the functions attributed to the episcopal office.

Franzelin attempts to show [7] that while the bishops were sometimes called πρεσβύτεροι, simple priests were never called ἐπίσκοποι. But the argument is not entirely conclusive, as usage varied in the primitive Church.[8] The functions attributed to bishops are a much better criterion.

The pastoral letters of St. Paul show that some of the disciples ordained by the Apostles exercised precisely those prerogatives by which the episcopate is distinguished from the priesthood, *i. e.* the power of ordaining priests and ecclesiastical jurisdiction. Thus Barnabas ordained

---

4 Sess. XXIII, can. 7: "*Si quis dixerit, episcopos non esse presbyteris superiores, . . . anathema sit.*"

5 *V. infra*, Thesis II.

6 Cfr. 1 Cor. III, 5; 2 John 1; 1 Pet. V, 1.

7 *De Ecclesia Christi*, thes. 16, 2nd ed., Rome 1907.

8 Cfr. H. Bruders, S.J., *Die Verfassung der Kirche bis zum Jahre 175 n. Christus*, pp. 360 sqq., Mayence 1904.

priests;[9] Titus was left for the same purpose in Crete;[10] Timothy was admonished not to impose hands lightly,[11] and so forth.

It was the will of Christ that the power which He had given to His Apostles should be transferred by them to their successors; consequently the episcopate is divinely instituted.

b) The episcopate is clearly marked in ancient Tradition as an independent, superior, and divinely instituted, monarchical office.

Nothing can be deduced in favor of our thesis from the *Didache,* the *Shepherd of Hermas,* or the letters of Clement of Rome, because in these sub-Apostolic writings the term ἐπίσκοπος, which we found in the New Testament, has not yet narrowed down to its more specific meaning. But we have an important witness in St. Ignatius of Antioch ($+$ 117), who clearly distinguishes three orders in the hierarchy. He says in his Epistle to the Magnesians: " I exhort you: — Be zealous to do all things in harmony with God, with the bishop presiding in the place of God, and the presbyters in the place of the council of the Apostles, and the deacons, who are most dear to me, entrusted with the service of Jesus Christ." [12] He attributes the superiority of the episcopal order to the fact that there is but one bishop in each diocese. " Be careful, therefore," he says, " to use one Eucharist, for there is one flesh of our Lord Jesus Christ, and one cup for union with His blood, one altar, as there is one bishop with the presbytery and the deacons." [13] That the episcopate exists by divine ordination is taught in the same writ-

---

9 Acts XIV, 22.
10 Tit. I, 5 sqq.
11 1 Tim. III, 1 sqq.; V, 22.

12 *Ad Magn.,* 6.
13 *Ad Philad.,* 4.

er's Epistle to the Ephesians. "The bishops," he avers, "who have been appointed throughout the world, are by the will of Jesus Christ. . . . For every one whom the Master of the house sends to do his business, we ought to receive as Him who sent him. Therefore it is clear that we must regard the bishop as the Lord himself." [14]

The testimony of St. Ignatius sufficiently refutes the assertion that the episcopate was but just springing into existence at the beginning of the second century. Bardenhewer sums up the argument from early Tradition as follows: "Hegesippus,[15] and soon after him Irenaeus,[16] draw up a list of Roman bishops, beginning with the Apostles. The existence of the episcopate about the middle of the second century is proved by overwhelming and explicit testimony. For the beginning of the second century we have the authority of St. Ignatius, the very text of whose letters precludes the possibility of a forgery. We nowhere hear of hindrances or difficulties in the way of the episcopate, or of quarrels or combats between bishops and priests. The episcopate is invariably introduced as a traditional institution of acknowledged legitimacy, which needs no proof." [17]

Among the many later Patristic testimonies we will mention only the famous dictum of St. Cyprian that "The bishop is in the Church, and the Church is in the bishop, and if any one is not with the bishop, he is not in the Church." [18]

---

[14] *Ad Ephes.*, III, 6.

[15] Cfr. Eusebius, *Hist. Eccles.*, IV, 22, 3.

[16] *Adv. Haer.*, III, 3.

[17] *Gesch. d. altkirchlichen Literatur*, Vol. I, p. 134, Freiburg 1902.

[18] *Ep.*, 66, 8: "*Unde scire debes, episcopum in ecclesia esse et ecclesiam in episcopo, et si quis cum episcopo non sit, in ecclesia non esse.*" (Cfr. De Augustinis, *De Re Sacrament.*, Vol. II, 2nd ed., pp. 440 sqq.)

Thesis II: The superiority of the episcopate over the priesthood is based mainly upon the power to confirm and ordain.

This proposition may be qualified as *"sententia certa."*

Proof. The Tridentine Council enumerates the following as specifically episcopal functions: "Bishops . . . administer the Sacrament of Confirmation, ordain the ministers of the Church, and can perform very many other things, over which functions others of an inferior order have no power." [19] The same holy Synod pronounces anathema against "anyone who saith that bishops are not superior to priests, or that they have not the power of confirming and ordaining, or that the power which they possess is common to them and priests." [20] Consequently, the superiority of the episcopal over the sacerdotal office is based principally upon the power of confirming and ordaining.

Since, however, the power of confirming can be granted to simple priests by papal dispensation,[21] the really distinctive and unique prerogative of the bishop, so far as

---

[19] Sess. XXIII, cap. 4: *"Episcopos sacramentum confirmationis conferre, ministros Ecclesiae ordinare atque alia pleraque peragere ipsos posse, quarum functionum potestatem reliqui inferioris ordinis nullam habent."* (Denzinger-Bannwart, n. 960).

[20] Sess. XXIII, can. 7: *"Si quis*

dixerit, episcopos non esse presbyteris superiores vel non habere potestatem confirmandi et ordinandi, vel eam quam habent illis esse cum presbyteris communem, . . . anathema sit."* (Denzinger-Bannwart, n. 967).

[21] *V.* Pohle-Preuss, *The Sacraments,* Vol. I, pp. 310 sqq.

the *potestas ordinis* is concerned, is his power to ordain priests. From this power spring all other episcopal prerogatives : — the bishop's position as the divinely appointed head of his diocese [22] and the center of unity both in faith and discipline; his character as a successor of the Apostles; his capacity of father of his priests and the faithful entrusted to their care; his right to represent his diocese at provincial, plenary, and ecumenical councils, etc.[23]

a) That bishops alone have the power to ordain priests is amply confirmed by Tradition.

Aërius of Sebaste, an Arian priest, whose former friend and rival Eustathius had been raised to the episcopal dignity, maintained that bishops and priests were absolutely equal in all things. St. Epiphanius ($+$ 403), in his " Medicine Chest," commonly called " *Haereses,*" refuted this contention as follows : " What sense is there in that? The order of bishops has for its chief purpose to produce new fathers, for its business is to propagate fathers in the Church. The other [*i. e.* the priesthood], unable to engender fathers, in the laver of regeneration brings forth sons of the Church, but not fathers and teachers. How would it be possible for [priests] to make other priests, as they have not the right to lay on hands?"[24]

St. John Chrysostom ($+$ 407) says : " Between bishops and priests there is hardly any difference, . . . by the power of ordination alone are the former superior [to the latter], and only this they seem to have more than the presbyters."[25]

[22] Cfr. Acts XX, 28: " *Spiritus sanctus posuit episcopos regere Ecclesiam Dei.*"

[23] Cfr. Berardi, *De Episcopo,* Bologna 1891.

[24] *De Haeres.,* 75, n. 3.

[25] *Hom. in I. Tim.,* 11.

Ecclesiastical practice agreed with this teaching. His‑ tory knows of no case in which the Church acknowledged the validity of higher orders when conferred by a simple priest. When St. Athanasius ($+$ 373) was accused of sacrilege for having permitted the consecrated chalice to be broken during a mass celebrated by a certain Ischyras, he proved that Ischyras had been invalidly ordained by the pseudo-bishop Colluthos, whereupon his enemies re‑ luctantly dropped the charge, because "the hands of Colluthos were without authority."[26] "Whence is this presbyter Ischyras?" the Saint asks. "Who ordained him? Colluthos, perhaps? . . . But it is known to all, and doubted by none, that Colluthos died as a presbyter, and his hands were without authority, and all ordained by him during the schism were sent back to the lay state."[27]

b) A difficulty arises from certain utterances of St. Jerome ($+$ 420), who exalts the priesthood at the ex‑ pense of the episcopate in such exaggerated terms that the Scotch Presbyterians boldly cite him as a witness to their non-prelatical form of church government. St. Jerome's attitude must be judged in the light of his per‑ sonal relations with Bishop John of Jerusalem and of the current practice of exalting the archdeacons at the ex‑ pense of priests in the administration of Church af‑ fairs.[28]

The strangest passage in the Saint's writings runs as fol‑ lows: *"Idem est ergo presbyter qui et episcopus, et antequam diaboli instinctu studia [i. e. factiones] in re‑ ligione fierent et diceretur in populis: Ego sum Pauli, ego Apollo, ego autem Cephae, communi presbyterorum*

---

26 Cfr. Pohle-Preuss, *The Sacra‑ ments*, Vol. II, p. 260.

27 *Apol. c. Arian.*, n. 12.

28 Cfr. Schwane, *Dogmengeschich‑ te*, Vol. II, 2nd ed., pp. 851 sqq., Freiburg 1895.

*consilio ecclesiae gubernabantur. . . . Sicut ergo presby-
teri sciunt se ex Ecclesiae consuetudine ei, qui sibi prae-
positus fuerit, esse subiectos, ita episcopi noverint se magis
consuetudine quam dispositionis dominicae veritate presbyteris esse maiores et in commune debere Ecclesiam
regere, imitantes Moysen, qui quum haberet in potestate
solum praeesse populo Israel, septuaginta elegit, cum quibus populum iudicaret."* [29] St. Jerome here has in view
the *potestas iurisdictionis* rather than the *potestas ordinis*
of bishops. He demands a more democratic administration of church affairs and greater power for the priesthood. But his chief complaint is directed against the
usurpations of the deacons: *"Audio quendam in tantam
erupisse vecordiam, ut diaconos presbyteris, i. e. episcopis
anteferret. Apostolus perspicue docet eosdem esse presbyteros quos episcopos. . . . Quod autem postea unus
electus est, qui caeteris praeponeretur, in schismatis remedium factum est."* [30] St. Jerome was undoubtedly justified in protesting against the arrogance of these deacons;
but he was wrong in belittling the episcopal office in favor
of the priesthood. In spite of these utterances, however,
Catholics have never suspected him of being a follower of
Aërius. For he unequivocally admits that the bishops
alone have the power to ordain,[31] and his very assertion
that the bishops are superior to priests "more through
custom than by divine institution" shows that at heart he
believed in the divine institution of the episcopate.[32]

Thesis III: The rite of episcopal consecration is a true Sacrament.

[29] *In Tit.*, I, 5.
[30] *Ep. ad Evangel.*, 146, n. 1.
[31] *Ibid.*: *"Quid enim facit exceptâ ordinatione episcopus, quod
presbyter non faciat?"* (Migne,
P. L., XXII, 1193).

[32] Cfr. Tixeront, *History of Dogmas*, Vol. II, pp. 325 sq., St. Louis
1914; Billuart, *De Sacramento Ordinis*, diss. 4, art. 1, obj. 2; De Augustinis, *De Re Sacrament.*, Vol. II,
2nd ed., pp. 449 sqq.

This proposition embodies a theological conclusion.

Proof. Scholastic writers disagree with regard to the sacramental character of episcopal consecration. Peter Lombard, Alexander of Hales, Blessed Albertus Magnus, St. Bonaventure, St. Thomas,[33] Duns Scotus, and others deny, while William of Auxerre, Durandus, Paludanus, Navarrus, Cardinal Cajetan, and Gabriel Biel affirm it. The later Schoolmen, with the sole exception of Dominicus Soto, defended the affirmative view so vigorously that Peter Soto did not hesitate to say that it was *"certâ fide tenenda,"*[34] and Cardinal Bellarmine characterized it as *"certissima."*[35] To-day our thesis is universally accepted by Catholic divines as a *conclusio theologica.* The arguments in its favor are, indeed, quite convincing.

a) That there is a Sacrament of Order was demonstrated above[36] from St. Paul's Epistles to Timothy. Now, according to the unanimous interpretation of the Fathers and Doctors of the Church, the Apostle speaks in that Epistle of the ordination of bishops.[37] Consequently, the ordination of bishops, or episcopal consecration, is a true Sacrament.

[33] St. Bonaventure, *In Sent.,* IV, dist. 24, qu. 3; St. Thomas, *Summa Theol., Supplement.,* qu. 40, art. 5.
[34] *De Instit. Sacerd.,* sect. 4.
[35] *De Ord.,* c. 5.
[36] *V. supra,* Ch. 1, Sect. 1.
[37] 1 Tim. IV, 11 sqq.

St. John Chrysostom says: " [St. Paul] here speaks not of presbyters, but of bishops; for the presbyters did not ordain the bishop." [38] St. Thomas takes the same view. He says in his commentary on the second Epistle to Timothy: " ' Which is in thee by the imposition of my hands,' that is to say, by whom he was ordained a bishop, in which imposition of hands the grace of the Holy Ghost was given him." [39]

This argument cannot be shattered by the assertion that St. Paul, in imposing hands on Timothy, merely ordained him to the priesthood, and that the episcopal dignity was added later and is an entirely non-sacramental complement. Timothy had the power of ordaining bishops, and this power could not have come to him by a mere Apostolic command, but must have been based on the episcopal character, which is inseparably bound up with the Sacrament of Orders.[40]

If episcopal consecration were not a true Sacrament and if it did not imprint a character on the soul of the recipient, the hierarchic distinction between the episcopate and the priesthood could not be of divine institution. The Church can take away what she herself has given (e. g. the dignity of an abbot, ecclesiastical jurisdiction); but she cannot take away the power of conferring Holy Orders. An excommunicated bishop can ordain validly even against her will, whereas no ordinary priest can ordain even with papal permission. It follows that episcopal consecration imprints on the soul a sacramental character and is, therefore, a true Sacrament.

b) The Fathers, whenever they treat of the

38 *In I. Tim.*, IV, 14.

39 *Expos. in II. Tim.*, cap. I, lect. 3: " ' *Quae est in te per impositio-nem manuum mearum* ': *a quo scil. ordinatus erat episcopus, in qua manus impositione data est ei gratia Spiritus sancti.*"

40 *V. supra*, Ch. I, Sect. 3, No. 2.

Sacrament of Holy Orders, have in mind principally episcopal consecration, because they regard the bishop as *the* priest *par excellence.*

Cardinal Bellarmine says [41] that to deny the sacramentality of episcopal consecration would endanger the Patristic argument for the existence of the Sacrament of Holy Orders, because the Fathers as a rule base their discussion of the subject on this rite. Nor is there any lack of express testimony in support of our thesis. St. Augustine, for instance, says concerning the readmission of the Donatistic bishops: "The Baptism they give is not theirs, but Christ's. The invocation made upon their heads when they were consecrated bishops is the invocation of God, not of Donatus. I do not receive him as a bishop upon whose head, at ordination, Donatus was invoked. In an erring and deserting soldier the crime is his own, whereas the character is that of the emperor." [42]

c) The Tridentine Council proves the existence of the Sacrament of Holy Orders from the consecration of Timothy at the hands of St. Paul.

The Council says: "Whereas, by the testimony of Scripture, . . . it is clear that grace is conferred by sacred ordination, . . . no one ought to doubt that Order is truly and properly one of the seven Sacraments of holy

41 *De Ord.,* c. 5.

42 *Serm. ad Caesar. Eccl. Plebem,* n. 2 (Migne, *P. L.,* XLIII, 691): "*Baptismus non est ipsorum, sed Christi. Invocatio nominis super caput ipsorum, quando ordinantur episcopi, invocatio illa Dei est, non Donati. Non eum suscipio episcopum, si quando est ordinatus, super caput eius Donatus est invocatus. In errante et deserente milite crimen est desertoris, character autem non est desertoris, sed imperatoris.*"— Other testimonies quoted by Bellarmine, *De Ord.,* c. 3 and 5.

Church; for the Apostle says: ' I admonish thee that thou stir up the grace of God, which is in thee by the imposition of my hands." [43] Immediately afterward the holy Synod declares that " bishops . . . principally belong to this hierarchical order," and that " they are superior to priests." [44] Whence we may argue: As ordination to the priesthood is a Sacrament, [45] consecration to the episcopate must be a Sacrament *a fortiori*. This argument derives force from the fact that the Council pronounces anathema against those who maintain that " vainly do the bishops say [at ordination] : ' Receive ye the Holy Ghost.' " [46]

d) The objections of certain Scholastics can be easily refuted, nay, to some extent turned against their own position.

Their principal argument may be stated thus: All orders are directed towards the Holy Eucharist as their goal and exist for its sake. Now, since the bishop's power over the Body of Christ does not exceed that of the priest, he receives no new character with regard to the Eucharist, and therefore episcopal consecration is not a Sacrament. [47]

43 Sess. XXIII, cap. 3: " *Quum Scripturae testimonio . . . perspicuum sit, per sacram ordinationem . . . gratiam conferri, dubitare nemo debet, ordinem esse vere et proprie unum ex septem sacramentis; inquit enim Apostolus: Admoneo te, ut resuscites gratiam,"* etc. (Denzinger-Bannwart, n. 959).

44 *Ibid.,* cap. 4: " *Episcopos ad hunc hierarchicum ordinem praecipue pertinere . . . eosque presbyteris superiores esse.*" (Denzinger-Bannwat. n. 960).

45 *V. supra,* Sect. 2.

46 Sess. XXIII, can. 4.— Cfr. E. Furtner, *Das Verhältnis der Bischofsweihe zum hl. Sakrament des Ordo,* Munich 1861.

47 Cfr. St. Thomas, *Summa Theol., Suppl.,* qu. 40, art. 5: " *Ordo potest accipi dupliciter. Uno modq secundum quod est sacramentum, et sic ordinatur omnis ordo ad Eucharistiae sacramentum. Unde quum episcopus non habeat potestatem superiorem sacerdote, quantum ad hoc episcopatus non erit ordo.*"

Answer. The premise upon which this argument rests is open to dispute. But even if it were sound, we could retort that the bishop actually *has* greater power with regard to the Eucharist than the priest, *because he can communicate the power of consecration to others.*

Another objection of the early Schoolmen was this: No order can be truly sacramental that is so dependent upon another that the omission of one renders the other invalid. If episcopal consecration imprinted the sacramental character, a deacon could be raised to the episcopate without having first been ordained to the priesthood. But such proceeding would be invalid. Hence the episcopal consecration is not a Sacrament.

Answer. Whether a deacon could be validly consecrated without being first ordained, is a point in dispute. Setting this aside, let us regard the logic of the argument. Would it not be equally consistent to argue thus: If Confirmation imprints a character, an unbaptized person, who lacks the baptismal character, could be validly confirmed; this, however, is impossible; consequently Confirmation is not a Sacrament. There is confusion here between an indispensable prerequisite and the essence of the thing. The baptismal character is an indispensable prerequisite for Confirmation. In the same way the character of the priesthood is an indispensable prerequisite for episcopal consecration. Neither postulate affects the essence of the respective Sacrament.

Again, it is inconsistent to admit the sacramental character of the diaconate, nay to ascribe a character to the four minor orders, and to deny it to episcopal consecration. Does not the administration of Confirmation and Holy Orders, which is reserved to bishops, require greater power than the administration of Baptism, preaching, and serving Mass, which belong to the lower orders?

It is objected, finally: The Church knows but seven

orders, and seven sacramental ordinations corresponding to them, *viz.:* the four minor orders, the subdiaconate, the diaconate, and the priesthood. If the episcopate were a separate sacramental order, the title "*De Septem Ordinibus,*" over Session XXIII, cap. 2, of the Decrees of Trent would be wrong.

Answer. That there are seven orders is by no means so certain as that there are seven Sacraments. Many canonists and theologians do not hesitate to speak of eight orders. The title "*De Septem Ordinibus*" was not composed by the Fathers of the Tridentine Council, but added later. Nor would it decide the question at issue even if it were authentic. The chapter thus inscribed treats the episcopate as a separate and distinct order. This fact does not necessarily render the title "*De Septem Ordinibus*" false. For the priesthood can be conceived as a genus with two species, *viz.:* the *sacerdotium maius* or *primi ordinis, i. e.* the episcopate, and the *sacerdotium minus* or *secundi ordinis, i. e.* the priesthood proper. The bishop is essentially a priest, but he is at the same time the highest priest (*summus sacerdos*) in the diocese. Nevertheless there are, theologically speaking, not seven or eight Sacraments of Holy Orders, but only one.[48] The lower orders are simply so many stages leading up to the priesthood, which, in turn, culminates in the episcopate.[49]

Other questions pertaining to the episcopate, especially as regards the power of jurisdiction, belong to Fundamental Theology and Canon Law.

---

[48] *Conc. Trident.,* Sess. XXIII, c. 2: "*unum ex septem sacramentis.*"

[49] Cfr. St. Thomas, *Summa Theol., Suppl.,* qu. 37, art. 1, ad 2: "*Divisio ordinis non est totius integralis in suas partes neque totius universalis, sed totius potestativi, cuius haec est natura, quod totum secundum completam rationem est in uno, in aliis autem est aliquâ participatione ipsius.*" Cfr. De Augustinis, *De Re Sacrament.,* Vol. II, 2nd ed., pp. 422 sqq.; Palmieri, *De Romano Pontifice,* 2nd ed., pp. 84 sqq., Rome 1897.

SECTION 2

The priesthood, like the episcopate, is a distinct order, superior to the diaconate and instituted by Christ; and the rite of ordination to the priesthood is a true Sacrament.

Thesis I: The priesthood is a distinct order, divinely instituted, and superior to the diaconate by the power of consecration and absolution.

This proposition is *de fide*.

Proof. The Council of Trent defines: "If anyone saith that in the Catholic Church there is not a hierarchy, instituted by divine ordination, consisting of bishops, priests, and ministers, let him be anathema." [1] And again: "If anyone saith that there is not in the New Testament a visible and external priesthood, or that there is not any power of consecrating and offering the true Body and Blood of the Lord and of forgiving and retaining sins, . . . let him be anathema." [2]

---

[1] Sess. XXIII, can. 4.

[2] Sess. XXIII, can. 1: *"Si quis dixerit, non esse in Novo Testamento sacerdotium visibile et exter-* *num vel non esse potestatem aliquam consecrandi et offerendi verum corpus et sanguinem Domini et peccata remittendi et retinendi, . . .*

94

The distinction between the priesthood and the episcopate, and the superiority of the former over the diaconate, follows from what has been said of the prerogatives of bishops.[3]

That there is a priesthood distinct from the episcopate is attested by St. Ignatius of Antioch, as we have seen.[4] That this distinction does not appear in the earlier Patristic writings is owing to the fact that πρεσβύτερος was used interchangeably with ἐπίσκοπος.[5] In view of the law of historic continuity it is safe to assume, however, that an institution which was fully developed at the beginning of the second century, in principle existed already in the first. Consequently, the priesthood dates from the first century of the Christian era, and because of the powers with which it is endowed, can have been instituted by none other than our Divine Lord Himself.

Πρεσβύτερος as a technical term to designate the intermediary stage between bishop and deacon, had passed through a process of development already at the time of St. Ignatius. The stages of this process were probably as follows: " In itself the name πρεσβύτεροι designated the presiding officers in general; but long before this signification became generally accepted, popular usage had coined the name διάκονοι for the lowest class of church officials. For these the faithful first required a clear designation because they were in close contact with them every day. Thus, after this new name had become current, the πρεσβύτεροι were divided into διάκονοι and non-διάκονοι. The latter were then called ἐπίσκοποι or ποιμένες. When at the close of the Apostolic age (67–110), this terminology proved inadequate, the word ἐπίσκοπος,

anathema sit." (Denzinger-Bannwart, n. 961).

3 V. supra, Sect. 1.

4 V. supra, pp. 82 sq.

5 Cfr. Schanz, Die Lehre von den hl. Sakramenten, pp. 663 sqq., Freiburg 1893.

which, in contradistinction to πρεσβύτεροι, was generally employed in the singular number, became the technical term for the chief shepherd of a diocese; the middle class continued to be called ποιμένες or πρεσβύτεροι. The circumstance that πρεσβύτεροι was a technical term among Jews and pagans, helped to give this word the preference over others still in use for the aforesaid middle class of officials and thus to make it the *terminus technicus* for this class." [6]

Thesis II: Ordination to the priesthood is a true Sacrament.

This also is *de fide*.

Proof. The sacramentality of sacerdotal ordination, though never expressly defined as an article of faith, is guaranteed by the ordinary teaching office of the Church.

a) The Messianic priesthood prefigured in the Old Testament [7] is realized in the New. Christ commissioned His Apostles and their successors to offer the Eucharistic sacrifice and to forgive sins. From the beginning of the Christian era to the present day, priests as well as bishops have been ordained for both these functions (consecration and absolution). It follows that ordination to the priesthood possesses a character which can be imprinted only by a true Sacrament.

b) Ecclesiastical Tradition up to St. Cyprian,

6 H. Bruders, S.J., *Die Verfassung der Kirche bis 175 n. Chr.*, pp. 384 sq., Mayence 1904; cfr. Pesch, *Praelect. Dogmat.*, Vol. I, 4th ed., pp. 194 sqq., Freiburg 1909.

7 Cfr. Isaias LXVI, 21; Mal. I, 11; III, 3.

Tertullian, and St. Ignatius of Antioch confirms the existence of priests as a class distinct from and superior to the deacons.

Some of the later Fathers, notably St. Gregory of Nyssa, St. Chrysostom, St. Jerome, and St. Augustine, expressly designate the ordination rite for priests as a Sacrament and put it on a level with Baptism.[8] Moreover, with the sole exception of the Protestants, all Christian sects regard ordination to the priesthood as a Sacrament. They cannot have invented this belief; it must have come to them from the Catholic Church, to which they all at one time belonged.

c) The two arguments just given from Scripture and Tradition may be strengthened by a third, drawn from the teaching of Trent. The Council defines that "Order, or sacred ordination, is truly and properly a Sacrament instituted by Christ."[9] Now, one may without heresy (though not without error) doubt the sacramental character of the ordination rite for bishops and deacons. If the ordination rite for priests were not a true Sacrament, there would be no certainty of faith that a Sacrament of Holy Orders exists.

" Hence," concludes Benedict XIV,[10] " all theologians infer that it must be received as of divine faith that at

8 *V. supra*, pp. 59 sq.

9 Sess. XXIII, can. 3.

10 *De Synodo Dioeces.*, VIII, 9, 2: " *Hinc omnes theologi inferunt fide divinâ tenendum, saltem ordinationem sacerdotum esse verum et proprium sacramentum. Ad veritatem enim praedictae definitionis universalis necesse est, ut ea ad minimum complectatur ordinem praestantissimum, quale est sacerdotium.*"

least ordination to the priesthood is truly and properly a Sacrament. For in order that the aforesaid universal definition [of Trent] be true, it must necessarily include at least the foremost order, *i. e.* the priesthood."

Furthermore, the ordination rite for priests, according to all existing formularies, communicates the Holy Ghost. Now the Council of Trent pronounces anathema against those who deny that the Holy Ghost is given in sacred ordination when the bishop says, " Receive ye the Holy Ghost." [11] This means that the invisible rite is accompanied by and produces invisible grace.[12] Consequently, ordination to the priesthood is a true Sacrament.

Finally, the Council solemnly defines that " a character is imprinted by that ordination," and that " he who has once been a priest cannot again become a layman." [13] The imprinting of a character is a specifically sacramental effect. Hence ordination to the priesthood must be a true Sacrament.

The Church acts upon this belief *in praxi* when she refuses to deprive excommunicated or suspended priests of the power of consecration. Neither can she deprive any priest of that other sacerdotal power of forgiving sins, though she can and often does make its exercise invalid by withdrawing the necessary jurisdiction.

---

11 Sess. XXIII, can. 4: *". . . per sacram ordinationem dari Spiritum sanctum ac proinde episcopos non frustra dicere: Accipe Spiritum sanctum."*

12 *V. supra*, pp. 72 sqq.

13 Sess. XXIII, can. 4: *". . . per eam [ordinationem] imprimi characterem et eum, qui semel sacerdos fuit, laicum rursus fieri non posse."*

SECTION 3

THE DIACONATE

Deacons (*diaconi,* διάκονοι), in the technical sense of the term, are men who minister to bishops and priests in the discharge of their official duties.[1] Their functions, according to the Roman Pontifical, are "to serve at the altar, to baptize, and to preach." [2]

The Catholic teaching on the diaconate may be set forth in two theses, as follows:

Thesis I: The diaconate is a distinct order instituted by Christ, and the lowest among the three hierarchical orders.

Both propositions are of faith.

Proof. In inculcating the divine institution of a hierarchy "consisting of bishops, priests, and *ministers,*" [3] the Tridentine Council by the latter term undoubtedly meant to include deacons. That the diaconate is subordinate to the episcopate and the priesthood follows from the fact that

---

1 Cfr. Phil. I, 1; 1 Tim. III, 8 sqq.— On the name "*diaconus*" and its history see H. Bruders, S.J., *Die Verfassung der Kirche bis 175 n. Chr.,* pp. 351 sqq.

2 "*Ministrare ad altare, baptizare et praedicare.*"

3 Sess. XXIII, can. 6: ". . . *quae constat ex episcopis, presbyteris et ministris.*"

the deacons "minister to the priesthood by virtue of their office." [4]

a) The origin of the diaconate is described as follows in the Acts of the Apostles: "In those days, the number of disciples increasing, there arose a murmuring of the Greeks against the Hebrews, for that their widows were neglected in the daily ministrations. Then the twelve calling together the multitude of the disciples, said: It is not reason that we should leave the word of God, and serve tables. Wherefore, brethren, look ye out among you seven men of good reputation, full of the Holy Ghost and wisdom, whom we may appoint over this business. . . . And they chose Stephen, . . . and Philip, and Prochorus, and Nicanor, and Timon, and Parmenas, and Nicolas. . . . These they set before the Apostles; and they praying, imposed hands upon them." [5] The table service in ancient times was intimately connected with the service of the altar.[6] Moreover, we see these seven deacons, especially Stephen and Philip, preaching the Gospel,[7] baptizing,[8] and ministering at divine worship.[9]

But does not the passage quoted prove that the diaconate is an Apostolic rather than a divine institution? This question can best be answered by

4 *Conc. Trident.*, Sess. XXIII, cap. 2: ". . . *qui sacerdotio ex officio deservirent.*"

5 Acts VI, 1 sqq.

6 Cfr. 1 Cor. XI, 21.

7 Acts VI, 8 sqq.; VIII, 5.

8 Acts VIII, 12, 38.

9 1 Tim. III, 8 sqq.

saying that an office that is always mentioned as organically connected with the priesthood,[10] and conferred by the imposition of hands,[11] must be of divine institution.

b) The Scriptural argument is strengthened by Tradition. The diaconate has always been sharply distinguished from the priesthood, more sharply, in fact, than the episcopate.

St. Clement of Rome, in his Epistle to the Corinthians, which was composed A. D. 96, when St. John the Evangelist was still alive, says: " The Apostles have received the message which they gave us from the Lord Jesus Christ; Jesus Christ was sent by God: hence Christ by God, and the Apostles by Christ,— these things are well ordained according to the will of God. . . . The Apostles ordained the first among their converts after examining their spirit, to be bishops and deacons.[12] Nor is this anything new. For Sacred Scripture says: ' I will constitute their bishops in justice and their deacons in faith.' We need not wonder that those to whom this office has been entrusted by God in Christ, have ordained those aforementioned." [13]

St. Ignatius of Antioch ($+$ 117), speaking of the divine constitution of the Church, says that it cannot exist without deacons. " Likewise let all respect the deacons as Jesus Christ, and also the bishop, who is the type of the Father, and the presbyters as the council of God and

10 1 Tim. III, 2 sqq.; Phil. I, 1.

11 Acts VI, 6.

12 εἰς ἐπισκόπους καὶ διακόνους.

13 Clem. Rom., Ep. ad Cor., c. 42, 1 sq.— The Scriptural passage quoted is Isaias LX, 17.— On the meaning of ἐπίσκοποι in the above-quoted text of St. Clement see Bardenhewer, Geschichte der altkirchlichen Literatur, Vol. I, p. 106, Freiburg 1902.

the college of the Apostles. Without these [three] the name of ' Church ' is not given." [14]

St. Polycarp (+ 166) says: " The deacons must be blameless before His righteousness, as the servants of God and Christ, and not of man." [15]

Bishops, priests, and deacons form as it were an inseparable triad also in later Patristic documents. Thus Clement of Alexandria (+ 217) says of the ecclesiastical hierarchy: " In the Church there is a gradation of bishops, priests, and deacons, which is, I believe, an imitation of the glory of the angels." [16]   Origen (+ 254), who was a simple priest, says of himself : " More is demanded of me than of the deacon; more of the deacon than of the layman; but he who occupies the citadel of the whole Church [i. e. the bishop] must give an account of the whole Church." [17]

Among Latin writers Tertullian [18] and St. Optatus of Mileve expressed themselves in similar words. Optatus (+ after 384), deploring the defection of so many Christians during the persecution of Diocletian, distinctly mentions deacons, priests, and bishops among the apostates.[19]

Thesis II: The ordination to the diaconate is a true Sacrament.

[14] *Ad Trall.,* 3.— Other similar texts from the writings of St. Ignatius *apud* Tepe, *Inst. Theol.,* Vol. IV, p. 579, Paris 1896.

[15] *Ep. ad Phil.,* c. 5.

[16] *Stromata,* VI, 13.

[17] *Hom. in Ierem.,* 11, n. 3.

[18] *De Praescr.,* c. 41.

[19] *De Schism. Donat.,* I, 13: " *Quid commemorem laicos, qui tunc in Ecclesia nullâ fuerunt dignitate suffulti? quid ministros plurimos?* *quid diaconos in tertio, quid presbyteros in secundo sacerdotio constitutos? Ipsi apices et principes omnium, aliqui episcopi illis temporibus . . . instrumenta divinae legis impie tradiderunt.*"— Cfr. De Smedt, " *L'Organisation des Églises Chrétiennes jusqu'au Milieu du IIIe Siècle,*" in the Report of the Intern. Scientific Congress for 1888, Vol. II, pp. 297 sqq.

This proposition, which is upheld by all Catholic theologians with the exception of Durandus [20] and Cajetan, is regarded as an article of faith by Vasquez.[21] Cardinal Bellarmine contents himself with calling it *"valde probabilis."* [22] We prefer to characterize it as *"sententia certa,"* with a firm basis in Scripture and Tradition.

a) Sacred Scripture, in speaking of the laying on of hands in the case of St. Stephen and his associates,[23] does not say that the rite bestowed grace. However, in view of the high moral demands made by St. Paul upon the newly created deacons,[24] it is safe to assume that the ceremony was accompanied by sacramental effects.

This probability becomes a certainty in the light of Tradition, which regards the ordination of the seven as the first ordination of deacons and a true Sacrament. " Behold, the sacred writer does not speak superfluously," says St. Chrysostom, " for he does not say in what manner, but simply that they were ordained by the imposition of hands and by prayer.[25] For this is ordination.[26] The hand of a man is imposed, but God effects the whole, and His hand it is which touches the head of the candidate to be ordained." [27]

---

20 *Comment. in Sent.,* IV, dist. 24, qu. 2.

21 *Comment. in S. Theol.,* III, disp. 238, c. 2.

22 *De Ord.,* I, 6.

23 Acts VI, 6.

24 1 Tim. III, 8 sqq.

25 ὅτι ἐχειροτονήθησαν διὰ προσευχῆς.

26 τοῦτο γὰρ ἡ χειροτονία ἐστίν.

27 *Hom. in Act. Apost.,* 14, n. 3. Many other Patristic texts of similar tenor will be found in De Augustinis, *De Re Sacrament.,* Vol. II, 2nd ed., pp. 463 sqq.

b) According to all extant rituals the Holy Ghost is communicated when the bishop lays his hands upon a candidate to make him a deacon.

The Pseudo-Apostolic Constitutions direct the bishop, when ordaining a deacon, to pray: "Almighty God, . . . turn Thy face towards this Thy servant, chosen to serve in the ministry of the diaconate, and fill him with the Holy Spirit and with power, as Thou didst fill Stephen." [28] According to the Sacramentary of Pope St. Gregory the Great the bishop says: "Send down upon him, we beseech Thee, O Lord, the Holy Ghost, that he may thereby be strengthened in the faithful discharge of the work of Thy ministry, through the bestowal of Thy sevenfold grace." [29]

In the Greek Church the bishop prays: "O Lord, our God, . . . pour out the grace which Thou didst grant to Stephen, Thy protomartyr, the first called by Thee for the discharge of this ministry. . . . Fill this Thy servant, whom Thou wishest to undertake the office of deacon, by the communication of Thy holy and life-giving Spirit, with all faith, charity, and holiness." [30]

Many similar texts have been collected by Martène [31] and Denzinger.[32]　All without exception connect the grace

[28] *Constitut. Apost.*, VIII, 17: "*Deus omnipotens,* . . . *ostende faciem tuam super servum tuum hunc electum tibi in diaconatus ministerium, et imple eum Spiritu sancto et virtute, sicut implesti Stephanum.*" (Migne, *P. G.*, I, 1115).

[29] "*Emitte in eum, Domine, quaesumus, Spiritum sanctum, quo in opus ministerii fideliter exequendi septiformis gratiae tuae munere roboretur.*" (Migne, *P. L.*, LXXVIII, 222).

[30] Goar, *Eucholog.*, p. 250: "*Domine, Deus noster,* . . . *gratiam Stephano protomartyri tuo in opus ministerii huius a te primum vocato concessam largire. . . . Ipse, Domine, servum tuum hunc, quem diaconi ministerium subire voluisti, sancti et vivifici Spiritus tui adventu omni fide et caritate et sanctificatione adimple.*"

[31] *De Antiquis Eccles. Ritibus,* Vol. II, pp. 35 sqq.

[32] *Rit. Orient.*, Vol. II, pp. 8, 69, 133, etc.

of the Holy Ghost with the imposition of hands in the ordination for the diaconate. Now the Council of Trent declares [33] that a rite in which the bishop says, "Receive the Holy Ghost," cannot be in vain. Consequently, the ordination rite for the diaconate communicates the Holy Ghost, and is a true Sacrament.[34]

Let it not be objected that the delivery of the book of Gospels is the "matter" of the diaconate, and that no such book existed at the time of the Apostles.[35] If this objection proves anything, it proves that the matter of ordination cannot consist in the *traditio libri evangeliorum*. We do not assert that it does, but hold with the majority of theologians that the matter of the Sacrament consists in the *impositio manuum*.

Another objection has been drawn from the fact that an ancient rite for the administration of minor orders and the blessing of deaconesses, as found in some rituals, contains an invocation of the Holy Ghost.[36] However, this rite was never in general use, is of post-Apostolic origin, and was abrogated in course of time. Hence it must have been of purely ecclesiastical institution. The Church, as we have learnt, can neither institute nor abrogate Sacraments.

[33] Sess. XXIII, can. 4.

[34] Cfr. Benedict XIV, *De Synodo Dioeces.*, VIII, 9, 2.— On the form of the ordination rite for the diaconate see Ch. I, Sect. 2, No. 2, p. 70 *supra*.

[35] Cfr. Acts VI, 6.

[36] Cfr. *Const. Apost.*, VIII, 20: "*Ipse nunc respice hanc ancillam electam ad ministerium et da ei Spiritum sanctum.*"

SECTION 4

That the subdiaconate and the four so-called *ordines minores* are ecclesiastical orders has never been denied. The only question is whether they are sacramental and directly instituted by Christ. The Church not having defined anything on this point, theologians are free to debate it pro and con. In matter of fact there is a long-standing controversy, which cannot, however, be decided on dogmatic grounds but must be fought out in the arena of history.

1. THE SUBDIACONATE NOT A SACRAMENTAL ORDO.—As the name itself indicates, a subdeacon (*subdiaconus,* ὑποδιάκονος) is one who ministers to a deacon.

The functions of a subdeacon according to the *Pontificale Romanum* are: " to prepare water for the ministry of the altar; to assist the deacon; to wash the altar cloths and corporals, and to present to him [the deacon] the chalice and paten for the use of the sacrifice." [1]

That the subdiaconate is not a Sacrament was main-

---

1 ". . . aquam ad ministerium altaris praeparare, diacono ministrare, pallas altaris et corporalia abluere, calicem et patenam in usum sacrificii eidem offerre." (*Pontific. Roman.*)

tained by Hugh of St. Victor, Peter Lombard, Durandus, and Cajetan. Other Scholastic writers regarded the subdiaconate as well as the four minor orders as sacramental. Of later authors, Vasquez[2] held that the subdiaconate is a Sacrament, whereas minor orders are not. However, since Morinus, Benedict XIV, and St. Alphonsus, the common opinion among Catholic theologians is that probably no order below deaconship is a true Sacrament.[3] This opinion rests on weighty arguments.

a) The subdiaconate was unknown before the third century, and consequently must owe its origin to the Church. As the Church cannot institute Sacraments, the subdiaconate is not a Sacrament.

a) The minor premise of this syllogism requires no proof. All the Sacraments, both in regard to matter and to form, have been directly instituted by Christ Himself.[4] Any rite instituted by human authority is at most a mere sacramental. This argument is not disproved by the contention[5] that the subdiaconate and the four minor orders have developed from, and must therefore have been virtually contained in, the diaconate. This fact, as Atzberger observes, " does not suffice to make them Sacraments; for if it was the Church that developed these orders from the diaconate, the rite of their administration cannot be sacramental, because all Sacraments owe their institution immediately to Christ." [6]

2 *Comment. in S. Theol.,* III, disp. 288, c. 2.

3 Among the few who hold that the orders below deaconship are a sacrament, are Glossner, De Augustinis, Billot, Sasse, and Egger.

4 V. Pohle-Preuss, *The Sacra-*

ments, Vol. I, pp. 97 sqq.

5 Cfr. Thomassin, *De Benef.,* P. I, l. 2, c. 30; Liebermann, *De Sacram. Ord.,* c. 1, §3; Dalponte, *Compendium,* p. 721, Trent 1890.

6 Sheeben-Atzberger, *Dogmatik,* IV, 3, 760.

β) The major premise can be demonstrated historically. No extant document prior to the third century speaks of the subdiaconate. Most likely this order was instituted by Pope Fabian (236–250).[7] "*Fabianus*," says the *Liber Pontificalis*, "*natione Romanus, . . . regiones* [*urbis Romae*] *divisit diaconibus et fecit septem subdiaconos, qui septem notariis imminerent, ut gesta martyrum in integrum colligerent.*"[8] This fact had not been entirely forgotten in the Middle Ages, for at the Council of Benevento (1091) Pope Urban II declared that while in exceptional cases subdeacons might be elected to the episcopate, the only sacred orders recognized by the primitive Church were the diaconate and the priesthood.[9] The *Decretum Gratiani* (1150) expressly says: "We read that levites [*i. e.* deacons] were ordained by the Apostles, chief among them being St. Stephen; the subdeacons and acolytes were in course of time appointed by the Church."[10] This theory was adopted by Peter Lombard,[11] and St. Thomas, seemingly forgetful of his own teaching, says in his *Opusculum* against William of Saint-Amour that ". . . there were in the primitive Church only two sacred orders, the priesthood and the diaconate, but

7 Euseb., *Hist. Eccl.*, VI, 29.

8 *Liber Pontificalis*, ed. Duchesne, I, 148.

9 Can. 1: "*Nullus deinceps in episcopum eligatur nisi qui in sacris ordinibus religiose vivens inventus est. Sacros autem ordines dicimus diaconatum et presbyteratum; hos siquidem solos primitiva legitur Ecclesia habuisse, super his solum praeceptum habemus Apostoli. Subdiaconos vero, quia et ipsi altaribus deserviunt, opportunitate exigente concedimus, sed rarissime.*" (Hardouin, *Concil.*, Vol. VI, p. 1695).

10 *Decr. Grat.*, dist. 21: "*Levitas autem* [*diaconos*] *ab Apostolis ordinatos legimus, quorum maximus fuit beatus Stephanus: subdiaconos et acolythos procedente tempore Ecclesia constituit.*" (Ed. Friedberg, col. 67).

11 *Sent.*, IV, dist. 24, n. 9: "*Ecce de septem Ecclesiae gradibus breviter elocuti, quid ad quemquam pertineat, insinuavimus. Quumque omnes spirituales sint et sacri, excellenter tamen canones duos tantum sacros ordines appellari censent, diaconatus scil. et presbyteratus* [*maior et minor*], *quia hos solos primitiva Ecclesia legitur habuisse. . . . Subdiaconos vero et acolythos procedente tempore Ecclesia sibi constituit.*"

the Church later on instituted for herself minor orders." [12]

How are we to explain the fact that the subdiaconate, despite its purely human institution, " is classed among the greater orders by the Fathers and sacred councils "? [13]

The answer is that the subdiaconate, like the hypodiaconate among the Greeks, was always regarded as a minor order in the ancient Latin Church, and that its elevation to the rank of a major order, with the obligation of celibacy, is the work of the Church in later times.[14] It is possible approximately to determine the time when this change occurred. Peter Cantor, writing about 1197, says that the subdiaconate had "lately been made a sacred order." [15] Early in the thirteenth century, Pope Innocent III, recalling the above-mentioned decree of Urban II, authoritatively declared that the subdiaconate must be counted among the major orders, and that a subdeacon may be elected to the episcopacy without a dispensation.[16]

b) The ordination rite for the subdiaconate lacks both matter and form, and therefore cannot be a Sacrament.

The essence of the Sacrament of Holy Orders consists in the imposition of hands as the *matter,* and the invocation of the Holy Ghost as the *form.* The rite of ordaining a subdeacon contains neither of these two ceremonies, and

---

12 *Contra Impugn. Dei Cultum,* c. 4, concl. 6: ". . . *sicut etiam in primitiva Ecclesia fuerunt duo soli ordines sacri, scil. presbyteri et diaconi; et tamen postea Ecclesia minores sibi ordines instituit."*— The term "minor orders" in this connection evidently includes the subdiaconate.

13 *Conc. Trident.,* Sess. XXIII, c. 2: "*Subdiaconatus ad maiores or-*dines a patribus et sacris conciliis refertur."

14 *V. supra,* Ch. II, Sect. 2.

15 *De Verbo Mirifico,* c. 57: "*Prima autem manus impositio debetur diaconibus ordinandis, de novo enim institutum est subdiaconatum esse sacrum ordinem."* (Migne, *P. L.,* LXXVIII, 482).

16 *Decret. Greg.,* l. I, tit. 14, c. 9:

consequently lacks both matter and form. The words " *Accipe Spiritum sanctum,*" upon which the Tridentine Council [17] lays such stress, are entirely wanting in the ordination rite of the subdiaconate.[18]

Cardinal Bellarmine holds that the subdiaconate is a Sacrament because it cannot be repeated. But his reasoning is not conclusive. No blessing is strictly speaking capable of repetition. Thus the benediction of a church, or of an altar, or of an abbot, cannot be repeated, though none of them are sacramental.[19] From the fact that a Sacrament imprints a character we may legitimately infer that it can be received but once; [20] but it will not do to reverse the argument.

Moreover, the subdeaconship may, with papal dispensation, be conferred by an ordinary priest, whereas the three major orders can be conferred only by a bishop.[21]

2. THE FOUR MINOR ORDERS.—There are in the Western Church four minor orders: that of porter, lector, exorcist, and acolyte. The Eastern Church has only two: hypodeacon and lector.

" *In quibus verbis innuitur, quod Urbanus ad statum primitivae Ecclesiae se referens, in quo subdiaconatus ordo sacer minime dicebatur, instituit, ut de subdiacono, nisi utilitatis causa . . . non posset electio celebrari. Verum quum hodie subdiaconatus inter sacros ordines computetur. . . . statuimus, ut subdiaconus in episcopum valeat libere eligi, sicut diaconus et sacerdos.*" (Ed. Friedberg, col. 28).

[17] Sess. XXII, can. 4.

[18] The cogency of this conclusion is not weakened by the fact that the Greeks since time immemorial administer the hypodiaconate by the imposition of hands and invocation of the Holy Ghost, for they expressly rank the subdiaconate with the lectorate as a mere minor order. (Goar, *Euchotog.,* p. 427).

[19] Cfr. St. Thomas, *Comment. in Sent.,* IV, dist. 24, qu. 1, art. 1.

[20] Cfr. *Conc. Trident.,* Sess. VII, can. 9.

[21] *V. infra,* Ch. II, pp. 120 sqq.— On the ordination rite for the subdiaconate see Gihr, *Die hl. Sakramente,* Vol. II, 2nd ed., pp. 304 sqq., Freiburg 1903.

Minor orders are conferred by the delivery to the candidate of the appropriate instruments, in accordance with the ritual given in the *Statuta Ecclesiae Antiqua,* a document which originated in Gaul about the year 500.[22]

Lacking historical knowledge, Blessed Albertus Magnus, St. Thomas, St. Bonaventure, Duns Scotus, Paludanus, and other Scholastics maintained the sacramentality of minor orders.   They were followed by Bellarmine, Estius, Gonet, Billuart, Gotti, and several modern authors, notably Glossner, De Augustinis, Billot, Sasse, and Egger. Against these writers Hugh of St. Victor, Peter Lombard, Durandus, Cajetan, Vasquez, Morinus, St. Alphonsus, and the majority of present-day theologians contend that the four minor orders are not sacramental.   This position seems to us the only tenable one, for two reasons.

a) The four minor orders did not exist in the Apostolic age, but were instituted one by one, as the need for them arose, in the course of the third century, and hence are of purely ecclesiastical origin.

Tertullian,[23] it is true, incidentally speaks of a " lector," but not as belonging to the clergy.   Where he enumerates the different ecclesiastical orders, he mentions but three, *viz.:* the episcopate, the priesthood, and the diaconate.[24]

The first mention of the complete series of orders is found in a letter of Pope Cornelius (251–253) to Fabius of Antioch.   The Pontiff states that there are among

22 Cfr. Boudinhon, *Cath. Encyclopedia,* Vol. X, pp. 332 sq.; Gihr, *op. cit.,* pp. 297 sqq.

23 *De Praescript.,* c. 41: " *Ordinationes eorum* [*i. e. haereticorum*] *temerariae, leves, inconstantes. . . .*

Alius hodie episcopus, cras alius; hodie diaconus, qui cras lector; hodie presbyter, qui cras laicus."

24 *De Bapt.,* 17; *De Fuga,* 11; *De Monog.,* 11.

the Roman clergy forty-two priests, seven deacons, seven subdeacons, forty-two acolytes, and fifty-two exorcists, lectors, and porters.[25]   While it is not likely that Cornelius himself had instituted the four minor orders mentioned in his letter, they are nowhere enumerated fully and in proper sequence before his time.   St. Cyprian (+ 258) speaks of exorcists, lectors, and acolytes, but makes no mention of porters.

Note that in the early Church the number of minor orders was not fixed and that occasionally ecclesiastical offices are mentioned which are not orders at all, *e. g., custos martyrum, notarius, defensor, psalmista, fossarius,* etc.[26]

De Augustinis attributes great importance to the canons of the Fourth Council of Carthage, holding that the rites which they describe [27] reflect the discipline of the latter part of the fourth century.   In matter of fact, however, these canons are spurious and were composed in or near the city of Arles towards the beginning of the sixth century.[28]

In the ninth century, Amalarius, Archbishop of Treves, recognized the priesthood (with its two degrees) and the diaconate as divinely instituted hierarchical orders, and said: " The other orders were added to these.   The growth of the Church entailed an increase in ecclesiastical offices ; that the multitude might be properly served, lower officials were appointed to assist the higher ones." [29]

25 Eusebius, *Hist. Eccles.,* VI, 43, 11: " *Ille ergo Evangelii vindex* [*scil. Novatianus*] *ignorabat, unum episcopum esse oportere in Ecclesia catholica? In quo non ei latebat (quomodo enim illud nescire potuisset?) presbyteros quidem esse 42, septem autem diaconos totidemque subdiaconos, acoluthos 42, exorcistas et lectores cum ostiariis 52.*"

(Migne, *P. G.,* XX, 622).

26 Cfr. Palmieri, *De Rom. Pontifice,* 2nd ed., pp. 98 sq., Rome 1897.

27 Cfr. Denzinger-Bannwart, n. 150 sqq.

28 Cfr. F. Maassen, *Geschichte der Quellen und der Literatur des canonischen Rechts,* Vol. I, p. 382 sqq. Gratz 1870.

29 *De Div. Offic.,* II, 6: " *Ceteri*

What the Church has introduced she can abolish. The Greek Church in course of time did abolish all her minor orders [30] except the hypodiaconate and the lectorate. We do not find that the Latin Church ever protested against this change, which she would surely have done had it involved a mutilation of the Sacrament of Holy Orders or the suppression of any essential part thereof.

These and other considerations led Morinus to "regard the proposition that the subdiaconate and the four minor orders are not Sacraments as so certain and self-evident that no one can deny it who has given due consideration to the testimony of the Fathers." [31]

b) The weakness of the objections urged against our thesis is another argument in its favor.

The *Decretum pro Armenis* proves nothing because Pope Eugene IV did not intend to issue an *ex-cathedra* definition on the subject of the sacramentality of the four minor orders.[32] Moreover, the teaching embodied in that Decree would not lose its value even if the sacramental character of the subdiaconate and the four minor orders were denied. The Sacrament of Holy Orders is sufficiently safeguarded by insisting on the

ordines his adiecti sunt; crescente Ecclesiâ crevit officium ecclesiasticum: ut multitudini Ecclesiae subveniri posset, adiiciuntur inferiores in adiutorio praepositorum." (Migne, *P. L.*, CV, 1082).

30 Council of Antioch, 341; Council of Laodicea, 362.

31 *De Sacram. Ord.*, P. III, exercit. 11, c. 1: "*Propositionem, qua asseritur et subdiaconatum et*

quattuor minores ordines non esse sacramenta iudico tam esse certam et evidentem, ut qui ea [testimonia patrum] consideravit, ire contra vix queat."— On the history of the different orders the student may profitably consult Fr. Wieland, *Die genetische Entwicklung der sog. Ordines Minores in den ersten drei Jahrhunderten*, Freiburg 1879.

32 *V. supra*, p. 65.

sacramentality of its three highest grades.[33] The contrary attitude of St. Antoninus,[34] who is supposed to have been an intimate friend of Eugene IV, throws no light on our question, for he nowhere refers to the Council of Florence, at which the *Decretum pro Armenis* was passed, as a decisive authority. If it had been the intention of the Council to decide this question, how are we to explain the fact that the contrary opinion, as embodied in our thesis, obtained all but universal acceptance afterwards? Nor can anything be proved against our thesis from the decrees of Trent (1562). Even our opponents admit [35] that the Tridentine Council purposely omitted to give a decision on the subject. It matters not what the private opinions of the assembled theologians were.[36] It is not the private opinions of theologians but the official decisions of the Church by which we must be guided. The Council expressly teaches that all those ordinations (and consequently those alone) in which the bishop pronounces the words, "Receive the Holy Ghost," bestow grace and imprint the sacramental character.[37] These words are used only in the ordination rites for the episcopate, the priesthood, and the diaconate, and consequently, according to the mind of the Tridentine Council, these three orders alone are sacramental.

3. THE TONSURE.—The tonsure (*prima tonsura*), so called from the ceremony of cutting the hair, is neither an *ordo* nor a Sacrament, but merely a ceremony of initiation into the clerical state.

33 *V. supra*, Sect. 1–3.

34 *Summa Maior*, P. III, tit. 14, c. 16, § 1 and 3.

35 Cfr. De Augustinis, *De Re Sacrament.*, Vol. II, p. 480.

36 Cfr. Aug. Theiner, *Acta*, Vol. II, pp. 135 sqq.

37 *Conc. Trident.*, Sess. XXIII, can. 4.

"*Non est ordo,*" says St. Thomas, "*sed praeambulum ad ordinem.*" [38] Originally the tonsure formed part of the rite by which the first of the greater orders was conferred. Since about A. D. 700 it is given separately.

The tonsure may be traced on mosaic portraits of the saints as far back as the middle of the fifth century. The custom of cutting the hair as a mark of initiation into the clerical state seems to have arisen towards the end of the fourth or the beginning of the fifth century, in imitation of an ancient monastic practice. In the early part of the sixth century the tonsure was not yet generally prescribed. The Council of Agde (506) simply forbade clerics to wear their hair long (*comam nutrire*). Clerical tonsure became obligatory in the Middle Ages, and the Canon Law of the Church contains a number of severe penalties for those who refuse to wear it. The Council of Trent presupposes tonsure as a condition for the reception of the lesser as well as the greater orders.[39] By the act of receiving the surplice and having his hair cut a man becomes a cleric and is endowed with all the privileges pertaining to the clerical state, but he is not authorized to exercise any *ordo*.[40]

---

38 *Summa Theol., Supplement.,* qu. 40, art. 2.

39 Sess. XXIII, cap. 2: ". . . *ut qui iam clericali tonsurâ insigniti essent, per minores ad maiores* [*ordines*] *ascenderent.*"

40 On the tonsure see E. Taunton, *The Law of the Church,* London 1906, pp. 619 sq., *Cath. Encyclopedia,* Vol. XIV, p. 779; Ziegler, *De Tonsura Clericali,* Wittenberg 1718.

CHAPTER III

THE MINISTER

The bishop is the ordinary minister of all, especially the three sacramental orders, but the subdiaconate and the four minor orders can, with papal permission, be administered by an ordinary priest. We shall demonstrate this in the form of two theses.

Thesis I: The bishop is the ordinary minister of all, especially of the holy or greater, orders.

This thesis embodies an article of faith.

Proof. The *Decretum pro Armenis* (1439) says: "The ordinary minister of this Sacrament is the bishop." [1] The Council of Trent defines: "Bishops . . . ordain the ministers of the Church, and they can perform very many other functions over which those of an inferior order have no power." [2]

a) As the New Testament speaks neither of the subdiaconate nor of minor orders, we must

---

[1] *" Ordinarius minister huius sacramenti est episcopus."* (Denzinger-Bannwart, n. 701).

[2] Sess. XXIII, cap. 4: *" Episcopos . . . ministros Ecclesiae ordinare atqua alia pleraque peragere ipsos posse, quarum functionum potestatem reliqui inferioris ordinis nullam habent."* (Cfr. can. 7).

limit the Scriptural argument for our thesis to the three sacramental orders—the episcopate, the priesthood, and the diaconate.

The Bible, wherever it records an ordination to the priesthood, names either an Apostle [3] or one of the disciples as minister.[4] These, in administering the Sacrament, were guided by well-defined rules and regulations.[5] The fact that the power of ordaining is attributed exclusively to bishops shows that it belongs to them by divine institution. Cfr. Tit. I, 5: "For this cause I left thee in Crete, that thou . . . shouldst ordain priests in every city, as I also appointed thee." [6]

But what does the Apostle mean when he says that Timothy was ordained *cum impositione manuum presbyterii* (μετὰ ἐπιθέσεως τῶν χειρῶν τοῦ πρεσβυτερίου) ? That St. Paul himself was the consecrator appears from 2 Tim. I, 6. What are we to understand by the "*presbyterium*"? The term may mean either the abstract dignity of a presbyter, *i. e.* bishop, which Timothy received by his consecration, or the consecrating bishops.[7] In either case we have a confirmation of the doctrine that the conferring of Holy Orders is an episcopal prerogative.

b) An argument from Tradition may be construed from the data given *supra,* Ch. II, Sect. 1, Thesis II.[8]

---

3 Acts VI, 6; XIII, 13; 2 Tim. I, 6.

4 1 Tim. V, 22; Tit. I, 5.

5 Cfr. 1 Tim. III, 1 sqq.; Tit. I, 5 sqq.

6 Tit. I, 5: "*Huius rei gratia reliqui te Cretae, ut . . . constituas per civitates presbyteros, sicut et ego disposui tibi.*"

7 The last-mentioned opinion was held by St. Chrysostom.

8 *Supra,* pp. 84 sqq.

A careful distinction must be drawn between the election (*electio*) and the ordination (*ordinatio*) of higher clerics. The former may by custom or ecclesiastical sufferance be exercised by priests, nay even laymen. According to St. Jerome,[9] the presbyters of Alexandria, from St. Mark the Evangelist to Heraclas (+ about 246) and Dionysius (+ 256), enjoyed the privilege of choosing one from their midst for the episcopal see. Another example in point is that of St. Ambrose, who was proclaimed bishop of Milan by clergy and people. In Switzerland even to-day congregations choose their own pastors, who subsequently receive the *missio canonica* from the bishop.

Ordination to the priesthood, on the other hand, belongs exclusively to the bishops, and they are not bound, in exercising it, to act with the consent of the people or the secular power. " If anyone saith," declares the Council of Trent, " that . . . orders conferred by them [the bishops], without the consent or vocation of the people or of secular power, are invalid, . . . let him be anathema." [10]

c) In order to be licit, ordination must be conferred by the recipient's own bishop. The rite of episcopal consecration requires the assistance of two other bishops besides the consecrator.

a) The Tridentine Council merely confirmed an ancient rule [11] when it prescribed, under penalty, that " Every one should be ordained by his own bishop." [12] Under this rule

9 *Ep. ad Evangel.,* 146.

10 Sess. XXIII, can. 7; " *Si quis dixerit, . . . ordines ab ipsis [episcopis] collatos sine populi sive potestatis saecularis consensu aut vo-* catione irritos esse, . . . anathema sit."

11 Cfr. c. 16 of the First Nicene Council.

12 Sess. XXIII, cap. 8, *De Re-*

no bishop may ordain the subject of another, except on the strength of a dimissorial letter. This does not, however, apply to the Pope, who, having primacy of jurisdiction over the whole Church, can ordain whomever he pleases and give power to ordain to any bishop regardless of the claims of others. The juridical relation of a secular ordinand to his bishop is based upon a fourfold title,— *origo, domicilium, beneficium,* and *familiaritas.* Regulars are subject to the bishop in whose diocese their convent is located. But these details belong to Canon Law rather than to Dogmatic Theology.

β) Three bishops are required for an episcopal consecration. This is an ancient custom,[13] but being of purely ecclesiastical institution, does not affect the validity, but merely the licitness of the rite.[14] " In case of urgent necessity," the Pseudo-Apostolic Constitutions ordain that " a bishop may be ordained by one [other bishop]." [15] Church history affords many examples of papal dispensation from this rule. Thus Pope Gregory the Great permitted St. Augustine of Canterbury to consecrate another bishop without assistants because he was the only bishop in England.[16] It follows from this and similar cases that an episcopal consecration performed with papal dispensation by one bishop alone is undoubtedly valid. But what if the papal dispensation be lacking? Vas-

---

form.: " *Unusquisque . . . a proprio episcopo ordinetur.*"

13 Cfr. *Conc. Nicaenum I,* c. 4: " *Episcopus convenit maxime quidem ab omnibus, qui sunt in provincia, episcopis ordinari. Si autem difficile fuerit, . . . tribus tamen omnimodis in idipsum convenientibus, . . . celebratio ordinetur.*"

14 Morinus, Gonet, and Tournely hold that it affects both validity and licitness.

15 *Const. Apost.,* VIII, 27: " *Co-*

gente necessitate episcopus ab uno ordinari potest."

16 *Ep.,* IX, 64: " *Et quidem in Anglorum ecclesia, in qua adhuc solus tu episcopus inveniris, ordinare episcopum non aliter nisi sine episcopis potes.*" (Migne, *P. L.,* LXX, 1191). Other examples are cited by Billuart, *De Sacram. Ord.,* diss. 4, art. 3.

17 *Comment. in S. Theol.,* III, disp. 243, c. 5, n. 63.

quez [17] holds that such a consecration would be invalid, just as Confirmation would be invalid if administered by an ordinary priest without special permission from the Pope. Benedict XIV[18] takes the contrary view, which is shared by many theologians and appears to be the only tenable one. According to the rite of consecration only one of the three bishops present actually consecrates, the other two merely assist. It follows that the consecrating bishop alone administers the Sacrament, especially since he alone pronounces the prayer " *Propitiare, Domine,*" etc. Moreover, though Pope Gregory the Great, in his above-quoted letter to St. Augustine, expressly states that the presence of some other bishops is useful, he does not intimate that it is essential to the validity of the Sacrament. Finally, we know of several cases where the Church, in condemning an episcopal consecration performed by one bishop as illicit, expressly admitted its validity.[19]

Thesis II: An ordinary priest can, with papal dispensation, confer the subdiaconate and the four minor orders, but not the three major or sacramental orders.

This thesis comprises two distinct propositions, each of which may be qualified as *"communis."*

Proof. The expression *"minister ordinarius huius sacramenti,"* employed by Pope Eugene IV in his *Decretum pro Armenis,* implies the possibility of a *minister extraordinarius.* As in Confirmation, this extraordinary minister is the priest, not the deacon.

[18] *De Synodo Dioeces.,* XIII, 13, 4.

[19] Examples in point are the consecration of Syderius (see Synesius, *Ep. 67 ad Theophil.*), Evagrius (cfr. Theodoret, *Hist. Eccles.,* V, 23), and Armentarius (cfr. Billuart, *De Sacram. Ord.,* diss. 4, art. 3).

The Tridentine Council contents itself with the general statement that the episcopal power of confirming and ordaining is not shared by priests. It does not define which orders may be conferred by a priest when authorized to act as extraordinary minister.[20] Hence the question is open to dispute. As the prerogative of conferring the subdiaconate and minor orders is an altogether extraordinary one for a priest, its valid exercise depends on the permission of his superiors. It is contended that in former times bishops possessed the privilege of empowering ordinary priests to confer certain orders.[21] While this may be true, there can be no doubt that to-day this privilege is reserved to the Pope.[22]

a) All theologians agree that the Supreme Pontiff can authorize any priest to confer the subdiaconate and the four minor orders.

Whatever doubts may have formerly existed among theologians with regard to the subdiaconate,[23] have been dispelled by the conviction that this particular order is not a sacrament, but merely a sacramental.[24] The Church herself has constantly acted on this conviction. The Second Nicene Council (787) acknowledged the right of abbots to confer the lectorate upon their subjects, and long before that time Pope Gelasius (+ 496) warned priests not to confer the subdeaconship or the order of acolyte without papal permission,[25] thereby clearly indicating that they could validly perform these acts with pontifical au-

---

20 Sess. XXIII, cap. 4; can. 7.

21 Cfr. Hallier, *De Sacr. Elect. et Ordinat.*, P. II, sect. 5, c. 1, art. 2.

22 Cfr. *Decret. Gregor.*, l. III, tit. 40, c. 9.

23 Cfr. Tanner, *Theol. Scholast.*, disp. 7, qu. 3, dub. 2.

24 *V. supra*, Ch. II, Sect. 4.

25 *Ep. 9 ad Episc. Lucan.*, c. 6: "*Nec sibi meminerit ulla ratione concedi sine summo pontifice subdiaconum aut acolythum ius habere faciendi.*" (Thiel, I, 365).

thorization. Before the Tridentine Council certain Cistercian and Benedictine abbots are said to have exercised the privilege of conferring subdeaconship upon their subjects.[26] To-day the subdiaconate ranks among the major orders [27] and its administration is reserved exclusively to bishops. According to the Tridentine law, therefore, abbots may give only the tonsure and minor orders to their subjects.[28]

b) The question whether ordinary priests can, with proper authorization, confer major orders, has been answered differently by theologians at various periods in the Church's history.

That a priest can under no circumstances validly ordain a bishop is conceded by all. But can he be empowered to confer the priesthood? Aureolus,[29] Morinus,[30] and others answered this question in the affirmative. They based their opinion on a passage in St. Leo's letter to Bishop Rusticus of Narbonne,[31] in which the major orders conferred by certain " pseudo bishops " are declared under certain conditions to be valid.[32] The passage in question is rather obscure. The " pseudo bishops " to whom the Pope refers were probably priests or deacons who had received episcopal consecration uncanonically,[33] though validly.

Morinus attaches great importance to the fact that the priesthood was often conferred by so-called *chorepiscopi,* who, it is claimed, were not true bishops, but mere " coun-

26 Cfr. Navarrus, *Consil.,* l. V, *de Privil. Consil.,* 14.

27 *V. supra,* p. 109.

28 Sess. XXIII, c. 10, *De Reform.: " Abbatibus . . . non liceat in posterum . . . cuiquam, qui regularis subditus sibi non sit, tonsuram vel minores ordines conferre."*

29 *Comment. in Sent.,* IV, dist. 25, art. 1.

30 *De Sacr. Ordin.,* P. III, exerc. 4, c. 3 sqq.

31 *Ep.,* 167, 1.

32 Cfr. Schanz, *Die Lehre von den hl. Sakramenten,* p. 692.

33 Cfr. the above-quoted letter of

try bishops " after the manner of rural deans or arch-priests. But we know from the proceedings of a council held at Antioch, in 341, that at least some of these digni-taries were real bishops, resembling in rank and func-tions our auxiliary bishops.[34]

Can a priest with papal dispensation validly confer the diaconate? This question is more difficult to answer. The fact that the diaconate is a true Sacrament does not prove that it cannot be administered by a priest. Con-firmation is a Sacrament, and yet a priest can admin-ister it with proper authorization from the Supreme Pontiff. With this analogy in mind Huguccio ($+$ 1210) argued that a priest can confer the priesthood, a deacon the diaconate and minor orders, a subdeacon the subdia-conate, etc.[35] The *sententia communis* since St. Thomas and Duns Scotus is that a priest cannot validly ordain a deacon. " Though some abbots were occasionally per-mitted to confer minor, not holy orders," says the Roman Catechism, " no one doubts that this is the proper office of the bishop, for whom, and for whom alone, it is lawful to initiate [candidates] into the other orders called greater and holy." [36]

The most ancient documents agree in limiting the power of conferring the diaconate to bishops, and make no distinction between the ordinary and the extra-ordinary minister. From this fact it seems to fol-

Leo the Great, *Ep.* 167, 1: "*Nulla ratio sinit, ut inter episcopos ha-beantur, qui nec a clericis sunt electi nec a plebibus expetiti nec a provin-cialibus episcopis cum metropolitani iudicio consecrati.*"

34 Cfr. Labbe, *Concil.*, Vol. II, p. 577.

35 "*Nam ordinem, quem non ha-bet, nullus potest conferre, sed quem habet, potest.*"— On this false prin-ciple see *Katholik,* 1909, I, 319.

36 *Cat. Rom.*, P. II, cap. 7, qu. 25: "*Quamvis nonnullis abbatibus per-missum sit, ut minores et non sacros ordines interdum administrent, ta-men hoc proprium episcopi munus esse nemo dubitat, cui uni ex omni-bus, praeterea nemini, licet reliquis ordinibus, qui maiores et sacri di-cuntur, initiare.*" (Ed. 4a Ratisbon., p. 267).

low that the existing practice is of divine right, in which case even the Pope could not dispense from it. Yet the matter is not entirely clear. Eugene IV seems to admit that there is a *minister extraordinarius huius sacramenti,* and Innocent VIII in his Bull *" Exposcit "* [37] is said to have conferred the privilege of ordaining deacons upon all abbots of the Cistercian order, who made use of it in good faith as late as 1663.[38] But even such an extraordinary privilege would not settle the dogmatic problem with which we are concerned, for, as Father Chr. Pesch justly observes, "one pontifical act does not make a law or dogma." [39]

37 A. D. 1489.

38 See Vasquez, *Comment. in S. Theol.,* III, disp. 243, c. 4, n. 39; Berti, *De Theol. Discipl.,* l. 36, c. 13, § 4.

39 *"Unum factum pontificium non facit legem neque dogma."* (*Praelect. Dogmat.,* Vol. I, p. 296). On the power of ordination the student may consult Billuart, *De Sacr. Ord.,* diss. 3, art. 1; Souben, *Nouvelle Théologie Dogmatique,* Vol. VIII, pp. 72 sqq., Paris 1905.— On the two recently discovered Bulls of Boniface IX to the Abbot of St. Osyth, see *English Hist. Review,* Vol. XXVI, (1911), pp. 125–127; Catholic *Fortnightly Review* (St. Louis), Vol. XXIV, No. 5 and 7; *Australasian Catholic Record,* Vol. I, No. 4 (Oct., 1924), pp. 27 sqq.; *La Scuola Cattolica,* March, 1924.

CHAPTER IV

As regards the conditions required for the valid reception of Holy Orders, Dogmatic Theology is concerned solely with the fitness of the candidate; the question of his worthiness belongs to a different theological discipline.

SECTION 1

CONDITIONS OF VALID RECEPTION

To receive the Sacrament of Holy Orders validly, a person must be (1) of the male sex and (2) baptized.

1. THE RECIPIENT MUST BE OF THE MALE SEX.—Like the Jewish Synagogue, the Catholic Church has always maintained that men alone are qualified for the service of the altar. Our Lord called men to be His Apostles and these, in turn, selected men to succeed them. St. Paul expressly excludes the female sex from participation in liturgical and ecclesiastical functions.[1] "Let women keep silence in the churches. . . .

[1] 1 Cor. XIV, 34 sqq.; 1 Tim. II, 11 sq.

For it is a shame for a woman to speak in the church." [2] To this principle the Church has faithfully adhered. [4] If there ever was a woman who deserved the honors of the priesthood, it most assuredly was the Blessed Virgin Mary. But our Divine Lord Himself debarred her from the altar. [3] The female priests of the Montanists and Collyridians were an abomination in the eyes of the Church. Our modern women "evangelists" excite derision rather than anger.

The Apostolic institution of deaconesses proves nothing against our thesis. " We cannot be sure," says Father Herbert Thurston, S.J., [5] " that any formal recognition of deaconesses as an institution of consecrated women aiding the clergy is to be found in the New Testament." Their duty was to guard the doors and maintain order among those of their own sex in church, to instruct them privately in the faith, to discharge those charitable offices which were performed for men by the deacons, to accompany women when visiting a bishop or deacon, and to attend female converts during the administration of Baptism, which in the early days took place by immersion. The pseudo-Apostolic Constitutions, after enumerating these functions, distinctly say : " The deaconess gives no blessing, she fulfils no function of priest or deacon . . ." [6] That the deaconesses were blessed according

2 i Cor. XIV, 34 sqq.: " *Mulieres in ecclesiis taceant; . . . turpe est enim mulieri loqui in ecclesia.*"

3 Cfr. St. Epiphanius, *Haer., 79, 2.*

4 See E. Krebs, *"Vom Priestertum der Frau"* in *Hochland,* Vol. XIX, 8, pp. 196-215 (May, 1922).

5 In the *Catholic Encyclopedia,* Vol. IV, p. 651.

6 *Const. Apost.,* VIII, 28: " *Diaconissa non benedicit neque facit aliquid eorum, quae presbyteri aut diaconi faciunt, nisi quod ianuas cu-*

to a prescribed rite does not prove that they received an order. St. Epiphanius expressly says that their functions are in no wise sacerdotal.[7] The age limit prescribed by St. Paul [8] (sixty years) was reduced to forty by the Council of Chalcedon (451). The institute of deaconesses became extinct in the eighth century. History shows that " the Church as a whole repudiated the idea that women could in any proper sense be recipients of the Sacrament of Order." [9]

What we have said about deaconesses applies also to abbesses. The benediction of an abbess does not make her a member of the clergy, nor does it give her ecclesiastical jurisdiction over her subjects.

Such titles as *episcopa, presbyterissa,* πρεσβῦτις, which occur in ancient documents, apply either to deaconesses [10] or to the living wives of married men ordained to the episcopate or the priesthood.[11]

2. THE RECIPIENT OF HOLY ORDERS MUST BE BAPTIZED.—Baptism is an indispensable condition for the valid reception of all the Sacraments.[12] An unbaptized man cannot be ordained to the priesthood, and if the rite were performed over

stodit et presbyteris ministrat, quum mulieres baptizantur, idque propter decorem et honestatem."

[7] *Haer.,* 79, 3: " *Quamquam diaconissarum in ecclesia ordo est, non tamen ad sacerdotii functionem aut ullam huiusmodi administrationem institutus est, sed ut muliebris sexus honestati consulatur."*

[8] 1 Tim. V, 9.

[9] Thurston in the *Cath. Encyclopedia,* IV, 652.— On the institute of deaconesses see Pinius, *De Ecclesiae Diaconissis,* in the *Acta*

Sanctorum of the Bollandists, Sept., Vol. I, § 5. See Appendix III, p. 245.

[10] Cfr. Epiphanius, *Haer.,* 79, 4; *Decr. Grat.,* d. 32, c. 19.

[11] Cfr. Du Cange, *s. v.* " Presbytera; " K. H. Schäfer, *Kanonissen und Diakonissen, die kanonische Äbtissin,* Freiburg 1910.— On the fable of the female Pope see Döllinger, *Papstfabeln des Mittelalters,* Munich 1863; Thurston, *Pope Joan,* London 1915.

[12] V. Pohle-Preuss, *The Sacraments,* Vol. I.

him before he received Baptism, he would have to be unconditionally reordained. Reordination was expressly prescribed for the followers of Paul of Samosata by the First Nicene Council (325).[13]

Can baptized infants be validly ordained? Durandus and Tournely answered this question in the negative, but the common opinion is that Holy Orders, in this respect, is on a line with Baptism and Confirmation, and can be validly administered to infants. The *Supplementum* to the *Summa Theologica* of St. Thomas, which, though not written by the Angelic Doctor, undoubtedly expresses his views, says that " children and others who lack the use of reason can receive any Sacrament that does not require as a necessary requisite an act on the part of the recipient, but by divine institution confers some spiritual power." [14] Needless to say, the ordination of infants, as practiced in ancient times, and to some extent in the Middle Ages, was an abuse, which the Church combatted and finally succeeded in abolishing. The validity of such ordinations can no longer be doubted since Benedict XIV decided, May 4, 1745, that if a bishop, having legitimate authority, should confer holy orders upon an infant, " it is the unanimous sense of theologians and canonists that such an ordination would have to be regarded as valid, though illicit." [15] The Pontiff adds that a boy thus ordained

---

13 Cfr. *Decr. Gregor.*, l. III, tit. 43, c. 3.

14 *Summa Theol.*, *Suppl.*, qu. 39, art. 2: " *Omnia sacramenta, in quibus non requiritur actus suscipientis de necessitate sacramenti, sed potestas aliqua spiritualis divinitus datur, possunt pueri suscipere, et alii qui usu rationis carent.*"

15 *Inter Sollicitas*, § 20: " *Si fortasse contingeret ab episcopo legitimâ auctoritate suffulto non solum minores, sed etiam sacros ordines infanti conferri, concordi theologorum et canonistarum suffragio definitum est, validam sed illicitam censeri hanc ordinationem.*"

should be allowed, upon reaching manhood, to decide for himself whether he will lead a celibate life or not. In case he chooses to marry, he must abstain forever from the exercise of the functions attaching to his order.[16]

16 Cfr. Ballerini-Palmieri, *Op. Theol. Mor.*, 3rd ed., Vol. V, p. 712, Prati 1900; Benedict XIV, *Opera Inedita,* by Fr. Heiner, Freiburg 1904, pp. 402 ssq.

SECTION 2

CLERICAL CELIBACY

1. OBLIGATION.—The obligation of celibacy in the Latin Church binds bishops, priests, deacons, and subdeacons.   Holy Orders is a diriment impediment to marriage.[1]   The Tridentine Council defines: "If anyone saith that clerics constituted in sacred orders . . . are able to contract marriage, and that being contracted, it is valid, notwithstanding the ecclesiastical law, . . . let him be anathema." [2]

a) The law making sacred orders a diriment impediment to marriage, is not as old as the obligation of celibacy.   It can, however, be traced to the Second Council of the Lateran (1139).[3]   The heroic battle waged by Pope Gregory VII (1073–1085) for the independence and purity of the priesthood stands out prominently from the pages of history.   But the celibacy of the clergy was a binding ecclesiastical precept long before Gregory's time.   The Council of Elvira (about 300) imposed celibacy upon the

1 This topic is treated in Canon Law.

2 *Conc. Trident.*, Sess. XXIV, can. 9: " *Si quis dixerit, clericos in sacris ordinibus constitutos . . . posse matrimonium contrahere contractumque validum esse, non obstante lege ecclesiasticâ, . . . ana-*thema sit." (Denzinger-Bannwart, n. 979).

3 Canon 7: " *Statuimus, quatenus episcopi, presbyteri, diaconi . . . qui uxores sibi copulare praesumpserint, separentur; huiusmodi namque copulationem matrimonium non esse censemus.*"

three higher orders,— bishops, priests, and deacons, — commanding those who were married to abstain from intercourse with their wives under pain of deposition.[4] Pope Siricius, in 385, extended this law to the whole Latin Church.[5] As regards subdeacons, the practice varied in different countries and at different periods. In Rome the subdeacons were bound by the law of celibacy under Leo the Great (+ 461).[6] Pelagius II (+ 590) applied this rule to Sicily, but his successor, Gregory the Great (+ 604), permitted the deacons of that country to continue their relations with their wives, though under penalty of being excluded from higher orders. Subsequent popes, especially Urban II (1089), enforced stricter measures, until finally, with the adoption of the subdiaconate into the category of major orders, in the twelfth and thirteenth centuries, the obligation of celibacy for this order became universal.

b) In the Greek Church celibacy was generally observed by the clergy but not enforced as a canonical precept.

Justinian I (527–565) imposed celibacy upon bishops. Under his Code of Civil Law no one who had a living wife or children could be raised to the episcopate. The present discipline of the Greek Church is not based on

4 Canon 33: "*Placuit in totum prohiberi episcopis, presbyteris et diaconis vel omnibus clericis positis in ministerio abstinere se a coniugibus suis et non generare filios; quicunque vero fecerit, ab honore clericatus exterminetur.*"

5 Cfr. his Epistle to Himerius, c. 7: "*Quilibet episcopus, presbyter atque diaconus . . . iam nunc sibi omnem per nos indulgentiae aditum intelligat obseratum, quia ferro necesse est excidantur vulnera, quae fomentorum non senserint medicinam.*"

6 Cfr. this Pope's *Ep. ad Anastas. Thessal.*, 84, c. 4: "*Nec subdiaconis quidem connubium carnale conceditur, ut et qui habent uxores, sint tamquam non habentes, et qui non habent, permaneant singulares.*"

Justinian's legislation, but follows the Council of Trullo (692), which, while requiring bishops and monks to lead a celibate life, permitted presbyters, deacons, and subdeacons to continue to cohabit with their wives. But they are not allowed to remarry after ordination. Benedict XIV, in his Constitution "*Etsi pastoralis,*" of May 26, 1742, declared that the Roman Church does not forbid this practice among the Uniate Greeks.[7]

2. ORIGIN.—That the celibacy of the clergy is not a divine law but merely an ecclesiastical precept, is the unanimous teaching of theologians. But there is a difference of opinion regarding the origin of the practice. Gregory of Valentia, Vasquez, Bellarmine, Zaccaria, Phillips, Bickell, and others hold that clerical celibacy is an Apostolic institution, whereas Natalis Alexander, Tillemont, Tournely, Hefele, Probst, and Funk maintain that it originated later. The problem is purely historical, and the evidence seems to show that celibacy, as a precept, is of post-Apostolic origin.

We say, as a *precept,* not as a voluntary practice. Bickell's argument for the Apostolic origin of celibacy does not take due account of this distinction.[8]

An important incident in the history of clerical celi-

---

[7] On clerical celibacy the student may consult: Laurin, *Der Zölibat der Geistlichen nach kanonischem Recht,* Vienna 1880; L. Gaugusch, *Das Ehehindernis der höheren Weihe,* Vienna 1902; N. Milas, *Das Kirchenrecht der morgenländischen Kirche,* Zara 1897; A. de Roscovány, *Coelibatus et Breviarium,* 13 vols., Vienna 1861–1890.

[8] *Zeitschrift für kath. Theologie,* Innsbruck, 1879, pp. 26 sqq., 792 sqq.

bacy is the stand taken by St. Paphnutius, an Egyptian bishop, at the First Nicene Council. Socrates [9] and Sozomen [10] relate the incident substantially as follows: When in the course of the conciliary proceedings, it was moved that bishops, priests, and deacons should in future abstain from carnal intercourse with their wives, Paphnutius, an aged and venerable bishop, protested against the heavy burden to be thus imposed upon the clergy, quoting St. Paul's well-known declaration (Heb. XIII, 4) respecting the purity of the marriage bed. He said it would be sufficient if bishops, priests, and deacons, in accordance with tradition, were forbidden to marry after ordination. The Council adopted his suggestion and the project was abandoned.

St. Paphnutius was justified in appealing to tradition, for before 325, clerics in major orders were frequently permitted to marry. The Apostolic Constitutions [11] commanded bishops, priests, and deacons to be satisfied with one wife and forbade them to marry after ordination. The decree of the Council of Ancyra (314) allowing deacons to marry after ordination, is exceptional. Under the existing discipline a deacon was merely permitted to retain his wife in case he had been married before ordination. Clement of Alexandria ($+$ 217), after expressing veneration for a celibate life, says: " All the same, the Church fully receives the husband of one wife,[12] whether he be a priest, deacon, or layman,— provided only he uses his marriage blamelessly; and such a one shall be saved in the begetting of children." [13]   On the other hand there is Patristic testimony to prove that celibacy was voluntarily practised by the higher clergy

9 *Hist. Eccles.*, I, 11.
10 *Hist. Eccles.*, I, 23.
11 *Const. Apost.*, VI, 17.

12 τὸν τῆς μίας γυναικὸς ἄνδρα.
13 σωθήσεται δὲ διὰ τῆς τεκνογο·
νίας.   (*Strom.*, III, 12).

long before it was enjoined by law. Thus St. Epiphanius (+ 406) says: "The priesthood is recruited mainly from the ranks of celibates, or otherwise of the monks; but if suitable persons for the administration of that office cannot be found among the monks, the priests are usually chosen from among those who abstain from conjugal intercourse with their wives or are widowed after one marriage." [14] In another treatise St. Epiphanius complains that "in some places" priests, deacons, and subdeacons "continue to have children," and he argues against the practice as "opposed to the very notion of the priesthood." [15]

Vigilantius' cynical advice that the bishops should ordain none but married men, was met by St. Jerome (+ 420) with the declaration that celibacy was all but universally observed by the clergy.[16] In general we may say [17] that "while celibacy in the first three centuries was not yet a strict obligation imposed upon the clergy, it was quite generally observed." [18]

3. CONGRUITY.—Clerical celibacy recommends itself for its many intrinsic and extrinsic advantages.

a) Virginity and marriage are both holy, but virginity is superior to marriage, and hence more befitting those who are set apart for the sacred ministry. The Tridentine

14 *Expos. Fidei Cath.,* 21.

15 *Haer.,* 59, 4.— On this passage see Funk, *Kirchengeschichtliche Abhandlungen und Untersuchungen,* Vol. I, pp. 132 sqq., Paderborn 1897.

16 *Contra Vigilant.,* c. 1: "*Quid faciunt orientis ecclesiae, quid Aegypti et Sedis apostolicae, quae aut virgines clericos accipiunt aut continentes, aut si uxores habuerint, mariti esse desistunt?*"

17 Gihr, *Die hl. Sakramente,* Vol. II, 2nd ed., p. 476.

18 Cfr. F. A. Zaccaria, *Storia Polemica del Celibato Sacro,* Rome 1774; Jos. Müller, *Die Keuschheitsidee in ihrer geschichtlichen Entwicklung und praktischen Bedeutung,* Mayence 1897; H. Koch, "*Tertullian und der Zölibat,*" in the *Theologische Quartalschrift* of Tübingen, 1906, pp. 406 sqq.

Council pronounces anathema against all who say "that the married state is to be placed above the state of virginity or celibacy, and that it is not better and more blessed to remain in virginity or in celibacy than to be united in matrimony." [19] It is conditions, not persons, that are contrasted here, and hence it would be wrong to say that the preference given to celibacy implies disrespect for the married state. No doubt a good mother who raises her children in the fear of God leads a more meritorious life than an indifferent nun. On the other hand we must remember that our Divine Lord Himself extolled virginity as a precious gift,[20] and St. Paul describes it as the higher call.[21] The Fathers develop this teaching. Thus St. Chrysostom says: "The state of virginity is good, I agree; indeed, it is better than the married state, I confess. And if you ask, By how much better? I answer: By as much as heaven is better than earth, or angels are better than men." [22] St. Augustine calls the virginal life "the portion of the angels." [23] Nothing reflects greater honor upon a priest than the virtue of chastity. In temptations he is strengthened by the example of the Divine High Priest Jesus Christ and His Apostles. Prayer and the Holy Sacrifice supply him with inexhaustible graces to preserve the innocence of his exalted state.[24] He who has voluntarily devoted himself to

19 Sess. XXIV, can. 10: "*Si quis dixerit, statum coniugalem anteponendum esse statui virginitatis vel coelibatus et non esse melius ac beatius manere in virginitate aut coelibatu quam iungi matrimonio, anathema sit.*" (Denzinger-Bannwart, n. 981).

20 Cfr. Matth. XIX, 11 sq.

21 1 Cor. VII, 38, 40.

22 *De Virginitate*, c. 10; cfr. A. Moulard, *S. Jean Chrysostome, le Défenseur du Mariage et l'Apôtre de la Virginité*, Paris 1923, Part II.

23 *De Virginitate*, c. 12: "*Vir-*

ginalis integritas et per piam continentiam ab omni concubitu immunitas angelica portio est."

24 Cfr. St. Jerome, *Ep. 68 ad Pammach.*, c. 20: "*Christus virgo, virgo Maria utrique sexui virginitatis dedicavere principia. Apostoli vel virgines, vel post nuptias continentes. Episcopi, presbyteri, diaconi aut virgines eliguntur aut vidui aut certe post sacerdotium in aeternum pudici.*"

the service of God and consecrated his life to the administration of the Sacraments, must serve God with an undivided heart.[25]

b) The celibacy of the clergy is, moreover, blessed with great advantages (1) for the Church, (2) for the clergy, and (3) for the faithful.

(1) For the Church. The Catholic Church is the spouse of Christ and must be free from all undue influence on the part of the secular power. This freedom she can enjoy only with a celibate priesthood. Married clergymen would have neither the power nor the will to oppose the civil authorities if they attempted to enslave the Church, nor to combat successfully the allurements of nepotism.

(2) For the clergy. Celibacy permits the members of the clergy to devote themselves to their high calling with energy and concentration and to gain great honor and influence among the people. A priest has troubles enough without being burdened with the cares of a family. Fr. Thurston, in his paper to which we have referred, quotes the testimony of Dr. Mahaffy, a distinguished married clergyman and professor of Trinity College, Dublin: " From the point of view of preaching there can be little doubt that married life creates great difficulties and hindrances. The distractions caused by sickness and other human misfortunes increase necessarily in proportion to the number of the household; and as the clergy in all countries are likely to have large families, the time which might be spent in meditation on their discourses is stolen from them by other duties and other cares. The Catholic priest, when his daily round of outdoor duties is over, comes home to a quiet study, where there is nothing to disturb his thoughts. The family man is met at the door by troops of children welcoming his return and

25 Cfr. 1 Cor. VII, 5.

claiming his interest in all their little affairs. Or else the disagreements of the household demand him as an umpire, and his mind is disturbed by no mere speculative contemplation of the faults and follies of mankind, but by their actual invasion of his home." [26]   The Catholic priest, on the contrary, can devote his undivided care to his parishioners.

(3) The celibacy of the clergy, thirdly, is fraught with great advantages to the faithful. They are the priest's children, to whom he should devote all his thought and attention. The chastity of his state of life is apt to inspire them with respect and admiration. It is with confidence that they confess their sins to him.[27]   It is with ardor and enthusiasm that they learn from him the ideals of the Christian religion.

Against these important advantages the occasional lapses of individual priests, which have furnished such writers as Lea and the Theiners with material for their *chronique scandaleuse,* weigh but lightly in the balance, especially if we consider that marriage is by no means an infallible safeguard against incontinency. "We do not abolish Christian marriage," aptly observes Father Thurston, "because so large a proportion of mankind are not faithful to the restraints which it imposes on human concupiscence. No one in his heart believes that civilized nations would be cleaner or purer if polygamy were substituted for monogamy. Neither is there any reason to suppose that scandals would be fewer and the clergy more respected if Catholic priests were permitted to marry." [28]

26 Mahaffy, *The Decay of Modern Preaching,* London 1882, p. 42; Thurston in the *Catholic Encyclopedia,* Vol. III, p. 482.

27 Thurston, *l. c.*

28 *Idem ibid.,* p. 483.— On clerical celibacy and its importance for the Church and the salvation of souls see D. B. Zimmermann, *Der Priesterzölibat und seine Bedeutung für Kirche und Gesellschaft,* Einsiedeln 1898; N. Gihr, *Die hl. Sakramente,* Vol. II, 2nd ed., § 72; I. Souben, *Nouvelle Théologie Dogmatique,* Vol. VIII, pp. 84 sqq., Paris 1905; Jos. Antonelli, *Medicina Pastoralis,* Vol. I, 3rd ed., pp. 419 sq., Rome 1906.

Readings:— Besides the general works listed in the first volume of this treatise (*The Sacraments,* Vol. I, pp. 3 and 4) the student will do well to consult the *Supplementum* to the *Summa Theologica* of St. Thomas, qu. 34 sqq., and the commentators, especially Billuart, *De Sacramento Ordinis* (ed. Lequette, Vol. VII, pp. 313 sqq.) ; Vasquez, *Comment. in S. Theol.,* III, disp. 235 sqq.

Likewise, Peter Soto, *De Institutione Sacerdotum,* Dillingen 1568.— *Fr. Hallier, *De Sacris Electionibus et Ordinationibus ex Antiquo et Novo Iure* (in Migne's *Theol. Curs. Complet.,* Vol. XXIV).— *J. Morinus, *Commentarius de Sacris Ecclesiæ Ordinationibus,* Antwerp 1695.— C. Oberndorfer, *De Sacramento Ordinis,* 1759.—*P. Gasparri, *Tractatus Canonicus de Sacra Ordinatione,* Paris 1893.— Cardinal G. M. van Rossum, C.SS. R., *De Essentia Sacramenti Ordinis,* Freiburg 1914.—F. Gillmann, *Zur Lehre der Scholastik vom Spender der Firmung und des Weihesakraments,* Paderborn 1921.—J. Tixeront, *L'Ordre et les Ordinations,* an admirable and non-controversial statement of the Catholic doctrine concerning orders and jurisdiction, both from the theological and the historical point of view, Paris 1925; Engl. tr. by S. A. Raemers, *Holy Orders and Ordination,* St. Louis 1928.—Rouzic, *Les Saintes Ordres,* Paris 1926.

B. J. Otten, S.J., *A Manual of the History of Dogmas,* Vol. I, St. Louis 1917, pp. 42, 52, 81, 87, 168, 326, 347, 350, 355, 474; Vol. II (1918), 380 sqq., 476.

On the different orders see E. Furtner, *Das Verhältnis der Bischofsweihe zum hl. Sakramente des Ordo,* Munich 1861.— A. Kurz, *Der Episkopat der höchste vom Presbyterat verschiedene Ordo,* Vienna 1877.— Schulte-Plassmann, *Der Episkopat ein vom Presbyterat verschiedener, selbständiger und sakramentaler Ordo oder die Bishofsweihe ein Sakrament,* Paderborn 1883.— O. Zardetti, *Die Bischofsweihe,* Einsiedeln 1889.—*L. Soblowsky, *Episkopat und Presbyterat in den ersten christlichen Jahrhunderten,* Würzburg 1893.— L. Gobet, *L'Origine Divine de l'Épiscopat,* Fribourg 1898.—*St. von Dunin-Borkowski, *Die neueren Forschungen über die Anfänge des Episkopates,* Freiburg 1900.—*A. Michiels, *L'Origine de l'Épiscopat,* Louvain 1900.—G. Péries, *Épiscopat et Presbytérat,* Paris 1908.— Arthur König, *Der katholische Priester vor fünfzehn hundert Jahren: Priester und Priestertum nach Hieronymus,* Breslau 1890.— J. N. Seidl, *Der Diakonat in der katholischen Kirche, dessen hieratische Würde und geschichtliche*

Entwicklung, Ratisbon 1884.—H. Reuter, *Das Subdiakonat, dessen historische Entwicklung und liturgisch-kanonistische Bedeutung,* Augsburg 1890.—*F. Wieland, *Die genetische Entwicklung der sogen. Ordines Minores in den ersten drei Jahrhunderten,* Freiburg 1897.—*A. Bruders, S.J., *Die Verfassung der Kirche von den ersten Jahrhunderten der apostolischen Wirksamkeit an bis zum Jahre 175 n. Chr.,* Mayence 1904.

H. C. Lea's *Historical Sketch of Sacerdotal Celibacy,* Philadelphia 1867, is biased and unreliable; cfr. Aug. Vassal, *Le Célibat Ecclésiastique au Premier Siècle de l'Église,* Paris 1896, and in general on Lea's methods as a historian, P. M. Baumgarten, *Die Werke von Henry Charles Lea und verwandte Bücher,* Münster 1908 (English tr., *Henry Charles Lea's Historical Writings; A Critical Inquiry into Their Method and Merit,* New York 1909).

PART III

MATRIMONY

INTRODUCTION

1. DEFINITION.—Matrimony (marriage) may be taken to denote the action, contract, or formality by which the conjugal union is formed (*matrimonium in fieri*) or the union itself as an enduring condition (*matrimonium in facto esse*). The contract is the basis of the married state, as ordination is the basis of the priesthood.

Unlike the five other Sacraments, Holy Orders and Matrimony were instituted for the preservation of the race (in the supernatural and the physical sense), rather than for the sanctification of the individual.

a) As the Sacrament of Holy Orders consists in ordination, so the Matrimony consists in the contract which effects the marital bond. The latter may be regarded both as *res* and *sacramentum*.

Matrimony is defined by the Roman Catechism as *the conjugal union of man and woman between legitimate persons, which is to last during life.*[1]

[1] "*Viri et mulieris maritalis coniunctio inter legitimas personas, individuam vitae consuetudinem retinens.*" (P. II, c. 8, qu. 3). We use Donovan's translation. (*Catechism of the Council of Trent*, p. 292, Dublin 1908).

This definition comprises three essential elements:

a) Marriage is a legitimate contract. Persons who have no right to marry cannot enter into such a contract. Then, again, even between parties who are free to marry each other, not every contract is legitimate. Among baptized Christians the sacramentality of the marriage contract always depends on its legitimacy, and hence the validity of the one is conditioned by the validity of the other.

β) Every true marriage is essentially a *maritalis coniunctio, i. e.* a union of a man and a woman, entered into primarily for the purpose of begetting and rearing children. This object differentiates marriage from every other kind of legitimate union between human beings.

γ) Marriage takes place between rational beings, and hence the conjugal union is crowned and ennobled by a spiritual companionship (*" individua vitae consuetudo "*) which connotes the two essential properties of Matrimony, *i. e.* unity and indissolubility.

b) The objects of Matrimony may be deduced from its nature. They are three, to wit:

(1) The begetting and rearing of offspring in compliance with the divine command to "increase and multiply." [2]

(2) Mutual help and assistance, both bodily and spiritual, for God said in creating Eve, "It is not good for man to be alone: let us make him a help like unto himself." [3]

To these two objects has been added since the Fall of our first parents a third, namely,

---

[2] Gen. I, 28: *" Crescite et multiplicamini."*

[3] Gen. II, 18: *" Faciamus ei adiutorium simile sibi."*

(3) The regulation of the sexual instinct in accordance with the dictates of reason. "For fear of fornication, let every man have his own wife, and let every woman have her own husband." [4]

The two last-mentioned objects are, however, entirely secondary and subordinate to the first and primary end of marriage.

From what we have said it does not follow that a marriage between two persons who have resolved to live continently would not be a true marriage. The Blessed Virgin Mary, though living continently with St. Joseph, was nevertheless his true spouse. [5]

Granted that the third of the objects mentioned above does not appertain to the essence of marriage, and that the second is attainable without conjugal intercourse, the question remains: How can a marriage which excludes the primary purpose of Matrimony, *i. e.* the begetting of children, be a true marriage? [6]

There is a clear-cut distinction between a right (*ius*) and the use of it (*usus iuris*). The right to conjugal intercourse is essential for the validity of marriage; not so, however, the use of it. A man may become the owner of a house without being obliged to occupy it. Similarly, two persons may acquire the right to conjugal intercourse without being obliged to make use of it. " It

4 1 Cor. VII, 2: "*Propter for-nicationem autem unusquisque suam uxorem habeat, et unaquaeque suum virum habeat.*"

5 Cfr. Pohle-Preuss, *Mariology,* 2nd ed., St. Louis 1916, pp. 87 sqq.

6 J. Freisen (*Geschichte des ka-nonischen Eherechtes bis zum Ver-fall der Glossenliteratur,* Paderborn 1888) maintains that it cannot.

is not the destruction of virginity that constitutes Matrimony," says St. Ambrose, " but the marital contract." [7]

2. THE BLESSINGS OF MARRIAGE.—To the three objects of Christian marriage correspond three distinct blessings. By the blessings of marriage we mean those things which make it a source of goodness, thereby rendering it pleasing to God and useful to men.

The three blessings of Matrimony are:

(1) Offspring brought up and educated for God (*bonum prolis*);

(2) Faith or fidelity of husband and wife to each other (*bonum fidei*);

(3) The Sacrament, that is, the indissolubility of the marriage tie, which symbolizes the indivisible union of Christ with His Church (*bonum sacramenti*).

The *bonum prolis* involves three obligations: (a) the procreation of children; (b) their physical care; (c) their mental and religious training. Against these obligations they sin who (1) prevent conception by unlawful means, such as contraceptives or abortion; (2) who disown or neglect their children; and (3) who fail to have them baptized and instructed in the Catholic religion.

The obligations of the married as regards fidelity (*bo-*

[7] *De Inst. Virg.*, c. 6, n. 41: " *Non enim defloratio virginitatis facit coniugium, sed pactio coniugalis.*" For other explanations see Benedict XIV, *De Syn. Dioeces.*, XIII, 22, 13; cfr. St. Thomas, *Summa Theol.*, *Suppl.*, qu. 48, art. 1.— Freisen partially retracted his error in the *Archiv für katholisches Kirchenrecht*, 1892, pp. 369 sqq. He is refuted by Pesch, *Praelect. Dogmat.*, Vol. VII, 3rd ed., pp. 365 sqq.

num fidei) are to render conjugal rights to each other and to avoid all sins against the sixth and ninth commandments.

The blessings of marriage as a Sacrament are peculiar to *Christian* Matrimony, which supernaturally ennobles and perfects both the procreation of children and their bringing up, as also the mutual fidelity of husband and wife, and imparts all graces necessary for the prevention of incontinency. At the same time the *bonum sacramenti* imprints upon the matrimonial contract the supernatural stamp of Christ's mystic union with His Church, and thereby elevates the two properties of every ideal marriage — *i. e.* unity and indissolubility — to the supernatural sphere.[8]

The existence of these blessings proves that marriage is morally licit. This conclusion is confirmed by another consideration. Marriage, being based on the divinely created difference of sex, is a law of nature. It was confirmed by God Himself,[9] and hallowed by our Lord Jesus Christ when He participated in the wedding feast at Cana in Galilee.

The Catholic Church has an additional reason for regarding marriage as sacred and supernaturally meritorious: in her eyes every true marriage between Christians is a Sacrament.[10]

St. Augustine and a few other Patristic writers spoke of marriage as though it involved uncleanness and im-

---

8 Cfr. St. Augustine, *De Genesi ad Liter.*, IX, n. 3; *Decretum pro Armenis,* in Denzinger's *Enchiridion Symbolorum et Definitionum,* 10th edition revised by O. Bannwart, S. J., Freiburg 1908, n. 702.

9 Gen. I, 27 sq.

10 Cfr. the *Caput " Firmiter "* of the Fourth Lateran Council: *" Non solum autem virgines et continentes, verum etiam coniugati per rectam fidem et operationem bonam placentes Deo ad aeternam merentur beatitudinem pervenire."* (Denzinger-Bannwart, n. 430).

morality. But these authors did not mean to deny that
Christian marriage is pleasing in the eyes of God. They
merely wished to censure inordinate concupiscence, which
is an effect of original sin.

3. DIVISION OF THIS TREATISE.—Christian
marriage is a natural, a moral, and a juridical
union, and hence belongs to three separate and
distinct theological disciplines, namely, Dogmatic Theology, Moral Theology, and Canon
Law. We deal with it here in its dogmatic aspects only.

Besides the Church the State is interested in marriage and has the right to regulate its effects so far as they
come within the secular sphere. Hence marriage is to a
certain extent subject to civil authority, provided the precepts of God and His Church are duly complied with.[12]
Moral Theology considers marriage in its ethical relations, showing what is permitted and what is forbidden in
regard to matrimonial engagements, the reception of the
Sacrament, and the married state. Present-day moralists
ought to lay greater stress on the advantages of marriage
as a nursery of virtue,— an aspect which has, unfortunately, been somewhat neglected.
Canon Law is concerned with Matrimony in as far as
it falls under the discipline of the Church.

Dogmatic Theology deals with Matrimony as
an object of faith.
The dogmatic teaching of the Church on Matrimony is summarized by the Council of Trent [11]

11 Sess. XXIV. Can. 1–12.   12 Codex I. C., can. 1016.

in those of its decrees which relate to the sacramental character of Christian marriage, its properties, the power of the Church to set up diriment impediments, and the superiority of virginity over the married state.[13] Other important doctrinal questions regarding the minister of the Sacrament and the precise nature of its matter and form, have been left open to debate.

GENERAL READINGS :—Peter Lombard, *Sent.,* IV, dist. 26 sqq.— St. Thomas, *Summa Theol., Suppl.,* qu. 41–68.— Bellarmine, *De Sancto Matrimonii Sacramento.*— P. Ledesma, *De Magno Matrimonii Sacramento,* Salamanca 1592.— Th. Sanchez, *De Sancto Matrimonii Sacramento,* Genoa 1602.— B. Pontius, *De Sacramento Matrimonii,* 1624.— Chr. Schardt, *De Matrimonio,* 1734.— Tournely, *De Sacramento Matrimonii.*— H. Klee, *Die Ehe; eine dogmatisch-archäologische Abhandlung,* 2nd ed., Mayence 1835.— J. Carrière, *Praelect. Theol. de Matrimonio,* Paris 1837.— Perrone, *De Matrimonio Christiano,* 3 vols., Rome 1861.— M. Heiss, *De Matrimonio,* 5th ed., Rome 1861.— B. Rive, S.J., *Die Ehe in dogmatischer, moralischer und sozialer Beziehung,* Ratisbon 1876.— Palmieri, *De Matrimonio Christiano,* Prati 1897.— M. Rosset, *De Sacramento Matrimonii Tractatus Dogmaticus, Moralis, Canonicus, Liturgicus et Iudicialis,* 6 vols., Fribourg 1896.— A. Devine, C.P., *The Sacraments Explained,* 3rd ed., pp. 431–515, London 1905.— W. Humphrey, S.J., *The One Mediator, or Sacrifice and Sacraments,* pp. 223–237, London 1890.— S. J. Hunter, S.J., *Outlines of Dogmatic Theology,* Vol. III, pp. 403–423.— Wilhelm-Scannell, *A Manual of Catholic Theology,* Vol. II, 2nd ed., pp. 510–532, London 1901.— A. Lehmkuhl, S.J., art. "Marriage, Sacrament of" in Vol. IX of the *Catholic Encyclopedia.*—P. J. Gannon, S.J., *Holy Matrimony,* London, 1928.

13 On the latter point see celibacy, *supra,* pp. 130 sqq.

CHAPTER I

MARRIAGE BETWEEN CHRISTIANS A TRUE SACRAMENT

SECTION 1

NATURE OF THE SACRAMENT AND ITS DIVINE INSTITUTION

Our chief task in this section will be to show from Divine Revelation (1) that marriage between Christians is a Sacrament and (2) that the Sacrament is inseparable from the contract.

Thesis I: The act or formality by which the conjugal union is established among baptized persons is a true Sacrament of the New Law.

This is an article of faith.

Proof. Certain ancient and medieval sects (Encratites, Manichæans, Priscillianists, Albigenses) regarded Matrimony as immoral. The Protestant "Reformers," notably Luther, denied its sacramental character and called it "a worldly thing." Against these heretics the Council of Trent defined: "If anyone saith that Matrimony is not truly and properly one of the seven Sacraments of the evangelic law, instituted by Christ the Lord, but that it has been invented by men in the Church, and that it does not confer grace, let him be anathema." [1]

The Council finds this doctrine "intimated" in St. Paul's Epistle to the Ephesians,[2] but bases its main argument on Tradition.

a) In Eph. V, 25–32 the Apostle admonishes husbands: "Love your wives, as Christ also loved the Church, and delivered himself up for it, that he might sanctify it, cleansing it by the laver of water in the word of life. . . . So also ought men to love their wives as their own bodies. . . . For this cause shall a man leave his father and mother, and shall cleave to his wife, and they shall be two in one flesh. This is a great mystery, but I speak in Christ and the Church." [3]

The Apostle here attributes to Matrimony the three essential notes of a Sacrament, to wit: (1) an external sign, (2) internal grace, (3) institution by Jesus Christ. Hence Christian marriage is a true Sacrament.

1 Sess. XXIV, can. 1: *"Si quis dixerit, matrimonium non esse vere et proprie unum ex septem legis evangelicae sacramentis a Christo Domino institutum, sed ab hominibus in Ecclesia inventum neque gratiam conferre, anathema sit."* (Denzinger-Bannwart, n. 971).

2 Cfr. Sess. XXIV, *Prooemium:* *" Paulus apostolus innuit . . ."*

3 *" Viri, diligite uxores vestras, sicut et Christus dilexit Ecclesiam, et seipsum tradidit pro ea, ut illam sanctificaret, mundans lavacro aquae in verbo vitae. . . . Ita et viri debent diligere uxores suas ut corpora sua. . . . Propter hoc relinquet homo patrem et matrem suam, et adhaerebit uxori suae, et erunt duo in carne una.* [Gen. II, 24]. *Sacramentum hoc magnum est, ego autem dico in Christo et in Ecclesia."*

The external sign is the matrimonial contract, which is represented by St. Paul as a symbol of the union between Christ and His Church. This mystic union, inasmuch as it "sanctifies" and "cleanses" the Church and all her members, is essentially supernatural and productive of grace, and hence Christian marriage, too, must be supernatural and a means of sanctification for those who receive it.

On no other hypothesis can the phrase, " This is a great mystery," [4] be interpreted intelligently. How could the conjugal union between a man and a woman be a great mystery if it did not communicate grace? How could it symbolize the mystic union between Christ and His Church, had not the Lord Himself raised it to the supernatural sphere, in other words, made it a true Sacrament? Thus understood, the term *sacramentum* regains its primitive meaning.

The argument from Eph. V, 25–32 may be briefly formulated thus: A sacred sign which produces internal grace is a true Sacrament. Now Christian marriage is a sacred sign which produces internal grace, because St. Paul calls it a great mystery and a symbol of Christ's union with His Church. Consequently, Christian marriage is a true Sacrament.

As we have seen in a previous volume of this series,[5] the Sacraments of the New Law, unlike the symbols of the Ancient Covenant, not merely signify and prefigure grace, but actually cause or produce it *ex opere operato*. Hence, if Matrimony is a true symbol of the

---

[4] Τὸ μυστήριον τοῦτο μέγα ἐστίν.
[5] Pohle-Preuss, *The Sacraments*, Vol. I, 2nd ed., 1917, pp. 121 sqq.

mystic union between Christ and His Church, it must cause or produce grace in the souls of those who receive it.

According to Luther and Calvin, St. Paul, in speaking of "a great mystery," meant the mystic union of Christ and His Church, not the matrimonial contract adumbrated in the quotation from Gen. II, 24. But the context excludes this interpretation. The Apostle says: "*propter hoc relinquet homo patrem et matrem suam et adhaerebit uxori suae et erunt duo in carne una: sacramentum hoc* [*i. e. coniunctio maritalis*] *magnum est, ego autem dico in Christo et in Ecclesia* [εἰς Χριστὸν καὶ εἰς τὴν ἐκκλησίαν,— that is, in relation to Christ and the Church]." Every legitimate marriage, therefore, is a symbol of the mystic union between Christ and His Church, and hence a great mystery. Adam cannot have meant his own marriage with Eve, as he had neither father nor mother, but evidently spoke with an eye to his future descendants.

Estius objects that if marriage as such symbolized the mystic union of Christ with the Church, it must have been a Sacrament among the pre-Christian Jews and gentiles, or else the Pauline text does not prove it to be a Sacrament at all.

We answer: Though every legitimate marriage is a symbol of Christ's mystic union with His Church, Christian marriage alone is a *perfect* symbol of that union, because it alone produces the grace which it signifies, whereas marriage in Paradise and among the Old Testament Jews and the gentiles of the pre-Christian era was merely an inefficacious symbol.[6]

When did our Lord institute the Sacrament of Matri-

6 Cfr. Tepe, *Institutiones Theologicae*, Vol. IV, pp. 612 sqq., Paris 1896.

mony? This question is answered differently by different
authors. Some say, at the marriage feast of Cana in
Galilee; others, after the Resurrection;[7] a third group
of theologians believes that marriage did not become a
Sacrament until our Lord restored its pristine indissolubility, as recorded in Matth. XIX, 8 sqq.[8]

b) The main argument for the sacramentality
of Christian marriage is derived by the Tridentine Council from the teaching of the Fathers
and early councils, and from the universal belief
and practice of the Church.

α) The argument from prescription is contained in the analogous argument for the septenary number of the Sacraments, as developed in
Pohle-Preuss, *The Sacraments,* Vol. I, pp. 33 sqq.
In particular the following facts should be noted:

No one denies that, since the Protestant Reformation,
Matrimony has been regarded as a Sacrament throughout the Catholic world. Going back another century, we
come upon the statement of the Council of Florence
(A. D. 1439), that "the seventh of the Sacraments is
Matrimony, which is a symbol of the union of Christ with
the Church."[9] How Matrimony was regarded at the
beginning of the twelfth century is evident from the fact
that it was included in the list of Sacraments drawn up
at that time.[10]

---

7 Cfr. Acts I, 3.

8 Cfr. Billuart, *De Matrimonio,*
diss. 1, art. 3.

9 *Decr. pro Armenis: "Septimum
est sacramentum matrimonii, quod
est signum coniunctionis Christi et*
Ecclesiae." (Denzinger-Bannwart,
n. 702).

10 Cfr. the profession of faith sub-
mitted by Michael Palæologus to the
Council of Lyons, A. D. 1274 (Denzinger-Bannwart, n. 465).

The Scholastics unanimously adopted this list.[11]   A few glossators and canonists (Gaufridus, Henry of Ostia, Bernard of Pavia) appear to deny the sacramental character of Matrimony; but in reality they merely assert that Matrimony fails to produce sacramental grace if a pecuniary fee is paid to the officiating priest, because in their opinion this involves simony.   They do not mean to deny that marriage is a true Sacrament.   The objection they raised was solved by the Angelic Doctor as follows: Matrimony is both a Sacrament and an office of nature; to give money for it as an office of nature is permissible; not so, however, as a Sacrament.[12]

As the schismatic Greeks, Russians, and Bulgarians all acknowledge the sacramentality of marriage, this dogma must antedate the great schism of the ninth century. By the same token it can be traced back to the fifth century, because the ancient sects of the Nestorians, Copts, and Armenians, which broke loose from the mother Church as early as 431,[13] retain belief in the Sacrament of Matrimony.   This belief is confirmed by the ancient rituals, e. g. the Sacramentary of Pope Gelasius, who died in 497.[14]

As for the first four centuries of the Christian era, they show no trace of a surreptitious introduction of the doctrine.   On the contrary, certain representations found in the catacombs prove that " in the second century, Christian marriage was not merely a civil function, but

11 Cfr. Pesch, *Praelectiones Dogmaticae*, Vol. VII, 3rd ed., pp. 354 sqq.

12 *Summa Theol.*, 2a 2ae, qu. 100, art. 2, ad 6: " *Dicendum est quod matrimonium non solum est Ecclesiae sacramentum, sed etiam naturae officium. Et ideo dare pecuniam pro matrimonio, inquantum est naturae officium, licitum est; inquantum vero Ecclesiae sacramentum, illicitum.*"

13 Cfr. Schelstrate, *Acta Orient. Eccles.*, Vol. I, pp. 126, 156, 388 sqq.

14 On the teaching of the Oriental sects, see Denzinger, *Ritus Orient.*, Vol. I, pp. 150 sqq., Würzburg 1865.

was already regarded as a Sacrament, to be entered upon before the Church, to be united to the offering of the Holy Sacrifice, and the reception of Holy Communion, and finally to be sealed by the benediction of the priest." [15] On some of the early monuments our Lord is depicted as standing between the bride and the groom, blessing them or crowning them with a wreath.[16]

Hence belief in the sacramental character of Matrimony is as old as the Church, which is merely another way of saying that it comes to us through the Apostles from our Lord Himself.[17]

β) With the exception of St. Augustine, the early Fathers intimate rather than express their belief in the sacramentality of marriage. But all without exception insist on its sanctity, and hence it is contrary to Patristic teaching to say, as Luther did, that Matrimony is "a worldly thing." [18]

St. Augustine expressly calls Christian marriage a Sacrament and ranks it with Baptism and Holy Orders. " It is certainly not fecundity only," he says, " the fruit of which consists of offspring, nor chastity only, whose bond is fidelity, but also a certain Sacrament which is recommended to believers in wedlock, wherefor the Apostle says, ' Husbands, love your wives, even as Christ also loved the Church.' Of this Sacrament the substance undoubtedly is this, that the man and the woman who are

---

15 A. S. Barnes, *The Early Church in the Light of the Monuments,* London 1913, p. 141.

16 F. X. Kraus, *Realenzyklopädie der christl. Altertümer,* Vol. I, pp. 283 sqq., Freiburg 1879.

17 Cfr. Nicole and Arnauld, *Per-*

petuité de la Foi, Vol. V, l. 6, c. 1 (on this work see Pohle-Preuss, *The Sacraments,* Vol. II, p. 55, n. 3); C. M. Kaufmann, *Handbuch der christl. Archäologie,* pp. 442 sq., Paderborn 1905.

18 *Von Ehesachen,* 1530.

joined together in wedlock should remain inseparable as long as they live, and that it should be unlawful, except for the cause of fornication, for one consort to be parted from the other. For this [principle] is faithfully observed in Christ and the Church, that living together they be not separated by a divorce. And so complete is the observance of this Sacrament in the city of our God, on His holy mountain,— that is to say, in the Church of Christ,— by all married believers, who are undoubtedly members of Christ, that although women marry and men take wives for the purpose of begetting children, it is never permitted to put away even an unfruitful wife for the sake of having another to bear children. . . . Thus between the conjugal pair, as long as they live, the nuptial bond [19] remains, which can be cancelled neither by separation nor by union with another. But this fact tends only to aggravate the crime, not to strengthen the covenant, as the soul of an apostate, which renounces as it were its marriage union with Christ, does not, even though it has cast away its faith, lose the Sacrament of faith [Baptism] which it received in the laver of regeneration." [20]

19 " Quiddam coniugale " (= quasi character; v. infra, Sect. 3, no. 3).

20 De Nupt. et Concup., I, 10, 11: " Quoniam sane non tantum foecunditas, cuius fructus in prole est, nec tantum pudicitia, cuius vinculum est fides, verum etiam quoddam sacramentum nuptiarum commendatur fidelibus coniugatis, unde dicit Apostolus: Viri, diligite uxores vestras, sicut et Christus dilexit Ecclesiam. Huius procul dubio sacramenti res est, ut mas et femina connubio copulati, quamdiu vivunt, inseparabiliter perseverent, nec liceat, exceptâ causâ fornicationis, a coniuge coniugem dirimi. Hoc enim custoditur in Christo et Ecclesia, ut vivens cum vivente nullo divortio separetur. Cuius sacramenti tanta observatio est in civitate Dei nostri, in monte sancto eius, hoc est in Ecclesia Christi, quibusque fidelibus coniugatis, qui sine dubio membra sunt Christi, ut quum filiorum procreandorum causa vel nubant feminae vel ducantur uxores, nec sterilem coniugem fas sit relinquere, ut alia foecunda ducatur. . . . Ita manet inter viventes quiddam coniugale, quod nec separatio nec cum altero copulatio possit auferre. Manet autem ad noxam criminis, non ad vinculum foederis, sicut apostatae anima velut de con·

In another passage the same holy Doctor compares Matrimony with Holy Orders: "The good that is secured by marriage . . . consists in the . . . chastity of the married fidelity, but in the case of God's people [the Christians] it consists moreover in the holiness of the Sacrament, by which it is forbidden, even after a separation has taken place, to marry another as long as the first partner lives, . . . just as priests are ordained to draw together a Christian community, and even though no such community be formed, the Sacrament of Orders still abides in those ordained, or as the Sacrament of the Lord, once it is conferred, abides even in one who is dismissed from his office on account of guilt, although in such a one it abides unto judgment." [21]

Other Fathers, while not so explicit in their pronouncements regarding the sacramental character of Matrimony, emphasize its sanctity. Thus St. Ambrose declares that marriage was hallowed by Christ, but its sanctifying power is lost by those who dishonor it. "We know," he says, "that God is as it were the head and protector of marriage, who does not permit that another's marriage bed be defiled; and further that one guilty of such a crime sins against God, whose law he violates and whose bond of grace he loosens. Therefore, since he sins against God, he loses his participation in the heavenly Sacrament." [22]

---

iugio Christi recedens etiam fide perdită sacramentum fidei [baptisma] non amittit, quod lavacro regenerationis accepit."

21 *De Bono Coniug.*, c. 24, n. 32: *"Bonum igitur nuptiarum . . . est in fide castitatis, quod autem ad populum Dei pertinet, etiam in sanctitate sacramenti, per quam nefas est etiam repudio discedentem alteri nubere, dum vir eius vivit, . . . quemadmodum si fiat ordinatio cleri ad*

plebem congregandam, etiamsi plebis congregatio non subsequatur, manet tamen in illis ordinatis sacramentum ordinationis et, si aliquâ culpâ quisquam ab officio removeatur, sacramento Domini semel imposito non carebit, quamvis ad iudicium permanente."— Cfr. P. Schanz, *Die Lehre von den hl. Sakramenten*, pp. 729 sqq., Freiburg 1893.

22 *De Abraham*, I, 7, 59: *"Cognoscimus velut praesulem custodem-*

Origen says: " God Himself has fused the two into one, so that they are no longer two after the man has married the woman. Inasmuch, however, as God is the author of this union, grace resides in those who are united by God. Well aware of this, St. Paul declares that Matrimony, according to the word of God, is a grace, just as a chaste unmarried life is a grace." [23]

That marriage was sanctified in a particular manner by our Lord at Cana, is a thought expressed by many of the Fathers. Thus St. Cyril of Alexandria says: " [Christ] was present, not to feast, but to work a miracle and thereby to sanctify the very foundation of human procreation, in so far, namely, as the flesh is concerned." [24]

The most ancient Patristic writers treat Christian marriage as a sacred thing. Tertullian writes to his wife: " How shall we describe the happiness of those marriages which the Church ratifies, the sacrifice strengthens, the blessing seals, the angels publish, the Heavenly Father propitiously beholds." [25] St. Ignatius of Antioch (d. about 117) says: " Speak to my sisters that they love the Lord, and be content with their husbands in flesh and in spirit. In the same way enjoin on my brothers, in the name of Jesus Christ, to love their wives as the Lord loved His Church. . . . It is right for men and women who marry to be united with the consent of the bishop (μετὰ γνώμης τοῦ ἐπισκόπου), that the marriage may be according to the Lord, and not according to lust." [26]

---

que coniugii esse Deum, qui non patiatur alienum torum pollui, et si quis fecerit, peccare in Deum, cuius legem violet, gratiam solvat. Et ideo, quia in Deum peccat, sacramenti coelestis amittit consortium." (Migne, *P. L.*, XIV, 465).

23 *In Matth.*, tom. 14, n. 16 (Migne, *P. G.*, XIII, 1230).

24 *In Ioa.*, c. 2, 2, 1 sq. (Migne,

P. G., LXXIII, 223).

25 *Ad Uxorem*, II, 9: " *Unde sufficiamus ad enarrandam felicitatem eius matrimonii, quod Ecclesia conciliat et confirmat oblatio et obsignat benedictio, angeli renuntiant, Pater rato habet.*" (Migne, *P. L.*, I, 1302).

26 *Ep. ad Polycarpum*, c. 5, n. 1 and 2, ed. Funk, I, 251; Kirsopp

Thesis II: Among Christians every legitimately contracted marriage is *eo ipso* a Sacrament, and, vice versa, whenever the Sacrament of Matrimony is received, there is a legitimate nuptial contract.

This proposition may be qualified as *"communis et certa."*

Proof. Among the Old Testament Jews and the gentiles of the pre-Christian epoch, marriage was not a Sacrament, but merely a contract, as it still is between non-baptized persons to-day. Between Christians, however, Matrimony is always a Sacrament.

How does the contract become a Sacrament? Is the sacramental sign added to the contract by the blessing of the priest, or is the contract itself intrinsically raised to the rank of a grace-producing sign?   Christ was free to choose either of these two methods; which one He did adopt can be determined only from Revelation.

If the marriage contract became a Sacrament by the addition of some external sign, it would be possible for baptized Christians to make a marital contract without receiving the Sacrament of Matrimony.

Lake, *The Apostolic Fathers*, Vol. I, p. 273.— On the Patristic argument for the sacramentality of Matri= mony, see J. Müllendorf in the *Zeitschrift für katholische Theologie*, Innsbruck, 1878, pp. 633 sqq.; Palmieri, *De Matrimonio Christiano*, thes. 7, Prati 1897.

That this *is* possible was formerly held by three groups of theologians.

(1) The so-called " court theologians " of the Gallican and Josephinist school (Antonio de Dominis,[27] Launoy,[28] J. N. Nuytz, J. A. Petzek, M. M. Tabaraud, J. A. Theiner, and Th. Ziegler) held that the Sacrament is constituted by the blessing of the priest and that the contract is merely a necessary requisite. This theory was avowedly contrived for the purpose of withdrawing matrimonial causes from the jurisdiction of the Church and handing them over to the State.

(2) Cano,[29] Sylvius, Estius, and Tournely regarded the contract as the matter and the sacerdotal blessing as the form of the Sacrament.[30] The contract itself, if legitimately concluded, is valid, they said; but it is not a Sacrament until completed by the nuptial blessing of the priest.

(3) Vasquez,[31] Hurtado, Platel, Billuart, Gonet, Holtzclau (of the Wirceburgenses) and other writers denied that the priestly blessing constitutes the sacramental form of Matrimony. They held that the sacramentality of the marriage contract depends on the presence or absence, in the souls of the contracting parties, of the intention of doing what the Church does. According to this school it is optional with the contracting parties whether, in giving the matrimonial consent, they receive a Sacrament or not.

All these theories are untenable because a marriage contract between baptized persons is *eo ipso* a Sacrament.

a) This truth is demonstrable from Revelation.

27 *De Republ. Eccles.*, I, 3, c. 2.
28 *De Regia in Matrim. Potest.*, Vol. I, p. 2, c. 4.
29 *De Locis Theol.*, l. VIII, c. 5.

30 *V. infra,* Ch. II, Sect. 1.
31 *De Sacram. in Gen.*, disp. 138, c. 5.

According to St. Paul, it is always a great mystery (*i. e.* a Sacrament) [32] among Christians when "a man leaves father and mother and cleaves to his wife." [33]   As this happens in every legitimate marriage, it follows that every legitimate marriage between Christians is a true Sacrament.

Though the Fathers did not treat this question expressly, they taught that marriage between baptized persons is a sacred thing, a great mystery, the most perfect symbol of the mystic union of Christ with His Church, and therefore indissoluble and monogamic ; and in so teaching they implicitly inculcated the inseparability of the contract from the Sacrament.   Their teaching was scientifically developed by the Schoolmen.   " The words in which the matrimonial consent is expressed," says *e. g.* St. Thomas, " constitute the form of this Sacrament; not the sacerdotal blessing, which is a sort of sacramental." [34]

Melchior Cano ($+$ 1560) was the first Catholic theologian to assert that the contract is merely the matter of the Sacrament, whereas the sacerdotal blessing constitutes its form.   He admitted that his assertion was contrary to the teaching of all his predecessors.   In matter of fact it is not only singular, but wrong, as can be shown from the official utterances of popes and councils before and after Cano's time,— utterances which, though not ex-cathedra decisions, unmistakably indicate the mind of the Church.

b) Thus the Council of Florence (1439) de-

---

32 *V. supra*, Thesis I.

33 Gen. II, 24.

34 *Summa Theol., Suppl.*, qu. 42, art. 1, ad 1: " *Verba, quibus consensus exprimitur matrimonialis* [*i. e. contractus*], *sunt forma huius sacramenti, non autem benedictio sacerdotalis, quae est quoddam sacramentale.*"

clares: "The seventh Sacrament is that of Matrimony. The efficient cause of Matrimony [*i. e.* as a Sacrament] invariably is the mutual consent expressed by words in the present tense." [35] From this definition we argue: The "mutual consent" of the contracting parties admittedly constitutes the marriage contract. If this same consent is the efficient cause of the Sacrament, contract and Sacrament must be identical.

This teaching is at least indirectly confirmed by the Council of Trent when, speaking of Christian marriage, it says: "If anyone saith that Matrimony is not truly and properly one of the seven Sacraments of the evangelic law, . . . let him be anathema." [36] Every marriage between Christians is a true Sacrament; consequently contract and Sacrament coincide.

We find this conclusion expressly drawn in a letter of Pope Pius VI. "It is an article of faith," he says, "that Matrimony, which before the advent of Christ was nothing but a sort of indissoluble contract, after His coming became one of the seven Sacraments of the New Law, instituted by Christ our Lord, as . . . the Council of Trent has defined under pain of excommunication." [37]

Pius IX resolutely defended the proposition that

---

[35] *Decr. pro Armenis:* "*Septimum est sacramentum matrimonii. Causa efficiens matrimonii regulariter est mutuus consensus per verba de praesenti expressus.*" (Denzinger-Bannwart, n. 702).

[36] Sess. XXIV, can. 1: "*Si quis dixerit, matrimonium non esse vere et proprie unum ex septem legis evangelicae sacramentis, . . . anathema sit.*"

[37] *Epist. ad Episc. Motulensem:* "*Dogma fidei est, ut matrimonium, quod ante adventum Christi nihil aliud erat nisi indissolubilis quidam contractus, illud post Christi adventum evaserit unum ex septem Novae Legis sacramentis a Christo Domino institutum, quemadmodum . . . Tridentinum sub anathematis poena definivit.*"

"among Christians there can be no marriage which is not at the same time a Sacrament, . . . and consequently the Sacrament can never be separated from the marital contract." [38] The contrary teaching of Professor Nuytz of Turin was condemned in the Syllabus.[39]

Leo XIII, in his Encyclical letter "*Arcanum divinae sapientiae*," of Feb. 10, 1880, declares that "in Christian marriage the contract is inseparable from the Sacrament, and therefore the contract cannot be true and legitimate without being a Sacrament as well." He adds: "For Christ our Lord added to marriage the dignity of a Sacrament; but marriage is the contract itself, whenever that contract is lawfully concluded. . . . Hence it is clear that among Christians every true marriage is, in itself and by itself, a Sacrament, and that nothing can be farther from the truth than to say that the Sacrament is a certain added ornament or outward endowment which can be separated and torn away from the contract at the caprice of man." [40]

In the light of can. 1012 of the new Code it is plain that the separability of the contract from the Sacrament may no longer be maintained by Catholics.

---

38 Allocution of Sept. 27, 1852: "*Inter fideles matrimonium dari non posse, quin uno eodemque tempore sit sacramentum . . . ac proinde a coniugali foedere sacramentum separari nunquam posse.*"

39 Prop. 73: "*Vi contractus mere civilis potest inter Christianos constare veri nominis matrimonium, falsumque est, aut contractum matrimonii inter Christianos semper esse sacramentum aut nullum esse contractum, si sacramentum excludatur.*" (Denzinger-Bannwart, n. 1773).

40 "*Exploratum est in matrimonio christiano contractum a sacramento non esse dissociabilem atque ideo non posse contractum verum et legitimum consistere, quin sit eo ipso sacramentum. Nam Christus Dominus dignitate sacramenti auxit matrimonium; matrimonium autem est ipse contractus, si modo sit factus iure. . . . Itaque apparet omne inter Christianos iustum coniugium in se et per se esse sacramentum nihilque magis abhorrere a veritate quam esse sacramentum decus quoddam adiunctum aut proprietatem allapsam extrinsecus, quae a contractu disiungi ac separari hominum arbitratu queat.*" (Denzinger-Bannwart, n. 1854).

c) Though the main question is thus decided, theological controversies regarding exceptional cases continue.

a) One of the questions most hotly debated among theologians is whether the marriage of an unbaptized couple becomes a Sacrament when both husband and wife embrace the Christian faith.

Vasquez, Mastrius, Simmonet, and a number of Thomist theologians answer this question negatively on the ground that only the original contract can be raised to the dignity of a Sacrament, not its subsequent approbation.

Capreolus, Henriquez, and Bellarmine, on the other hand, hold that in such a case the original contract becomes a Sacrament by a renewal of consent on the part of the contracting parties, and that this act assumes the functions of the sacramental sign and constitutes a renewal of the contract on a Christian basis.

Sanchez, Tanner, and the majority teach that the reception of Baptism suffices to elevate what was originally a mere marriage of nature to the dignity of a Sacrament. This theory is far more plausible than the other two, for if it were necessary to renew the consent, the omission of this formality would result in a marriage which was not a Sacrament,— a conclusion inadmissible in the light of the Patristic, conciliar, and papal teaching set forth above. Hence the reception of Baptism is sufficient to reconstitute the bond of pagan wedlock and impress upon it the Christian stamp, and such converts receive the sacramental graces of Matrimony together with those of Baptism.

β) The case is more complicated when only one of the two contracting parties embraces Christianity, or when an unbaptized marries a baptized person — presuming, of course, that the diriment impediment of *disparitas cultus* has been removed by a dispensation. Does the baptized party in that case receive the Sacrament?

Dominicus Soto, Perrone, Palmieri, Pesch, and others hold that such a marriage is a true Sacrament, for two reasons: first, because the Church claims jurisdiction over it, and secondly, because at least one of the contracting parties is capable of receiving the sacramental grace of Matrimony.

Sanchez, Tanner, Hurter, Tepe, Atzberger, and others deny the cogency of this argument and assert that the matrimonial tie binds both contracting parties in precisely the same way. This seems to us the more acceptable view. ("*Matrimonium non debet claudicare.*") [41]

γ) Another debated question is whether marriage contracted by proxy or by letter is a true Sacrament. A marriage contracted in either one of these two ways is undoubtedly valid as a contract, and since the contract among Christians is inseparable from the Sacrament, such a marriage is a true Sacrament, and Cano and Cajetan erred in asserting that it requires an oral ratification by the contracting parties to raise it to sacramental dignity. Marriage by proxy has always been regarded as valid under the Canon Law, and the Tridentine Council merely added a new condition when it ordained that the representatives of both parties must sign the marriage contract in presence of the pastor and the required witnesses.

41 Cfr. De Augustinis, *De Re Sacramentaria,* Vol. II, 2nd ed., pp. 633 sqq. Cfr. *Codex Iuris Can.,* can. 1088, § 1.

MATTER AND FORM

1. FALSE THEORIES.—From what was said in the preceding Section it follows that we must reject all those theories which seek the matter and form of the Sacrament of Matrimony elsewhere than in the mutual consent of the contracting parties.

a) Thus Melchior Cano teaches that the mutual consent of the contracting parties, whether manifested by words or signs, constitutes merely the matter of the Sacrament, its form being the benediction pronounced by the priest.

That this view is false follows from the reflection that, if the sacerdotal blessing were for some reason omitted, there would, in Cano's hypothesis, be a valid matrimonial contract but no Sacrament. Moreover, the Council of Trent recognized the validity of clandestine marriages contracted in places where the *" Tametsi"* had not been promulgated. By a clandestine marriage we understand one contracted secretly without the coöperation of the pastor and the required witnesses. The Council said that all such marriages, when freely contracted where the *" Tametsi"* had not been published, were *" rata*

et vera," unless formally nullified by the Church.[1]   Note
that, according to Tridentine as well as present-day usage,
a legitimate marriage among Christians is always a Sacrament, whether blessed by a priest or not.   The words
pronounced by the priest, *"Ego vos in matrimonium
coniungo,"* contribute nothing to the validity of the Sacrament.   This formula occurs in none of the ancient rituals,[2]
and is omitted whenever a marriage is contracted with the
merely passive assistance of the pastor.   The object of this
formula, therefore, is merely to acknowledge the marriage as publicly and solemnly contracted *in facie Ecclesiae*[3] and to declare its sacramental nature.[4]

b) Vasquez does not go quite so far astray as
Cano when he teaches that the matter of the
Sacrament is constituted by the bodies of the contracting parties, in so far as they are mutually
surrendered for the sacred purposes of wedlock.
While it is quite true that both the contract and
the Sacrament have the bodies of the contracting
parties for their object, Vasquez is mistaken in

1 Sess. XXIV, cap. 1, *De Reform.
Matrim.*: *" Tametsi   dubitandum
non est, clandestina matrimonia
libero contrahentium consensu facta
rata et vera esse matrimonia, quamdiu Ecclesia ea irrita non fecit, et
proinde iure damnandi sunt illi, ut
eos S. Synodus anathemate damnat,
qui vera ac rata esse negant, . . .
nihilominus,"* etc.

2 Cfr. Martène, *De Antiq. Eccles. Rit.*, l. I, c. 9, art. 3.

3 Hence the term, *solemnizatio matrimonii.*

4 Cfr. St. Bonaventure, *Com-*

ment. in Sent., IV, dist. 28, qu. 5:
*" Ad esse matrimonii ista duo suf-
ficiunt, scil. legitimitas in personis et
unitas in consensu. Ad solemnitatem
vero et decorem et honestatem requiritur et parentum traditio et sacerdotum benedictio; haec tamen ita
sunt ad decorem sacramenti, ut tamen sint de necessitate praecepti."*—
Merely as a curiosity we will mention Catharinus' view that the form
of the Sacrament is contained in the
virtually persisting words of Adam,
recorded in Gen. II, 24. On the
present practice see *Codex Iuris
Can.*, can. 1094, 1098.

regarding these as the proximate matter of the Sacrament. In reality the proximate matter (*materia proxima sive ex qua*) is the matrimonial contract itself. The bodies of the contracting parties are merely the remote matter (*materia remota sive circa quam*).

It needs no special argument to prove that the sacramental form, too, must be contained somewhere in the matrimonial contract. The question is, where? The form might conceivably be sought (though I do not believe any theologian has ever looked for it there) in the formal signification of the words embodying the matrimonial consent, assuming the matter to be contained in the material sound. This assumption would be analogous to that of the Scotists regarding Penance, and equally unconvincing. The same must be said of Navarrus' view that the matter of Matrimony is to be found in the internal consent and the form in the external assent of the contracting parties.[5] The external assent is merely the outward expression of the internal consent. Moreover, the matter (as well as the form) of a Sacrament must be perceptible by the senses.

2. THE TRUE THEORY.—The only tenable theory is that of Bellarmine, Suarez, Sanchez, and other authors,—that both the matter and the form of the Sacrament are contained in the matrimonial contract itself, being the words of consent spoken by the contracting parties, or the signs used instead. These words or signs constitute

[5] Navarrus, *Manuale,* c. 22, n. 20.

the matter of the Sacrament in so far as they signify the mutual surrender of the bodies (*traditio*), and its form in so far as they signify the acceptance (*acceptatio*) of the same.

It is easy to see the mutual relation of these two functions. The *traditio* is something undetermined and receives its determination from the *acceptatio*. "These two," says Suarez, "namely, *traditio* and *acceptatio,* so concur in the matrimonial contract that the *traditio* underlies and forms the basis of the *acceptatio,* which, in its turn, completes the contract. Thus it happens that the mutual consent of the contracting parties . . . has the nature of matter in as far as it contains the mutual *traditio,* and the nature of form in as far as it effects the mutual *acceptatio*." [6] Though the words, " I take you for my lawful husband (wife) " directly signify and effect the marital union (*nexus maritalis*), they indirectly signify and effect sanctifying grace, because every marriage between Christians, by virtue of the divine institution of Matrimony, is necessarily a symbol of the mystical union of Christ with His Church.[7]

---

[6] Suarez, *De Sacram. in Genere,* disp. 2, sect. 1, n. 4: " *Haec duo, scil. traditio et acceptatio, ita in contractu concurrunt, ut traditio supponatur acceptationi et in illa inchoetur, per hanc vero consummetur contractus. Atque hinc fit, ut consensus utriusque coniugis, . . . quatenus mutuam traditionem continent, habeant rationem materiae, quatenus vero efficiunt mutuam acceptationem, habeant rationem formae.*"

[7] V. Sect. 1, *supra.*

SECTION 3

SACRAMENTAL EFFECTS

1. INCREASE OF SANCTIFYING GRACE.—The first effect of Christian marriage is an increase of sanctifying grace.

" If anyone saith," defines the Tridentine Council, " that Matrimony . . . does not confer grace, let him be anathema." [1]

Whenever the Council speaks of grace conferred by a Sacrament, it means *sanctifying* grace. Matrimony, being a symbol of Christ's union with His mystic spouse, necessarily presupposes the state of sanctifying grace, and hence its first and principal effect can be none other than to augment that grace.

It follows that Matrimony is, by its very concept, a Sacrament of the living.

If it is received in the state of mortal sin, there are two possibilities: Either the unworthy recipient is conscious of the state of his soul, or he is unconscious thereof. In the former case he commits a sacrilege by receiving the Sacrament *informe* or *ficte,* as it were under false pretences, and thereby deprives himself of its graces, at least so long as the obstacle (*obex gratiae*) is not removed by an act of perfect contrition or the worthy reception of Penance. In the latter case he is unconscious of being in the state of mortal sin, and hence acts in good faith

---

1 Sess. XXIV, can. 1: *" Si quis dixerit, matrimonium . . . . neque gratiam conferre, anathema sit."*

168

and may, if he has imperfect contrition, receive sanctifying grace *per accidens*.

2. THE SACRAMENTAL GRACE OF MATRIMONY. —Besides increasing sanctifying grace, matrimony confers certain special graces. This is evident *a priori* from a consideration of the great importance of this Sacrament for family, State, and Church, as well as the onerous nature of the duties and burdens which it imposes.

The " sacramental grace " of Matrimony probably consists in a claim based upon and confirmed by sanctifying grace, which claim entitles the recipient to the actual graces (*gratiae actuales*) necessary for faithfully performing the duties of the married state. The Tridentine Council says: " The grace which might perfect that natural love [of husband and wife for each other] and confirm that indissoluble union and sanctify the married, Christ Himself . . . merited for us by His Passion; as the Apostle Paul intimates, saying: ' Husbands, love your wives as Christ loved the Church.' . . . Impious men of this age, in their foolish rage, have not only harbored false notions touching this venerable Sacrament, but, introducing . . . a carnal liberty," etc.[2]

An analysis of this teaching enables us to distinguish a twofold class of graces conferred by Matrimony: some impart strength for the faithful performance of the duties of the married state, others serve as

2 Sess. XXIV, *Prooem.*: " *Gratiam vero, quae naturalem amorem perficeret, et indissolubilem unionem confirmaret coniugesque sanctificaret, ipse Christus . . . suâ nobis passione promeruit. Quod Paulus Apostolus innuit dicens: Viri, diligite uxores vestras, sicut Christus dilexit Ecclesiam . . . Impii homines huius saeculi insanientes non solum perperam de hoc venerabili sacramento senserunt, sed . . . libertatem carnis introducentes,*" etc. (Denzinger-Bannwart, n. 969).

a medicine against the temptations of the flesh. To the former class belong the perfection of the natural love which husband and wife have for each other, after the pattern of Christ's love for His mystical spouse; conscientiousness in the begetting and rearing of children; prudence in daily intercourse; patience and trust in God; mutual forbearance, etc. The latter class comprises those actual graces that counteract the threefold concupiscence to which human flesh is heir since the Fall.[3]

3. THE QUASI-CHARACTER OF MATRIMONY.— Another effect peculiar to Matrimony is the marriage bond (*vinculum matrimoniale*), which symbolizes the one and indissoluble union of Christ with His mystic spouse, the Church. This effect strongly resembles the sacramental character imprinted by Baptism, Confirmation, and Holy Orders,[4] and hence is often called *quasi-character*.

Bellarmine[5] and Sanchez[6] regard the marriage bond as a sort of permanent Sacrament. But this view is

3 Cfr. St. Bonaventure, *C. in Sent.*, IV, dist. 26, art. 2, qu. 2: " *Ex hac gratia fit remedium contra triplicem inordinationem concupiscentiae et nascitur triplex bonum matrimonii. Concupiscentia enim inclinat ad multas, quia luxuriosus non est unâ [muliere] contentus; et matrimonio datur gratia homini, ut soli uxori velit coniungi et ita pronitas ad multas excluditur per copulam singularem. Concupiscentia etiam inclinat ad delectationem, non ad utilitatem, quia luxuriosus non quaerit nisi satisfactionem appetitivae seu appetitus sensitivi: datur ergo gratia in matrimonio, ut non cognoscat uxorem nisi propter prolem, et ita excluditur delectatio per copulam utilem. Item concupiscentia fastidium generat post impletionem, unde luxuriosus, postquam cognovit unam, illam respuit et vadit ad aliam; in matrimonio vero datur gratia, ut semper velit esse cum una et ita excluditur variarum concupiscentia per copulam inseparabilem.*"— Needless to add, all these graces become efficacious only if husband and wife faithfully coöperate with them.

4 Cfr. Pohle-Preuss, *The Sacraments*, Vol. I, p. 95.

5 *De Matrimonio*, I, 6.

6 *De Matrimonio*, l. II. disp. 5.

untenable. The Sacrament proper (*sacramentum tantum*) in Matrimony is the transient act by which the conjugal contract is formed, just as the Sacrament of Baptism is the transient act of ablution. But the bond of wedlock is a permanent effect, bearing a striking resemblance to the character imprinted by Baptism, Confirmation, and Holy Orders, and hence must be regarded as *res et sacramentum,* and may justly be styled " quasi-character," especially in view of the fact that it renders the Sacrament incapable of repetition during the lifetime of both contracting parties. It would be wrong, however, to ascribe to Matrimony a sacramental character in the strict sense. The mark imprinted on the soul by this Sacrament, unlike the character imparted by the other three Sacraments mentioned, is not physical, but purely moral.

From the " quasi-character " of Matrimony flow the two properties of Christian marriage, *viz.:* unity (*unitas*) and indissolubility (*indissolubilitas*).[7]

READINGS.—D. McBride, *Christian Marriage a Sacrament,* Toronto 1920.

7 *Codex I. C.,* can. 1013, § 2.

CHAPTER II

SECTION 1

UNITY

The unity of marriage (*unitas matrimonii*) consists in this, that a man has only one wife and a woman only one husband. This ideal state is called *monogamy*.

Opposed to monogamy is *polygamy*. Polygamy may mean: (1) a plurality of wives or husbands in succession; (2) a plurality of husbands at the same time, more properly called *polyandry;* (3) a plurality of wives at the same time, which is polygamy in the strict sense of the term.

Successive polygamy, *i. e.* repeated marriage, is not destructive of the unity of wedlock. The same cannot be said of polyandry, nor of polygamy proper, though here, too, it is necessary to make a distinction. Polyandry (*polyandria simultanea*) is directly contrary to the law of nature, whereas polygamy (*polygamia simultanea*) is forbidden by a positive divine law, but not by the law of nature, at least not absolutely. The

Catholic teaching on these points can best be explained in the form of two theses.

Thesis I: Polyandry, *i. e.* a plurality of husbands at the same time, is no true marriage, but a crime against the law of nature.

This may be technically qualified as *"propositio certa."*

Proof. That polyandry is opposed to the law of nature is so evident that the Church takes the illicitness and invalidity of such marriages for granted.[1]

The profession of faith made by the Emperor Michael Palæologus at the Council of Lyons, A. D. 1274, contains this passage: "With regard to Matrimony [the Church] holds that a man may not have several wives at the same time, and that a woman is not permitted to have several husbands."[2] Polyandry, *i. e.* a plurality of husbands at the same time, is forbidden because it frustrates the primary object of marriage, *i. e.* the begetting of children, and thus destroys the *bonum prolis*. A woman who habitually has carnal intercourse with several men will rarely conceive.[3] Were such a relation permitted, the human race would soon become extinct. If (as sometimes happens) children are born of a polyandrous marriage, their parentage is often uncertain and it is generally speaking impossible to provide properly for their bodily and spiritual training. For these reasons polyandry is held in

---

1 Cfr. Rom. VII, 3.

2 "*De Matrimonio vero tenet [Ecclesia], quod nec unus vir plures uxores simul nec una mulier permittitur habere plures viros.*" (Denzinger-Bannwart, n. 465).

3 Cfr. St. Augustine, *De Bono Coniug.*, c. 17, n. 20: "*Plures enim feminae ab uno viro foetari possunt, una vero a pluribus non potest.*"

abhorrence by civilized nations, and even by the majority of uncivilized tribes.

Thesis II: Polygamy proper, *i. e.* having several wives at the same time, cannot be a valid marriage.

This proposition is *de fide*.

Proof. While Calvin, in his extreme rigorism, condemned the plural marriages of the Patriarchs as adulterous, Luther and Melanchthon erred in the opposite direction by declaring polygamy to be permissible under the New Testament and allowing the Landgrave Philip of Hesse to marry another woman while his legitimate wife was still alive.[4] The excesses committed by the Anabaptists of Münster are notorious. Mormonism is a menace to the American Republic.[*]

Against Luther the Council of Trent defined: "If anyone saith that it is lawful for Christians to have several wives at the same time, and that this is not prohibited by any divine law, let him be anathema."[5]

The unity of Christian marriage can be demonstrated from Scripture and Tradition.

a) Christ Himself restored monogamy, as it had existed in Paradise, and made it the only

---

4 Cfr. *Lutheri Opera*, ed. De Wette, V, 241: "*Quod circa matrimonium in lege Moysis fuit permissum, Evangelium non revocat aut vetat.*"

5 Sess. XXIV, can. 2: "*Si quis dixerit, licere Christianis plures simul habere uxores et hoc nullâ lege divinâ esse prohibitum, anathema sit.*"

* See C. S. Jones, *The Truth about Mormonism*, 1920.

valid form of Matrimony.   Cfr. Matth. XIX, 4
sqq.: "Have you not read that he who made
man from the beginning, made them male and
female?   And he said: For this cause shall a
man leave father and mother, and shall cleave to
his wife, and they two shall be in one flesh.
Therefore now they are not two, but one flesh.
What therefore God hath joined together, let no
man put asunder." [6]

When the Pharisees, in response to this
declaration, called our Lord's attention to the
fact that "Moses commanded to give a bill of
divorce," Jesus replied: "From the beginning it
was not so.   And I say to you that whosoever
shall put away his wife, and shall marry another,
committeth adultery." [7]

In the first of these texts our Lord establishes
monogamy as the law of the New Testament; in
the second, He condemns polygamy as adulterous.

St. Paul always speaks of monogamy as a matter of course (cfr. Rom. VII, 2 sqq.; 1 Cor. VII, 2
sq., 10 sq.; Eph. V, 31).

The Fathers unanimously uphold monogamy and condemn polygamy.   Theophilus of Antioch (+ about 186)

[6] Matth. XIX, 4 sqq.; " *Non legi-
stis, quia qui fecit hominem ab initio, masculum et feminam* (ἄρσεν
καὶ θῆλυ) *fecit eos et dixit: Propter hoc dimittet homo patrem et
matrem et adhaerebit uxori suae* (τῇ
γυναικὶ αὐτοῦ) *et erunt duo in carne
una* (οἱ δύο εἰς σάρκα μίαν). *Itaque iam non sunt duo, sed una caro.
Quod ergo Deus coniunxit, homo
non separet.*"

[7] Matth. XIX, 8 sq.: " *Ab initio
autem non fuit sic.   Dico autem vobis, quia quicunque dimiserit uxorem
suam . . . et aliam duxerit, moechatur* (μοιχᾶται)."

praises his fellow Christians for faithfully observing the unity of marriage.[8] Clement of Alexandria writes: " In restoring the ancient [practice], our Lord no longer permitted polygamy, . . . but only monogamy, because of the begetting of children and the care of the home, for which the wife is given [to man] as a helpmate." [9]

In the West, Tertullian valiantly championed the unity of marriage. Minucius Felix describes the domestic life of the Christians of his day as in full agreement with the law of monogamy.[10]

The teaching of the later Fathers and ecclesiastical writers differed in no wise from that of their predecessors. The constant practice of the Roman See, therefore, rests upon a solid doctrinal basis.[11]

b) In demonstrating the Catholic doctrine theologians generally emphasize the fact that the Creator meant marriage to be monogamous from the beginning, and consequently the conjugal union between Adam and Eve in Paradise must be looked upon as the pattern exemplar for all their descendants.

The Christian law of monogamy, as we have seen, is simply a restoration of the original condition of marriage. Hence Pope Nicholas the First, that valiant champion of the marriage bond, was justified in writing: " To have two wives at the same time is repugnant to the orig-

8 *Ad Autolyc.,* 1. III, n. 15 (Migne, *P. G.,* VI, 1142).

9 *Stromata,* III, 12 (Migne, *P. G.,* VIII, 1183).

10 Tertullian, *Apologeticus,* c. 46: " *Christianus uxori suae soli masculus nascitur.*"— M. Felix, *Octavius,* c. 31: " *Unius matrimonii vinculo libenter inhaeremus; cupiditatem procreandi aut unam scimus aut nullam.*"

11 Cfr. J. Sasse, *De Sacramentis Ecclesiae,* Vol. II, pp. 390 sqq., Freiburg 1898.

inal state of the human race, and forbidden by the Christian law." [12]

The unity of marriage, as established in Paradise, was maintained up to the time of the Deluge. Lamech, a great grandson of Cain, was the first of the Patriarchs to have two wives. For so doing he was generally regarded as a transgressor of the law. After the Flood, because of the lack of males, God permitted the Jews (and probably also the gentiles) to have several wives. Traces of this dispensation are clearly discernible in the Mosaic law. Hence Calvin was wrong when he denied the licitness and validity of polygamous marriages during this period and accused the Patriarchs and their descendants down to the time of Christ of living in adultery. A divine dispensation in favor of polygamy is plainly evident from Deut. XXI, 15 sqq., where we read: "If a man have two wives, one beloved and the other hated, and they have had children by him, and the son of the hated be the firstborn, and he meaneth to divide his substance among his sons, he may not make the son of the beloved the firstborn, and prefer him before the son of the hated," etc. The intimate friendship with which Yahweh honored Abraham, Jacob, and David, who were all polygamists, shows that He tolerated the practice. The use of the term "concubine" (*pellex*, πάλλαξ) in the Old Testament does not prove that a woman so designated was not a lawful wife. It simply indicates that she did not enjoy equal civil rights with her husband's chief or favorite wife. These "concubines" may be likened to the morganatic wives of modern princes.[13]

---

12 *Ad Consulta Bulgarorum*, c. 51: "*Duas tempore uno habere uxores nec ipsa origo humanae conditionis admittit nec lex Christiano-rum ulla permittit.*" (Migne, *P. L.*, CXIX, 999).

13 On the use of the term "*concubina*" in Canon Law see Pesch,

That it required a divine dispensation, or perhaps we had better say, toleration, to make polygamy lawful, is expressly stated by Pope Innocent III.[14] We know that the Mosaic concession was revoked by Christ, not only for His faithful followers, but for infidels and pagans as well, and that no polygamist can be baptized unless he dismisses all his wives except one — the first.[15]

c) The fact that polygamy was tolerated in the Old Testament raises the question whether, and in how far, the practice can be said to be contrary to the moral law of nature.

Polygamy, unlike polyandry,[16] is not intrinsically immoral, else God could never have permitted it. This consideration has led Catholic philosophers and theologians to unite on the proposition that polygamy is opposed to the natural law, not primarily but secondarily. The meaning is: Though the objects of matrimony may be attained in a polygamous union, they cannot be reached with nearly the same perfection as in a monogamous marriage, and hence the law of nature counsels the latter, while it discountenances the former. It is evident that both the *bonum prolis* and the *bonum fidei* can be attained in a polygamous marriage, since one man can cohabit with and be true to several wives and provide for the children born to him. But it is equally patent that a plurality of wives is not conducive to domestic peace and happiness nor to the proper control of concupiscence, and that polygamy degrades the female sex. The most that

Praelect. Dogmat., Vol. VII, 3rd ed., pp. 415 sqq.
   [14] *Cap. " Gaudemus," De Divort.: " Nulli unquam licuit simul plures uxores habere nisi cui fuit divinâ* *revelatione concessum."*
   [15] On monogamy as the ideal form of marriage see Billuart, *De Matrimonio,* diss. 5, art. 1.
   [16] V. Thesis I, *supra.*

can be said against polygamy, therefore, is that it greatly impedes the secondary end of marriage, and destroys the symbol of the mystic union of Christ with His Church so completely that the elevation of Matrimony to the dignity of a Sacrament would have been impossible had not plural marriage been definitively abolished.[17]

Thesis III: Whenever the marriage bond is broken by death, the surviving partner, under the divine law, is free to marry again.

This proposition may be qualified as *"doctrina catholica."*

Proof. Our thesis merely asserts that second or successive marriages, contracted after the death of husband or wife, are not contrary to the divine law. It does not assert that such marriages may not be forbidden by the Church.

In matter of fact the Church has the right to forbid remarriage, though she has never made use of it. While consistently upholding the principle that perfect monogamy is realized only where husband and wife remain faithful to each other, even in death, she has always permitted widowers and widows to remarry. This can be seen from many authentic declarations by popes and councils. Thus the First Nicene Council (325) commanded the converted Cathari to hold ecclesiastical communion with those who had married again (*digami*).[18] Clement IV (1267) caused to be inserted into the profession of

---

17 On polygamy from the ethical point of view see Jos. Rickaby, S. J., *Moral Philosophy* (Stonyhurst Series), pp. 270 sqq.; on the toleration of polygamy in the Old Testament, cfr. St. Thomas, *Supplement.*, qu. 65, art. 1; *Summa c. Gent.*, III, 24; IV, 78.

18 Cfr. Denzinger-Bannwart, n. 55: *" cum digamis communicabunt."*

faith demanded of Michael Palæologus a passage declaring second and third marriages valid and permissible.[19] Eugene IV in his decree for the Jacobites says: " We declare that a man can lawfully pass not only to a second, but to a third and fourth marriage, and to still others, provided there be no impediment," adding, however, that " It is more praiseworthy to abstain from remarriage and to lead a continent life." [20] This teaching was reinforced by Benedict XIV in two constitutions issued in 1742 and 1745, respectively.

a) St. Paul writes in his first Epistle to the Corinthians: "I say to the unmarried and to widows: it is good for them if they remain even as I. But if they have not self-control, let them marry; it is better to marry than to be on fire [with passion.]" [21] And again: "A wife is bound to her husband so long as he liveth; but if her husband die, she is free to marry whom she will; only [let it be]in the Lord." [22]

b) The Fathers taught that second marriage, while less perfect than continence, is not forbidden.

19 " *Soluto vero legitimo matrimonio per mortem coniugum alterius secundas et tertias deinde nuptias successive licitas [Ecclesia] esse dicit.*" (Denzinger-Bannwart, n. 465).

20 " *Declaramus non solum secundas, sed tertias et quartas et ulteriores [nuptias], si aliquod impedimentum non obstat, licite contrahi posse; commendatiores tamen dicimus, si ulterius a coniugio abstinentes in castitate permanserint.*" (*Decretum pro Iacobitis*, in Hardouin, *Conc.*, Vol. IX, col. 1028).

21 1 Cor. VII, 8 sq.: " *Dico autem non nuptis et viduis: bonum est illis si sic permaneant, sicut et ego. Quodsi non se continent, nubant; melius est enim nubere quam uri.*"

22 1 Cor. VII, 39: " *Mulier alligata est legi, quanto tempore vir eius vivit. Quodsi dormierit* (κοιμηθῇ = *mortuus fuerit) vir eius, liberata est: cui vult nubat, tantum in Domino.*"— Cfr. Al. Schäfer, *Erklärung der beiden Briefe an die Korinther*, pp. 152 sq., Münster 1903.

a) St. Ambrose says: " We do not prohibit second marriages, but neither do we praise them if often repeated." [23] Clement of Alexandria writes: " If the Apostle permits a man to pass to a second marriage because of incontinency, . . . such a one does not sin under the Testament — for there is no law to hinder him — but he fails to attain to that perfect ideal of life which is practiced according to the Gospel." [24] When St. Jerome was criticized for attacking bigamists, he replied: " Let my accuser blush for saying that I condemned first marriages, when he reads that I do not [even] condemn second and third, and, if I may say so, eighth marriage." [25] St. Augustine knows no reason for condemning successive marriages, seeing that they are allowed by St. Paul.[26]

Tertullian's Montanistic teaching on this head [27] found no defender among the Fathers.

β) It should be noted, however, that second marriages were frowned upon in the Orient. Councils held at Ancyra (314), Neocæsarea (314), and Laodicea, though acknowledging second marriages as valid, imposed a canonical fine on those who contracted them. Athenagoras (+ about 182) calls second marriage " decent adultery," [28] and says that the Christians of his time regarded it as " a sign of incontinence and a violation of the faith pledged

---

[23] " *Non prohibemus secundas nuptias, sed non probamus saepe repetitas.*" (*De Viduis*, c. 11).

[24] *Stromata*, l. III, c. 12 (Migne, *P. G.*, VIII, 1183).

[25] " *Erubescat calumniator meus dicens me prima damnare matrimonia, quando legit: Non damno digamos et trigamos et, si dici potest, octogamos.*" (*Ep. 48 ad Pammach.*,

n. 9; Migne, *P. L.*, XXII, 499).

[26] *De Bono Viduitatis*, c. 12: " *Quoties voluerit, viris mortuis nubat femina nec ex meo corde praeter scripturae sanctae auctoritatem quotaslibet nuptias audeo condemnare.*" (Migne, *P. L.*, XL, 439).

[27] In his treatise *De Monogamia*.

[28] εὐπρεπὴς μοιχεία. (*Legat.*, c. 33).

to the dead." [29] St. Basil ($+$ 379) vigorously de-
nounced second and third marriages [30] and demanded
severe canonical penalties for those who contracted them.
The Greek Church, under Nicholas I of Constantinople
(A. D. 920), declared fourth and, under certain conditions, even third marriages null and void. St. John
Chrysostom, though himself not disposed to encourage remarriage, took a more sensible view, and allowed it in
accordance with St. Paul's teaching. [31] This legislation
was approved by Pope John X, but is no longer strictly
enforced. [32]

29 Cfr. H. Kihn, *Patrologie*, Vol.
I, p. 177, Paderborn 1904.

30 He calls them "*castigata fornicatio*" and "*ecclesiae inquinamen-
tum.*" Cfr. *Ep. ad Amphiloch.*, 188,
can. 4; can. 50.

31 Cfr. A. Moulard, *St. Jean
Chrysostome, Le Défenseur du*
Mariage et l'Apôtre de la Virginité,
Paris 1923, Appendix.

32 Cfr. Palmieri, *De Matrimonio,*
pp. 10 sqq.—On the Encratites and
their teaching see J. Tixeront, *History of Dogmas,* Vol. I, pp. 190
sqq., St. Louis 1910.

SECTION 2

INDISSOLUBILITY

1. STATE OF THE QUESTION.—In order to explain the Catholic teaching on the indissolubility of the marriage bond, we must draw a distinction. To say that the *vinculum,* or marriage tie, is *intrinsically indissoluble* means that it cannot be dissolved by the contracting partners. To say that it is *extrinsically indissoluble* means that no earthly authority can annul it.

a) To this twofold indissolubility corresponds a twofold dissolubility.

A contract is intrinsically dissoluble if it can be revoked by those who have made it. *"Per quascunque causas res nascitur, per easdem dissolvitur,"* says an ancient legal adage. If the marriage contract were intrinsically dissoluble, husband and wife could separate whenever they wished. In matter of fact, the contract, as we shall see, is intrinsically indissoluble, and consequently cannot be revoked by the contracting parties. It may happen, however, that an intrinsically indissoluble contract can be annulled by a higher law or authority. Such a contract is extrinsically dissoluble. If a marriage is actually dissolved by divine ordinance or by the Pope, we know that this is merely a case of extrinsic

183

dissolubility, which does not affect the intrinsic indissolubility of the bond.[1]

b) Before expounding the Catholic teaching on the indissolubility of marriage, we must explain the division of Matrimony into *legitimum, ratum,* and *consummatum.*

(1) A legitimate marriage (*matrimonium legitimum*) is any marriage validly contracted between unbaptized persons (Jews, Mohammedans, pagans). Such a marriage is not sacramental.

(2) A ratified marriage (*matrimonium ratum*) is any marriage between Christians, whether consummated or not. It is always sacramental.

(3) A consummated marriage (*matrimonium consummatum*) is any marriage which has become perfect by conjugal intercourse.

2. Dogmatic Theses.—Marriage between baptized persons, whether consummated or not, is always intrinsically indissoluble, so far as the *vinculum* is concerned, and after it has been consummated, is indissoluble also extrinsically, that is to say, no human authority can annul it.

Thesis I: Every marriage between baptized persons, whether consummated or not, is intrinsically indissoluble.

This proposition may be qualified as *"saltem fidei proxima."*

1 Cfr. Palmieri, *De Matrimonio,* pp. 125 sqq.

Proof. The meaning is that a valid marriage between baptized persons cannot be dissolved by the mutual consent of the contracting partners. For either of them to contract another marriage, therefore, would involve adultery. Not even heresy, incompatibility of temper, or desertion would justify either party to dissolve the marriage. The Tridentine Council declares: "If anyone saith that on account of heresy, or irksome cohabitation, or the designed absence of one of the parties the bond of matrimony may be dissolved, let him be anathema." [2] This canon, which was directed mainly against Luther and Bucer, does not, of course, forbid "separation from bed and board."

a) That marriage between baptized persons is intrinsically indissoluble appears from the fact that our Divine Lord abolished the Mosaic practice of granting a bill of divorce on the express ground that no man should put asunder what God has joined together.[3] St. Paul teaches: "To the married I give this charge—nay, not I, but the Lord—that a wife depart not from her husband (but if she have departed, let her remain unmarried, or be reconciled to her husband), and that a husband put not away his wife." [4]

---

2 Sess. XXIV, can. 5: "*Si quis dixerit, propter haeresim aut molestam cohabitationem aut affectatam absentiam a coniuge dissolvi posse matrimonii vinculum, anathema sit.*" (Denzinger-Bannwart, n. 975).

3 Matth. XIX, 6: "*Quod ergo Deus coniunxit, homo non separet.*"

4 1 Cor. VII, 10: "*Iis autem qui matrimonio iuncti sunt, praecipio,*

This is not merely good advice, but a divine command, which binds under pain of mortal sin.[5] Both to the Corinthians and to the Romans the Apostle speaks in general terms and nowhere makes a distinction between consummated and unconsummated marriages.

For the teaching of the Fathers see *infra*, Thesis II.

The Church has always enforced the indissolubility of the marriage bond between Christians.[6]

b) The allied question as to the matrimonial tie among non-baptized persons may be considered in the light both of positive divine law and of the law of nature.

a) In the former point of view, marriage was made intrinsically indissoluble by a positive precept in Paradise.

Adam, " under the influence of the Holy Ghost," [7] uttered the prophetic words: " Therefore a man shall leave father and mother, and shall cleave to his wife, and they shall be two in one flesh." [8] Our Lord quotes these words and immediately adds: " What therefore God hath joined together, let no man put asunder." [9] When the Pharisees retorted: " Why then did Moses command

non ego, sed Dominus: uxorem a viro non discedere. Quodsi discesserit, manere innuptam (μενέτω ἄγαμος) aut viro suo reconciliari. Et vir uxorem non dimittat."

5 Cfr. Rom. VII, 3: " *Igitur vivente viro vocabitur adultera (μοιχαλίς), si fuerit cum alio viro."*

6 Cfr. *Decret. Gregor.*, l. IV, tit. 19, c. 7: " *Sacramentum fidei, quod semel est admissum, nunquam amittitur; sed ratum efficit coniugii sa-cramentum, ut ipsum in coniugibus illo durante perduret."* This declaration of Innocent III has remained a guiding principle in the Canon Law of the Church.

7 " *Divini Spiritus instinctu,"* as the Tridentine Council puts it; Sess. XXIV, *Prooem.*

8 Gen. II, 24.

9 Matth. XIX, 6: " *Quod ergo Deus coniunxit, homo non separet."*

to give a bill of divorce and to put away?" Jesus said:
"In the beginning it was not so," [10] thereby giving them
to understand that marriage is by divine right both monogamic and intrinsically indissoluble.[11]

If marriage is intrinsically indissoluble by divine right,
then only God Himself, or some one commissioned by
Him for this purpose, can permit divorce. The Mosaic
command to which the Pharisees referred was clearly
a divine dispensation. Cfr. Deut. XXIV, 1: "If a
man take a wife, and have her, and she find not favor
in his eyes for some uncleanness (*propter aliquam foedi-
tatem*), he shall write a bill of divorce (*libellum repudii*),
and shall give it in her hand, and send her out of his
house (*dimittet*)." This text has been variously interpreted. Peter Lombard, St. Bonaventure, Dominicus
Soto, Estius, Sylvius, and other writers think that the
libellus repudii merely implied a separation from bed and
board. Bellarmine, Maldonatus, and the great majority,
including practically all modern theologians, on the contrary hold that it meant a true divorce. They base their
opinion on three principal grounds.[12]

(1) Our Lord Himself testifies that Moses permitted
the Jews to put away their wives because of "the hard-
ness of their hearts."[13]

(2) The Bible takes for granted that under the Old
Law a wife who was put away by her husband in virtue

10 Matth. XIX, 8: "*Ab initio
(ἀπ' ἀρχῆς) autem non fuit sic.*"
11 In this sense Pope Pius VI
wrote July 11, 1789: "*In tali
matrimonio [infidelium], siquidem
verum est matrimonium, perstare
debet omninoque perstat perpetuus
ille nexus, qui a prima origine divino iure matrimonio ita adhaeret, ut
nulli subsit civili potestati.*" (*Ep.*

ad Episc. Angriae, quoted by Rosko-
vány, *Matrim. in Eccles. Cath.,* Vol.
I, p. 291).
12 Cfr. St. Thomas, *Summa
Theol., Supplem.,* qu. 67, art. 3.
13 Matth. XIX, 8: "*Moyses ad
duritiam cordis vestri permisit
(ἐπέτρεψεν) vobis dimittere uxores
vestras.*"

of a *libellus repudii* could remarry as well as the husband.

(3) Had the *libellus repudii* not been a real divorce, how explain the Mosaic law which forbade a discharged wife to return to her first husband after having been repudiated by the second, or after his death? [14]

What was the "*aliqua foeditas*" on account of which a man could put away his wife? The meaning of this phrase is not quite clear. The Hebrew term עֶרְוַת דָּבָר , which the Septuagint renders by ἄσχημον πρᾶγμα, no doubt denoted something with which the Old Testament Jews were perfectly familiar. That it meant any reason whatever, *e. g.* inability to cook, as Rabbi Hillel and his school maintained, is highly improbable. Shamai's theory that the law referred to a violation of conjugal fidelity, is far more likely.

β) There remains the purely philosophical question whether the matrimonial bond is indissoluble under the law of nature.

It stands to reason that marriage, whether consummated or not, cannot be dissolved by the contracting parties at pleasure. The law of nature inculcates order and virtue no less rigorously than the positive divine law. Pope Pius IX in his famous Syllabus condemned the proposition that "The bond of matrimony is not indissoluble by the law of nature, and in certain cases divorce, in the strict sense of the term, may be sanctioned by civil authority." [15]

Our doctrine is more easily demonstrable of mar-

---

14 Deut. XXIV, 2 sqq.
15 Prop. 67: "*Iure naturae matrimonii vinculum non est indissolubile et in variis casibus divortium proprie dictum auctoritate civili sanciri potest.*" (Denzinger-Bannwart, n. 1767).

riages blessed with children than of such as have proved sterile. The bodily and spiritual care of children demands a home and life-long parental coöperation. One cannot advocate divorce without admitting all those serious inconveniences that flow from the principle of " free love," whereby the human race is reduced to the level of the poultry-yard.

The voice of reason is confirmed by experience. History teaches that all pure and strong nations have upheld the sanctity and indissolubility of the marriage tie, whereas the introduction of divorce has always signalized decay. Ancient Rome in its early days and under the emperors affords a good example for both assertions.

Unfruitful marriages, too, are indissoluble: first, because Matrimony by its very nature implies permanent and undivided community of life, and second, because the knowledge that a divorce can be had for the asking seriously imperils the family and the State.[16]

As the domestic and social evils of divorce can be greatly lessened by legal control, we have still to answer the question whether the natural law does not empower the State in exceptional cases (sterility, incurable insanity, adultery) to grant a divorce to unbaptized persons. Theologians are at variance on this point. Some[17] concede this power to the State, whereas others hold with St. Thomas[18] that no purely human authority can dissolve the marriage bond because the common good of society is superior to the individual welfare of its mem-

---

16 Cfr. the magnificent Encyclical " *Arcanum divinae* " of Leo XIII, issued Feb. 10, 1880, and contained in an excellent English translation in *The Pope and the People,* a collection of select letters and addresses by Leo XIII, published by the English Catholic Truth Society, new and revised edition, London 1912, pp. 41-46.— See also Jos. Rickaby, S. J., *Moral Philosophy,* pp. 276 sq.

17 E. g. Bellarmine, *De Matrimonio,* c. 4, and Sanchez, *De Matrimonio,* l. II, disp. 13, n. 4.

18 *Summa Theol., Suppl.,* qu. 67, art. 1.

bers, and the natural law cannot take into consideration
accidental evils, but must aim at that which is substantially good and safe.[19]　Hence, if a marriage were to be
dissolved in a State governed under the pure law of nature,
it could be done only by the highest authority, *i. e.* God,
and He would have to exercise this power, not by a general permission,— because this would open the door to
license and anarchy,— but individually in each case in
which, for weighty reasons, He is willing to dispense
from the secondary demands of the natural law.[20]

**Thesis II: No cause, not even adultery, can justify
the innocent, and much less the guilty partner in proceeding to a new marriage.**

This is *fidei proximum.*

Proof.　We have here merely an application of
our first thesis.　Most Protestants regard adultery as a sufficient ground for divorce.[21]　This error is shared by the "Orthodox," and to some extent even by the Uniate Greeks.　Among Latin
theologians it was defended by Cajetan, Ambrose
Catharinus, and Launoy.

The official teaching of the Catholic Church is
clearly set forth by the Tridentine Council:　"If
anyone saith that the Church has erred in that
she taught, and doth teach, in accordance with the
evangelical and Apostolic doctrine, that the bond
of matrimony cannot be dissolved on account of

19 Cfr. Billuart, *De Matrimonio,*
diss. 5, art. 2, § 1.

20 The indissolubility of Christian

marriage is well treated by Palmieri,
De Matrimonio, thes. 23.

21 Cfr. Luther, *Von Ehesachen,*

the adultery of one of the married parties, . . .
and that he is guilty of adultery who, having put
away the adulteress, shall take another wife, as
also she who, having put away the adulterer,
shall take another husband, let him be anathema." [22]

Though the above-quoted canon, strictly speaking, defines nothing more than that the Church is infallible in her
teaching on this point, that teaching itself is so clearly set
down as of faith that it cannot be denied without a dangerous approach to heresy. Pallavicini relates that in
formulating this canon the Council chose the milder among
two proposed phrases at the suggestion of certain prelates
who thought it would be unwise to brand the Greeks as
heretics.[23]

Separation from bed and board, on the other
hand, is permitted for good reasons. Eugene IV
says in his famous *Decretum pro Armenis:*
"Though it be permitted, because of fornication,
to obtain a separation *a toro,* it is not allowed to
contract a new marriage, because the bond of
legitimate wedlock is perpetual." [24] This teaching can be proved from Scripture and Tradition.

1530; Calvin, *Instit.,* IV, 19, 37.

22 Sess. XXIV, can. 7: *"Si quis
dixerit, Ecclesiam errare, quum do-
cuit et docet iuxta evangelicam et
apostolicam doctrinam propter adulterium alterius coniugum matrimonii
vinculum non posse dissolvi . . .
moecharique eum qui dimissâ adul-
terâ aliam duxerit, et eam quae di-
misso adultero alii nupserit, anathema sit."* (Denzinger-Bannwart, n.
977).

23 Pallavicini, *Hist. Concil. Trid.,*
XXII, 4, 27 sqq.

24 *" Quamvis autem ex causa fornicationis liceat tori separationem
facere, non tamen aliud matrimonium
contrahere fas est, quum matrimonii
legitimi vinculum perpetuum sit."*
(Denzinger-Bannwart, n. 702).

a) The scriptural argument may be stated in three propositions, to wit:

(1) Whenever Holy Scripture speaks of married people who have separated from each other, it brands the remarriage of either with a third person as adultery (Matth. X, 11 sq.; Luke XVI, 18).

(2) Where there is a just cause for separation (none can be more just than adultery) the Bible knows of but one alternative—the parties must either remain single or become reconciled. (1 Cor. VII, 10 sq.)

(3) The only thing that can dissolve the marriage bond is death (cfr. Rom. VII, 2 sq.; 1 Cor. VII, 39).[25]

α) This teaching would be contradictory if adultery were a legitimate cause for divorce, and hence the most elementary principle of hermeneutics demands that the two ambiguous texts from St. Matthew, which Protestants quote in favor of divorce, be interpreted in conformity with the Scriptural truths stated above.

The texts referred to are:

Matth. V, 32: "Whosoever shall put away his wife, excepting the case of fornication, maketh her to commit adultery, and he that shall marry her that is put away, committeth adultery."[26]

Matth. XIX, 9: "Whosoever shall put away his wife, except it be for fornication, and shall marry another,

---

25 The argument is developed in detail by Tepe, *Instit. Theol.*, Vol. IV, pp. 636 sqq., Paris 1896.

26 Matth. V, 32: "*Omnis, qui dimiserit uxorem suam, exceptâ fornicationis causâ (παρεκτὸς λόγου πορνείας), facit eam moechari, et qui dimissam duxerit adulterat.*"

committeth adultery; and he that shall marry her that is
put away, committeth adultery." [27]

Our opponents conclude from these texts, not only that
a man may *leave* his adulterous wife,— which is in conformity with Catholic teaching,— but that adultery dissolves the marriage bond, as if Christ had said: "He
who puts away his wife for fornication (adultery) and
marries another, does not commit adultery."

But this interpretation is manifestly false. Logic forbids us arbitrarily to shift a restriction from one member of a sentence to another. The phrase, *nisi ob for-
nicationem,* or *exceptâ fornicatione,* plainly refers to
dimittere, not to *ducere aliam.* Were I to say: "Whoever eats meat on Friday, except he have a dispensation,
and drinks to excess, commits a sin," I could not reasonably be understood to mean that he committed no
sin, who, having a dispensation permitting him to eat
meat on Friday, would drink to excess. To drink to
excess is always sinful. If a man, besides drinking ex-
cessively, were to eat meat on Friday, he would commit two separate and distinct sins. Similarly, Christ
means to say: To put away an adulterous wife is no sin,
but to marry another is adultery, while if a man were to
put away his innocent wife and then marry another, he
would be guilty of double adultery,— that is to say, he
would be responsible for the adultery committed by his
wife (*facit eam moechari*) and commit the same crime
himself. Hence, when our Lord speaks of dismissing a
wife for fornication, he does not mean divorce, but
merely a separation from bed and board, and the sense of
the two texts is: "Whosoever shall put away his wife

27 Matth. XIX, 9: "*Quicumque   aliam duxerit, moechatur et qui
dimiserit uxorem suam, nisi ob for-   dimissam duxerit, moechatur.*"
nicationem (μὴ ἐπὶ πορνείᾳ), et*

(which is justifiable if she be guilty of adultery), and marry another, commits adultery." [28]

The interpretation we have given is the only one that fits into, nay is demanded by, the context. The object of the whole passage (Matth. XIX, 3–9) is to revoke the Mosaic law permitting divorce, and to restore Matrimony to its pristine indissolubility. Had our Lord excepted adultery as a cause for divorce, He would have stultified Himself, for He says (Matth. XIX, 19) : " He that shall marry her that is put away, committeth adultery." How could this be if the adulterous woman did not remain the wife of her first husband? [29]

If we were to grant the Protestant interpretation for argument's sake, what would be the result? Would Matrimony be elevated from its former state of degradation to a position of security and permanence under the New Testament? No; on the contrary, it would sink beneath the level of the Mosaic law, for the adulterous wife as well as her husband would be empowered to contract another marriage, whereas a woman innocently put away by her husband would, according to 1 Cor. VII, 10 sq., be obliged to remain single unless she became reconciled to her husband. This would be putting a premium upon adultery and making the New Testament inferior to the Old, which punished adultery in both male and female with death.[30] To ascribe such legislation to Christ would be to deny His wisdom and holiness. The Apostles evidently did not understand our Lord's words in the sense which modern Protestants put

28 Cfr. Tepe, *Instit. Theol.*, Vol. IV, p. 636.

29 Cfr. St. Augustine, *De Coniug. Adult.*, I, 9, 9: "*Neque quisquam ita est absurdus, ut moechum neget esse qui duxerit eam quam maritus propter causam fornicationis abiecit, quum moechum dicat eum, qui duxerit eam, quae praeter causam fornicationis abiecta est.*"

30 Lev. XX, 10.

upon them, for they said to Him: " If the case of a man with his wife be so, it is not expedient to marry," [31] that is, if a man may not put away his wife for adultery, it is better not to marry.

β) This interpretation of the disputed texts is so evident and incontrovertible that we need not devote much space to certain other theories which have been suggested by Catholic theologians. Cardinal Bellarmine, *e. g.,* explains the clause *nisi ob fornicationem* in a purely negative sense, as if our Lord meant to say: " Whosoever shall put away his wife,— I am not now concerned with the case of fornication,— and shall marry another, committeth adultery." [32] This interpretation fails to do justice to the context.

Other writers suggest that the two Scriptural passages under consideration refer to marriage among the Jews, who under the Mosaic law rightly regarded adultery as a sufficient ground for divorce. This interpretation is plainly untenable.

The same must be said of Döllinger's theory that the term " fornication " (πορνεία) means unchaste conduct before marriage.[33] If this were so, Christ would have made a sin committed before marriage a diriment impediment.

Patrizi interpreted *fornicatio* literally and explained the disputed passages in St. Matthew's Gospel as follows: " No marriage can be dissolved, even by adultery, except the quasi-marriage of those who live in concubinage." [34] This suggestion is unacceptable: first, because *fornicatio* is a generic term which includes *adulterium* as a species, and second, because Christ expressly calls the al-

---

31 Matth. XIX, 10: " *Si ita est causa hominis cum uxore, non expedit nubere.*"

32 *De Matrimonio,* l. I, c. 16.

33 Döllinger, *Christentum und Kirche,* p. 392, Ratisbon 1868.

34 *De Interpret. Scriptur.,* l. I, c. 7, Rome 1844.

leged concubine "wife," [35] and brands her second marriage as "adultery." [36]

b) The Latin Fathers are unanimous in teaching that adultery is no ground for divorce, and we may therefore confine the Patristic argument to the Greek Fathers, in order to show that the lax practice of the schismatic Orientals belies their own past.

We begin with Hermas, because he wrote in Greek. "If a man have a faithful wife in the Lord," says the "Shepherd," "and finds her out in some adultery, does the husband sin if he lives with her? . . . 'What . . . shall the husband do if the wife remain in this disposition?' 'Let him put her away,' he said, 'and let the husband remain by himself (ἐφ' ἑαυτῷ). But if he put his wife away and marry another, he also commits adultery himself." [37]

St. Justin Martyr says: "Whoever marries a woman that has been put away by another, commits adultery." [38]

Clement of Alexandria writes: "When Sacred Scripture advises [a man] to take a wife, and never allows a withdrawal from marriage, it openly lays down the law:

35 Matth. XIX, 9: "uxorem suam, τὴν γυναῖκα αὐτοῦ."

36 For a fuller discussion of the New Testament teaching on the subject of divorce we must refer the student to Palmieri, De Matrimonio, pp. 178 sqq.; A. Ott, Die Auslegung der neutestamentlichen Texte über die Ehescheidung, Münster 1911; F. E. Gigot, Christ's Teaching Concerning Divorce in the New Testament, New York 1912.

37 Pastor Hermae, Mand. IV, i, 4-6: ". . . εἰ γυναῖκα ἔχῃ τις πιστὴν ἐν κυρίῳ καὶ ταύτην εὕρῃ ἐν μοιχείᾳ τινί, ἆρα ἁμαρτάνει ὁ ἀνὴρ συνζῶν μετ' αὐτῆς; . . . Τί οὖν, φημί, κύριε, ποιήσῃ ὁ ἀνήρ, ἐὰν ἐπιμείνῃ τῷ πάθει τούτῳ ἡ γυνή; 'Ἀπολυσάτω, φησίν, αὐτὴν καὶ ὁ ἀνὴρ ἐφ' ἑαυτῷ μενέτω· ἐὰν δὲ ἀπολύσας τὴν γυναῖκα ἑτέραν γαμήσῃ, καὶ αὐτὸς μοιχᾶται." (K. Lake, The Apostolic Fathers, Vol. II, p. 78, London 1913).

38 Apol., c. I, n. 15 (Migne, P. G., VI, 350).

Thou shalt not put away thy wife except for adultery. At the same time, however, [the Bible] declares it to be adultery if a person marries another while his or her partner is still alive. . . . It says: Whoever marries the wife that has been put away, commits adultery." [39]

Of such pseudo-marriages Origen says: "As the wife who has been put away is an adulteress, though she seems to be married to another man during the lifetime of her husband, so our Saviour has shown that the man who has seemingly married such a woman, is not to be called her husband, but rather an adulterer." [40]

St. Gregory of Nazianzus condemns the unjust divorce laws of his time as follows: "In this question I behold most people ill advised, and their law unjust and illogical. What justifies them in putting a curb on the woman, while they leave the husband unmolested? The wife that has disgraced the marriage bed of her husband is branded with the mark of adultery and punished with the severest penalties, whereas the husband who is unfaithful to his wife goes scot free. I do not approve of such a law, I do not commend such a custom. Men made this law, and therefore it is directed against the women." [41]

St. John Chrysostom composed a homily on the Mosaic bill of divorce, in which he says: "What is that law which Paul has given to us? The wife, he says, is bound by the law, and consequently may not separate from her living husband, or take another man besides him, or contract a second marriage. And behold how carefully he has weighed his words. He does not say: 'She shall cohabit with her husband as long as he lives,'

39 *Stromata*, l. II, c. 23 (Migne, P. G., VIII, 1095).

40 *In Matthaeum*, tom. 14, n. 23 (Migne, *P. G.*, XIII, 1246).

41 *Or.*, 37, n. 6.

but: 'The wife is bound by the law as long as her husband lives.' Hence, even if he gives her a bill of divorce, and she leaves his home and lives with another, she is bound by the law, and an adulteress. . . . Do not cite the [civil] laws made by outsiders, which command that a bill be issued and a divorce granted. For it is not according to these laws that the Lord will judge thee on the last day, but according to those which He Himself has given." [42]

Thesis III: A consummated marriage between Christians is both intrinsically and extrinsically indissoluble.

This proposition may be technically qualified as *"propositio certa."*

Proof. A marriage may be intrinsically indissoluble, yet extrinsically soluble.[43] A consummated marriage between unbaptized persons can be dissolved if one party embraces Christianity and is baptized, while the other either refuses to live with the baptized party, or will not cohabit with him or her in peaceful wedlock without injury to the Creator. (This is called the Pauline privilege or *casus Apostoli,* of which we shall have something more to say later on.) [44] A marriage legitimately contracted between baptized Christians, but not yet consummated (*matrimonium ratum tantum*), can be dissolved either by

42 *De Libello Repudii* (Migne, *P. G.,* LI, 218). On St. Chrysostom's teaching on Marriage see Λ. Moulard, *S. Jean Chrysostome, le Défenseur du Mariage et l'Apôtre de la Virginité,* Paris 1923, Part I.

Cfr. M. Denner, *Die Ehescheidung im Neuen Testament,* Paderborn 1910.

43 *V. Supra,* No. 1.
44 *V. infra,* Sect. 3.

solemn profession in a religious order or by decree of the Sovereign Pontiff.[45] We are dealing in this thesis with a consummated marriage (*ratum et consummatum*) between Christians, and we assert that such a marriage cannot be dissolved by any earthly power. We advisedly say, by any earthly power, because God could dissolve it, though we hold that He never does so.

The argument for our thesis may be briefly stated as follows: Had God meant to empower any earthly authority to dissolve a validly contracted and consummated marriage, He would surely have given this privilege to His Church, and not to the State, which in all probability can not even dissolve purely natural marriages. But the Church denies that she has this power. Consequently, no earthly authority can dissolve a consummated marriage between Christians.

Canon Law is full of provisions showing the mind of the Church in this matter. Even where the situation of the innocent party is almost unbearable, the Church forbids second marriage as adulterous if it is certain that the first marriage was both ratified and consummated. Pope Alexander III declares: "What the Lord says in the Gospel, that a man is not allowed to put away his wife except for fornication, must according to the true interpretation of Sacred Scripture be understood of those whose marriage has been consummated by carnal intercourse." [46]

[45] *V. infra,* Sect. 3.
[46] "*Sane quod Dominus in evan-* *gelio dicit, non licere viro nisi ob causam fornicationis uxorem suam*

The reason for this absolute indissolubility is that only of a properly consummated Christian marriage can it be said in the full sense of the phrase that husband and wife are " two in one flesh," [47] and that their union is a perfect symbol of Christ's mystic union with His Church, consummated by the Incarnation.[48]

dimittere, intelligendum est secundum interpretationem sacri eloquii de his, quorum matrimonium carnali copulâ est consummatum." (Denzinger-Bannwart, n. 395).

47 Gen. II, 24.

48 Cfr. St. Thomas, *Summa Theol., Suppl.,* qu. 61, art. 2, ad 1: " *Matrimonium ante carnalem copulam significat illam coniunctionem,* quae est Christi ad animam per gratiam, . . . sed post carnalem copulam significat coniunctionem Christi ad Ecclesiam quantum ad assumptionem humanae naturae in unitatem personae, quae omnino est indivisibilis."— For a fuller development of the doctrine set forth in our thesis see Palmieri, *De Matrimonio Christ.,* thes. 24.

SECTION 3

We have seen that Matrimony can be dissolved neither by mutual agreement nor by any human agency. The question arises: Can it be dissolved by a divinely constituted authority? The answer is: Yes, in certain exceptional cases.

Marriage between baptized persons, provided it has not yet been consummated, can be dissolved (1) by a dispensation from the Supreme Pontiff, and (2) by solemn profession in a religious order.

Marriages among pagans or infidels, whether consummated or not, can be dissolved by virtue of the Pauline privilege when one party becomes converted to the true faith and the other refuses to receive Baptism or to live in peaceful wedlock.

We shall explain this teaching in three separate theses.

Thesis I: The Pope can for important reasons dissolve an unconsummated marriage between Christians.

Proof. In the Middle Ages the doctrine embodied in this thesis was upheld by the canonists against the theologians, but to-day it is regarded as *"sententia communis et certa"* by all.

About the middle of the sixteenth century Ruardus Tapper (+ 1559) censured Cardinal Cajetan for defending this papal prerogative " against the common view of theologians and the express teaching of St. Thomas." Among later divines Tournely, Drouin, Collet, and Berlage took the same attitude, while canonists quite generally held the affirmative. Among the earlier theologians there was a sort of *dissensus negativus,* as they did not treat this subject at all. However, it has been proved from history that unconsummated marriages between Christians were occasionally dissolved by papal decree,[1] nay, more,— from Martin V to Leo XIII the popes have expressly claimed and exercised the prerogative of dissolving such marriages, and hence it is no longer permissible to speak of mistakes committed by individual pontiffs. The conduct of the Holy See in this matter is so constant and so deeply touches faith and morals that it cannot possibly be attributable to error. Consequently, the power of dissolving unconsummated marriages between Christians must be a legitimate function of the primacy.

Some writers deduce this prerogative from Matth. XVI, 19: "Whatsoever thou shalt loose on earth, it shall be loosed also in heaven." But this text proves too much and therefore proves nothing. Were we to allow the interpretation put upon it, we should have to admit that it proves

---

1 If only unconsummated marriages had been dissolved by papal decree, Dom. Soto might have been justified in writing: *" Factum pontificium non facit fidei articu-* *lum, sed opinionem canonistarum sunt secuti."* (*Comment. in Sent.,* IV, dist. 27, qu. 1, art. 4). But this was not the case.

the power of the Pope to dissolve consummated as well as unconsummated marriages, which is false. Hence we prefer to rest the argument on a different basis. The papal prerogative asserted in our thesis is not contrary to Scripture, Tradition, and the natural law; and, according to the unerring belief of the universal Church, belongs to the Sovereign Pontiff by virtue of the primacy.

There is nothing in Sacred Scripture or Tradition to prove the absolute (intrinsic and extrinsic) indissolubility of Christian marriage before it is actually consummated. The law of nature merely says that the marriage bond cannot be dissolved except by God or by a divinely constituted authority.[2] But the Pope, being the vice-gerent of Christ on earth, exercises his primatial power in the name of God, and the Church not merely tolerates this practice, but expressly approves of it. Surely the episcopate would have protested had the Holy See usurped a power to which it had no just claim. It is incompatible with the dogma of the Church's infallibility to assume that the entire Church, both *docens* and *discens,* grievously erred in such an important question of faith and morals, and hence we must conclude that the Supreme Pontiff actually has the power to dissolve unconsummated marriages between Christians.[3]

Thesis II: **An unconsummated marriage between Christians is dissolved by the solemn profession of either party in a religious order.**

We are here dealing with an article of faith.

2 *V. supra,* Sect. 2.

3 This thesis is more fully devel- oped by Palmieri, *De Matrimonio Christ.,* pp. 209 sqq. See *Codex I. C.,* can. 1119.

Proof. This exception from the rule of indissolubility was manifestly made in favor of the religious state, which, as such, is superior to wedlock.[4] Examples of marriages dissolved by solemn religious profession can be traced to the early days of Christianity. Theoretically our dogma was defined by the Council of Trent, as follows: "If anyone saith that Matrimony contracted, but not consummated, is not dissolved by the solemn profession of religion by one of the married parties, let him be anathema."[5] Hence solemn profession in a religious order stands in the same relation to unconsummated marriage as death does to consummated marriage. It is a kind of spiritual death, a relinquishment of the world and worldly things.[6] Note, however, that the marriage bond is not dissolved by mere entry into a religious order, but only by the act of solemn profession.

a) The proof of our thesis rests entirely on Tradition. In the twelfth century, what had long been a practice was embodied in a decretal of Alexander III, and in the thirteenth, was confirmed by a decision of Innocent III. Both documents form part of the *Corpus Iuris Canonici*.[7]

---

4 *V. supra*, pp. 130 sqq.

5 Sess. XXIV, can. 6: "*Si quis dixerit, matrimonium ratum non consummatum per solemnem religionis professionem alterius coniugum non dirimi, anathema sit.*" (Denzinger-Bannwart, n. 976).

6 Cfr. St. Thomas, *Summa Theol., Suppl.*, qu. 61, art. 2.

7 *Decret. Gregor.*, l. III, tit. 32, c. 2 and 14. The decretal of Innocent III reads as follows: "*Nos . . . nolentes a praedecessorum nostrorum vestigiis . . . declinare, qui re-*

Pope Alexander III recalls the example of certain saints who left their wives to embrace the religious state. As Alexander wrote in the year 1180, these saints must have lived before the twelfth century. St. Bede has preserved an early example in the story of Queen Edilthryda, who flourished in the seventh century.[8] Still more ancient is the story of the two courtiers related by St. Augustine in his Confessions.[9] The older Fathers [10] tell how St. Thecla abandoned her husband to serve God in the state of virginity.[11] Though the Acts of Paul and Thecla are not history but "a highly romantic work of imagination," [12] the reflexions based upon her supposed conduct by the Fathers prove that the primitive Church regarded the act of leaving husband or wife for God's sake as a new and higher spiritual marriage with the Divine Spouse. It was this belief, no doubt, which led to the opinion that the new bond dissolved the older and weaker

spondere consulti, antequam matrimonium sit per carnalem copulam consummatum, licere alteri coniugum reliquo inconsulto ad religionem transire, ita quod reliquus ex tunc legitime poterit alteri copulari." (Denzinger-Bannwart, n. 409). The older decretal of Alexander III runs thus: *" Post consensum legitimum de praesenti licitum est alteri, altero etiam repugnante, eligere monasterium, sicut sancti vocati de nuptiis vocati fuerunt, dummodo carnalis commixtio non intervenerit inter eos, et alteri remanenti (si commonitus continentiam servare noluerit) licitum est ad secunda vota transire: quia quum non fuissent una caro simul effecti, satis potest unus ad Deum transire et alter in saeculo remanere."* (Ed. Friedberg, II, col. 583 sq., 579; Denzinger-Bannwart n. 396).

8 *Hist. Eccles. Anglor.*, IV, 19;

cfr. Herder's *Kirchenlexikon*, Vol. IV, 2nd ed., pp. 125 sqq., Freiburg 1886.

9 *Confessiones*, VIII, 16, 15.

10 Cfr. Epiphanius, *Haer.*, 78, 16 (Migne, *P. G.*, XLII, 726); St. Ambrose, *De Virgin.*, II, 3, 19 (Migne, *P. L.*, XVI, 211).

11 St. Ambrose says (*l. c.*): *" Thecla doceat immolari, quae copulam fugiens nuptialem et sponsi furore damnata naturam etiam bestiarum virginitatis veneratione mutavit."*

12 Cfr. Bardenhewer-Shahan, *Patrology*, p. 102, Freiburg and St. Louis 1908. On the Acts of St. Thecla see Carl Holzhey, *Die Thekla-Akten, ihre Verbreitung und Beurteilung in der Kirche*, Munich 1905; J. P. Kirsch in the *Catholic Encyclopedia*, Vol. XIV, p. 564.

one, provided the latter had not yet become indissoluble by carnal intercourse.

b) There is a lively controversy among theologians as to whether the dissolution of an unconsummated marriage by solemn religious profession is based on the natural law, the law of the Church, or the divine law.

α) St. Thomas,[13] Bellarmine, Habert, Drouin, and others hold that it is based on the law of nature. They argue that so long as there is no violation of the rights of a third party (which is impossible when a marriage has not yet been consummated), the more perfect abolishes the less perfect state. However, this view is untenable for several reasons. In the first place it would seem that the married state, being prior to the religious state, negatives the latter. Second, the marriage bond and the religious state are by no means mutually exclusive, but may coexist, as *e. g.* when a father enters a religious order with the consent of his wife. Third, a truly religious life may be led not only in the regular orders, but likewise in approved congregations which demand no solemn profession. Thus the Society of Jesus, according to a constitution of Gregory XIII,[14] is a true religious order despite the fact that many of its members take only simple vows, which do not dissolve the bond of an unconsummated marriage. Fourth, the episcopate vies in perfection with the religious state, and yet episcopal consecration does not dissolve the marriage tie.

β) Suarez, Lessius, Sardagna, Lehmkuhl, Tepe, and other theologians hold that the dissolution of an uncon-

---

13 *Summa Theol., Suppl.,* qu. 53, art. 2; qu. 61, art. 2.

14 *"Ascendente Domino,"* May 25, 1584.

summated marriage by solemn religious profession is based entirely on ecclesiastical law. The Church, they say, has the power to clothe any religious profession with the character of solemnity. *" Voti solemnitas ex sola constitutione Ecclesiae est inventa,"* says Pope Boniface VIII.[15] Hence it is the Pope who, by virtue of the primacy, and acting through an ecclesiastical law, dissolves the marriage bond whenever one party to an unconsummated marriage makes solemn profession in a religious order.[16]

Against this theory stands the fact that the dissolution of the marriage bond by solemn religious profession is more ancient than the papal book of decretals and the Canon Law of the Church. The law is merely a positive formulation of a practice which existed in the primitive Church, and hence cannot be of purely ecclesiastical origin. Moreover, there must be some unalterable dogmatic truth underlying the Tridentine canon. If the law dissolving marriage in the case of solemn religious profession owed its existence to the Church, it could be revoked by the Church, which no theologian will dare to assert.

γ) Hence it is more probable to hold with Sanchez, Tournely, Billuart, Benedict XIV, Perrone, Palmieri, and De Augustinis, that the law by which an unconsummated marriage is dissolved when one of the parties makes solemn profession in a religious order, is of divine institution and that the Church has no other power with regard to this law than to determine the conditions under which it takes effect.[17]

---

15 *Sixti Decret.,* 1. III, tit. 15.

16 Cfr. Tepe, *Inst. Theol.,* Vol. IV, p. 646.

17 For a fuller treatment of this thesis consult Palmieri, *De Matrimonio Christ.,* pp. 205 sqq.; De Augustinis, *De Re Sacrament.,* Vol. II, 2nd ed., pp. 708 sqq.

Thesis III: A marriage between infidels or non-baptized persons, even though consummated, may be dissolved by virtue of the so-called Pauline privilege, if one party is converted to the faith, while the other refuses to live with the baptized in peaceful wedlock.

This doctrine may be qualified as *"sententia communis et certa."* (*C. I. C.,* can. 1120, § 1).

The " Pauline privilege," or *" casus Apostoli,"* as it is commonly called by canonists, applies only to marriages contracted between unbaptized infidels, Jews or pagans. As soon as one of the parties embraces Christianity and receives Baptism, even though the other remain unconverted, such a marriage falls under the jurisdiction of the Church. However, Baptism as such does not dissolve the marriage bond,[18] but merely gives the baptized party the right to contract a new marriage with a Christian, which latter *ipso facto* dissolves the previous marriage.[19]

Before the converted party to such a marriage can invoke the Pauline privilege, he or she must ascertain, (1) whether the unconverted party is willing to embrace the Christian religion, in which case the bond remains intact; (2) whether he or she is willing to live in peaceful wedlock without injury to the Creator (*sine contumelia Creatoris*). Only if both these questions are answered in the negative may the Pauline privilege be made use of and a new marriage contracted. Such a dissolution

18 Cfr. *Decr. Gregor.,* l. IV, tit. 19, c. 8: ". . . *quum per sacramentum baptismi non solvantur coniugia, sed crimina dimittantur."* (Denzinger-Bannwart, n. 407).

19 Cfr. Pesch, *Praelect. Dogmat.,* Vol. VII, 3rd ed., pp. 401 sq.; Palmieri, *De Matrimonio Christ.,* pp. 224 sqq.

of the marriage bond takes place " in favor of the faith " and by divine right.[20]

Proof.—a) The famous *privilegium Paulinum* is promulgated in 1 Cor. VII, 10 sqq., where the Apostle says:

"Iis autem, qui matrimonio [Christiano] iuncti sunt, praecipio non ego, sed Dominus, uxorem a viro non discedere; quodsi discesserit, manere innuptam aut viro suo reconciliari, et vir uxorem non dimittat. Nam ceteris (τοῖς δὲ λοιποῖς) *ego dico, non Dominus: Si quis frater uxorem habet infidelem* (ἄπιστον) *et haec consentit habitare cum illo* (συνευδοκεῖ οἰκεῖν μετ᾽ αὐτοῦ)*, non dimittat illam. Et si qua mulier fidelis habet virum infidelem et hic consentit habitare cum illa, non dimittat virum. . . . Quodsi infidelis discedit, discedat* (εἰ δὲ ὁ ἄπιστος χωρίζεται, χωριζέσθω)*: non enim servituti subiectus est* (δεδούλωται) *frater aut soror in huiusmodi; in pace* (ἐν δὲ εἰρήνῃ) *autem vocavit vos Deus."*

Anglice (according to the Westminster Version): "To the married I give this charge—nay, not I, but the Lord,—that a wife depart not from her husband (but if she have departed, let her remain unmarried, or be reconciled to her husband), and that a husband put not away his wife. But to the rest, it is I who speak, not the Lord: If any brother hath an unbelieving wife, and she

20 Cfr. *Decret. S. Officii, d. 11 Iulii 1886.*

is content to live with him, let him not put her away. And the wife that hath an unbelieving husband, who is content to live with her, let her not put away her husband. . . . (But if the unbeliever depart, let him depart; the brother or the sister is under no bondage in such cases, but God hath called you unto peace)."

That St. Paul in this passage concedes to the baptized party under certain conditions the right to dissolve the old and pass to a new marriage, is evident from the fact that he expressly opposes the marriage of unbelievers to marriage between Christians.

Among Christians, he says, if a wife depart from her husband, she must remain unmarried or be reconciled to him. In other words, Christian marriage is indissoluble. Not so among the unbaptized. If one party receives Baptism, and the other refuses to dwell peacefully with him or her, " let the unbeliever depart,"— for " the brother or the sister is under no bondage in such cases,"— that is to say, is free from the marriage bond, and consequently can contract another marriage. For if the neophyte remained bound by his former marriage, he would enjoy no privilege but, on the contrary, be condemned to lead a celibate life, like the separated parties to a Christian marriage.

St. Paul does not expressly discuss the case where the unconverted party is willing to dwell peacefully with the converted party, not, however, *sine contumelia Creatoris, i. e.* without injury to God and his or her own soul.[21]

---

21 Cfr. St. Thomas, *Summa Theol.,*   *verba blasphemiae prorumpens et*
Suppl., qu. 59, art. 5: "*. . . in   nomen Christi audire nolens.*"

But the very purpose of the Pauline privilege sufficiently indicates that such unsatisfactory cohabitation would be morally equivalent to a *discessio* and consequently could not stop the effect of the χωρίζεσθαι for the baptized party.[22] Moreover, in such cases it is not true that " the unbelieving husband is sanctified in the wife, and the unbelieving wife is sanctified in the believing husband." [23]

b) Whether or not the unconverted party is willing to live with the converted party,[24] can only be ascertained by an inquiry.

This inquiry, technically called *interpellatio,* is imposed by the Church as a strict obligation.[25] Whether its omission makes a new marriage invalid, is a controverted question. The affirmative view is championed by Brancatius and Perrone. Against them Ballerini maintains [26] that the mere fact that the unconverted party refuses to dwell peacefully with his or her converted partner is sufficient to render a new marriage valid, just as the mere fact that a husband or wife is dead is sufficient to insure the validity of a second marriage.

c) What if the inquiry demanded for the Pauline privilege is either physically or morally

---

22 Cfr. *Decret. Greg.,* l. IV, tit. 19, c. 7: " *Contumelia Creatoris solvit ius matrimonii circa eum, qui relinquitur.*" (Denzinger-Bannwart, n. 405).

23 1 Cor. VII, 14: " *Sanctificatus est enim vir infidelis per mulierem fidelem, et sanctificata est mulier infidelis per virum fidelem.*"— Cfr. Schäfer, *Erklärung der beiden Briefe an die Korinther,* pp. 130 sqq.; J. McRory, *The Epistles of St. Paul to* the Corinthians, Part I, pp. 92 sqq.; F. E. Gigot, *Christ's Teaching concerning Divorce in the New Testament,* pp. 121 sqq.

24 1 Cor. VII, 12 sq.: " *Si haec* [hic] *consentit* (συνευδοκεῖ) *habitare cum illo* [illa] . . ."

25 Cfr. *Decret. Congr. de Prop. Fide d. 5 Martii 1816. C. I. C.,* can. 1121.

26 *Opus Theol. Moral.,* ed. D. Palmieri, Vol. VI, 3rd ed., pp. 330 sq., Prati 1900.

impossible, as *e. g.* when the unconverted party is a prisoner of war or has removed to unknown parts? Is the baptized party in such a case condemned to lead a single life? According to Canon Law the Holy See has the power to dispense from the duty of interpellation if the unconverted party cannot be found.[27]

a) The Third Plenary Council of Baltimore (1884) decrees: "One who has contracted Matrimony with an infidel in the state of infidelity, and then becomes converted to the faith and baptized, cannot pass to a new marriage without first interrogating his infidel spouse concerning her (or his) will to live with him (or her) peacefully and without injury to the Creator. If the infidel party cannot be interpellated in accordance with the law, the Holy See must be asked for a dispensation."[28] A peculiar feature of this practice is that a new marriage contracted with papal dispensation is valid even if it turns out later that the unconverted party was ready at the time to dwell peacefully with the converted party or had himself embraced the faith. As this case is not covered by the Pauline privilege, some theologians (Benedict XIV, Perrone, Hurter, Braun) hold that in such circumstances the Pope can extend the Pauline privilege because in exceptional cases, which St. Paul did not foresee, there must exist a supreme authority which adapts the divine law to concrete conditions.[29]

---

27 *Const. Gregor. XIII, " Populis et nationibus,"* Jan. 25, 1585. *C. I. C.,* can. 1121, § 2.

28 " *Coniux qui iam matrimonium in infidelitate cum infideli contraxit, et conversus deinde ad fidem baptizatus fuit, nequit novum matrimonium inire, quin prius interpellet coniugem infidelem circa eius voluntatem cohabitandi pacifice et sine Creatoris iniuria. Quodsi coniux infidelis nequeat legitime interpellari, recurrendum est ad S. Sedem pro dispensatione.*" (*Acta et Decreta,* § 129, Baltimore 1886, pp. 65 sq.)

29 Cfr. Benedict XIV, *De Synodo Dioecesana,* l. XIII, c. 21, n. 4;

β) However, the practice of the Apostolic See in granting such dispensations can be more satisfactorily explained on the assumption that the Pope is not only empowered to interpret the Pauline privilege authentically, but likewise, by virtue of the primacy, to dissolve the legitimate marriages of infidels when either one or both parties embrace Christianity. That such a power is really vested in the Holy See may be inferred from the declaration of Urban VIII that "the marriages of infidels are not so firm that they cannot be dissolved when necessity urges," [30] and from the fact that a convert who has several wives may, if the first refuses to be converted, with papal permission retain any one of them who will embrace the faith.[31]

READINGS:—Gasparri, *Tract. Canonicus de Matrimonio*, 2 vols., Paris 1891.— Baier, *Die Naturehe in ihrem Verhälnis zur paradiesischen, vorchristlichen und christlich-sakramentalen Ehe*, Ratisbon 1884.—C. Boeckenhoff, *De Individuitate Matrimonii*, Berlin 1901.—Didon, *Die Unauflöslichkeit der Ehe und die Ehescheidung*, Ratisbon 1893.— Al. Cigoi, *Die Unauflöslichkeit der christl. Ehe und die Ehescheidung nach Schrift und Tradition*, Paderborn 1895.— J. Fahrner, *Die Geschichte der Ehescheidung im kanonischen Recht, I: Geschichte des Unauflöslichkeitsprinzips und der vollkommenen Scheidung der Ehe*, Freiburg 1904.— Scharnagl, *Das feierliche Gelübde als Ehehindernis in seiner geschichtlichen Entwicklung*, Freiburg 1908.

Archiv für kath. Kirchenrecht, Vol. 51, pp. 209 sqq.

30 "*Infidelium matrimonia non ita firma censeri, quin necessitate suadente dissolvi possint.*" (Quoted by Chr. Pesch, *Praelect. Dogmat.*, Vol. VII, 3rd ed., p. 399).

31 Constitution "*Romani Pontifices*," of Aug. 2, 1571.— The Holy Office, on Aug. 1, 1759, issued the following instruction for the missions of Cochin-China: "*Si gentilis con-versus ante susceptionem baptismi habebat plures uxores et prima recusat amplecti fidem, tunc legitime potest quamlibet ex illis retinere, dummodo fidelis fiat.*"— For further information on the Pauline privilege see Gasparri, *Tract. Canonicus de Matrimonio*, Vol. II, n. 1083 sqq., Paris 1891; A. Lehmkuhl, S.J., in the *Catholic Encyclopedia*, Vol. V, p. 60; E. Taunton, *The Law of the Church*, p. 483, London 1906.

CHAPTER III

THE MINISTER

The contracting parties to a marriage administer the Sacrament to each other. The priest is merely the minister of the (accidental) celebration and the representative and chief official witness of the Church. This explains why his presence is prescribed by ecclesiastical law.

a) That the contracting parties administer the Sacrament to each other is evident from the fact that contract and Sacrament coincide [1] and that both the matter and the form of Matrimony are contained in the contract.[2]

Contract and Sacrament being identical, he who makes the contract *eo ipso* administers the Sacrament. Again, as matter and form of the Sacrament are contained in the contract, whoever furnishes the matter and form, effects the Sacrament. It is the express teaching of the Church that the Sacrament of Matrimony is effected solely [3] by the mutual consent [4] of the contracting parties. Conse-

---

[1] *V. supra*, Ch. I, Sect. 1, Thesis II.

[2] *V. supra*, Ch. I, Sect. 2.

[3] *Solus consensus.* Cfr. *Resp. Nicolai I. ad Consult. Bulgar.*, c. 3 (Denzinger-Bannwart, n. 334); *De-*

cret. Gregor., 1. IV, tit. 1, c. 23 (Denzinger-Bannwart, n. 404).

[4] *Mutuus consensus.* Cfr. *Decr. pro Armenis* (Denzinger-Bannwart, n. 702).

quently the contracting parties are the sole ministers of the Sacrament. It is on this assumption that the Tridentine Council declared clandestine marriages (*i. e.* marriages performed without a priest and the required witnesses) to be *vera et sacra,* provided the Church does not enjoin a special form of celebration as a condition of validity.

Berlage's opinion [5] that the priest is the ordinary, whilst the contracting parties are the extraordinary ministers of the Sacrament, is untenable, (1) because the form of a Sacrament can not be arbitrarily changed, and (2) because Nicholas I and Innocent III have expressly declared that the only thing required for the validity of marriage, and hence of the Sacrament, is the consent of the contracting parties. Very properly, therefore, is Matrimony called "the lay Sacrament."

b) If, as we have seen, the sacramental form of marriage does not consist in the benediction given by the priest, the priest cannot be the minister of the Sacrament.

How, then, are we to regard the part which he takes in the celebration of marriage?

(1) The priest is the official representative of the Church, to whose external forum Christian marriage belongs on account of its juridical effects;

(2) He is the official chief witness (*testis autorizabilis*), upon whose presence, since the Council of Trent, both the licitness and the validity of marriage ordinarily depend;

(3) He is the (sole) minister of the solemn ceremonies with which the Church surrounds marriage, not only the

5 *Dogmatik,* Vol. VII, p. 827, Münster 1864.

ecclesiastical recognition (*solemnizatio matrimonii*), which
he expresses in saying, " I join you together in Matrimony; " but also the nuptial blessing, which is one
of the Church's most beautiful and significant sacramen-
tals.

Yet all these ceremonies are non-essential, as appears
from the fact that they may, nay under certain conditions
must, be omitted and that they have varied in different
ages and countries. In the primitive Church the bride
concealed her face under a red veil to symbolize her
fidelity and submission to her husband, just as nuns
wear a white veil as an emblem of fidelity and obedience
to their mystic spouse.[6] The very word *nuptiae* is derived from *nubere,* to veil or conceal. At one time it was
customary for the bridal couple to carry burning candles
as a sign of conjugal chastity.[7] The bride, if she was
a virgin, wore a crown of flowers, which later developed
into the bridal wreath. Among the Greeks, in consequence of this custom, marriage is still called " the crowning of the bride." Another ancient custom was to tie
the bride and groom together with a ribbon as a warning
that they must not break the bond of conjugal unity.
The blessing of the wedding ring, too, is an ancient
ceremony. St. Isidore of Seville says that " the wedding
ring is worn upon the fourth finger because a vein is believed to run from that finger to the heart." [8]

6 Cfr. St. Ambrose, *De Virginitate,* c. 5, u. 26.

7 St. Peter Chrysologus (+ 450),
Serm., 22 (Migne, *P. L.,* LII, 262).

8 In the old English marriage
service it was the custom for the
bridegroom to put the ring on the
thumb of his bride, saying, " In the
name of the Father," then on the
next finger saying, " And the Son,"
then on the third saying, " And the
Holy Ghost," and finally on the
fourth with the word " Amen." On
the fourth finger it remained, because, as the Sarum rubric comments, " a vein proceedeth thence to
the heart." "Even if the whole
story is physiologically false, the
lesson remains, the lesson of love,
mutual love, taught and expressed
by the ring. This is the love husband and wife should have in ruling
the domain of home. Anyway, why
is the ring on the fourth finger?
Let the cynics answer." (F. X.
Doyle, S J., *The Home World,* p.
44 sq., N. Y. 1922).

CHAPTER IV

THE RECIPIENT

The contracting parties are not only the ministers, they are also the recipients of the Sacrament. The conditions of valid reception are four:

(1) The recipients must be baptized;[1]

(2) They must be of different sex;[2]

(3) There must be no diriment impediment in the way of their marriage;

(4) They must have the intention of doing what the Church does, *i. e.* contracting a Christian marriage.[3]

In order that a marriage be licit as well as valid, the Church furthermore requires:

(1) Freedom from forbidding impediments (*impedimenta prohibentia*);

(2) Compliance with all other ecclesiastical precepts;

(3) The state of sanctifying grace.[4]

The detailed explanation of these requirements belongs to Moral Theology and Canon Law.

a) Are all men obliged to receive the Sacrament of Matrimony?

1 *V. supra*, p. 157.　　3 *V. supra*, p. 158.
2 *V. supra*, p. 140.　　4 *V. supra*, pp. 168 sqq.

If Matrimony were necessary for salvation, all men would be obliged to marry, regardless of whether Matrimony were a Sacrament or not. However, no such obligation (*praeceptum matrimonii*) can be proved either from the law of nature or from the positive divine law.

The law of nature obliges a man to do those things, and those only, which are necessary to attain his final end. Marriage is not necessary for this purpose, except *per accidens, e. g.* for those who are unable to live chastely outside of the married state.

But does not the individual owe it to the community in which he lives, to the State, to society,— to marry and beget offspring? The duties we owe to society, we owe to existing society, not to the society of the future. Marriage serves to beget future citizens, towards whom we have no duties because they do not yet exist.

True, the State has an interest in marriage because without a sufficient number of marriages the human race would become extinct. But the State has no right to compel any individual to marry in order to forestall such a calamity. Marriage is a matter of the heart, and compulsory legislation would lead to tyranny and rouse popular opposition.

Sanchez says: " Formerly, when men were few, [God] obliged individuals; now that they have multiplied, he merely obliges the State in a general way to compel its subjects to marry in case of necessity." [5] This assertion is untenable. How could the State make marriage obligatory? It is simply impossible. Nor is anything gained by attributing this right to the law of nature in the abstract. For to say that the obligation of marrying

---

5 *De Matrimonio*, l. I, disp. 3, n. 3: " *Olim quum pauci homines erant, obligabat [voluntas Dei] singulos, nunc autem illis multiplicatis tan-* *tum obligat rempublicam in communi, ut necessitate occurrente compellat subditos.*"

does not bind all men, but merely some (a restriction demanded by the inequality in the number of men and women) is equivalent to saying that nobody in particular is obliged to marry, or at most the community at large, which, as such, cannot marry.

We may add that a law compelling people to marry would be utterly superfluous. The sexual instinct is so strongly developed in the majority of men, and marriage offers so many advantages, that it is morally impossible that all men should prefer a single life.[6] As a matter of fact the race has steadily multiplied from Adam and Eve down to the present day without any law compelling people to marry.

b) But how about the positive divine command (Gen. I, 28): "Increase and multiply and fill the earth"? These words were obviously addressed, not to our first parents alone, but to all their descendants. As an argument for compulsory marriage, however, they prove nothing. Our Lord Himself and St. Paul frequently extol virginity above marriage.[7] God would contradict Himself if He recommended the single life to some after imposing the obligation of marriage on all. Hence if, as some believe, Gen. I, 28 contained a universal command, that command must have lost its obligatory force as soon as the Creator's purpose in giving it was attained, that is to say, as soon as the earth became peopled with human beings. In matter of fact God's words to Adam

---

6 Cfr. St. Thomas, *Summa Theol., Suppl.,* qu. 41, art. 2: " *Ex tali inclinatione non obligatur quilibet homo per modum praecepti; alias quilibet homo obligaretur ad agriculturam et aedificatoriam, et ad huiusmodi officia quae sunt necessaria communitati humanae; sed inclinationi naturae satisfit, quum per diversos diversa de praedictis com-plentur. Quum ergo ad perfectionem humanae multitudinis sit necessarium aliquos contemplativae vitae inservire, quae maxime per matrimonium impeditur, inclinatio naturae ad matrimonium non obligat per modum praecepti, etiam secundum philosophos.*"

7 *V. supra,* pp. 130 sqq.

and Eve were meant as a benediction; they form part of the general blessing pronounced upon all living creatures. The words " Increase and multiply " are on a level with " subdue the earth and rule over the fishes of the sea," etc. They embody a vocation, not a command. For our first parents, of course, this vocation involved the duty of marrying, because their failure to do so would have frustrated the express purpose of the Creator. This does not, however, apply to all their descendants.

What if the human race were threatened with extinction,— would marriage in that case be obligatory on all? This question is purely theoretical because such an eventuality is not likely to occur. Without attempting an answer, we will simply call attention to St. Augustine's [8] declaration that there would be no universal obligation to marry even if the human race were about to die out, but that even in that case it would be more advisable for men to lead a virginal life in order that the predestined number of the elect might be attained as soon as possible.

READINGS :—I. Pleyer, *De Ministro Sacramenti Matrimonii*, 1759. —Th. M. Filser, *Ueber den Ausspender des Ehesakramentes*, 1844.—A. Fischer, *Der Spender der sakramentalen Gnade bei den unter Christen geschlossenen Ehebündnissen*, 1845.—W. Sulerzyski, *Wer ist Minister bei dem Sakrament der Ehe?* 1881.

8 *De Bono Coniugali*, l. X.

CHAPTER V

In this chapter we purpose to show, (1) that the Church possesses control over Christian marriage; (2) that this control is based on a positive divine law and can be exercised independently of the secular power; (3) that the Church has the exclusive right to establish diriment impediments.

SECTION 1

THE CHURCH HAS CONTROL OVER THE SACRAMENT OF MARRIAGE

1. THE DOGMA.—The contracting parties, the officiating priest, and the required witnesses are by no means the only persons who have a part in the administration of Matrimony. The Pope and the bishops, as representatives of the Church to whom our Lord has entrusted the administration of all the Sacraments,[1] also play an important rôle.

One of the palmary rights of the Church in connection with marriage is to establish and to dispense from diriment impediments.

Luther and Protestants generally admit those

---

1 Cfr. 1 Cor. IV, 1.

impediments which are mentioned in Leviticus, but deny that the Church has the power to establish others. This attitude is entirely consistent on the part of men who do not regard Matrimony as a Sacrament.

Against the Protestant Reformers the Council of Trent defined: "If anyone saith that the Church could not establish impediments dissolving marriage, or that she has erred in establishing them, let him be anathema." [2] Luther's pet theory is expressly condemned in canon 3 of the same Session: "If anyone saith that those degrees only of consanguinity and affinity which are set down in Leviticus can hinder matrimony from being contracted, and dissolve it when contracted, and that the Church cannot dispense in some of those degrees or establish that others may hinder and dissolve it, let him be anathema." [3]

2. PROOF OF THE DOGMA.—The Church is infallible, indefectible, and holy; and hence, if she attributes to herself and exercises a right, that right undoubtedly belongs to her. Now it is a fact that, constantly asserting her claim, she has established diriment impediments since the fourth

---

[2] Sess. XXIV, can. 4: "*Si quis dixerit, Ecclesiam non potuisse statuere impedimenta matrimonium dirimentia vel in iis constituendis errasse, anathema sit.*" (Denzinger-Bannwart, n. 974).

[3] Sess. XXIV, can. 3: "*Si quis dixerit, eos tantum consanguinitatis et affinitatis gradus, qui Levitico exprimuntur, posse impedire matrimonium contrahendum et dirimere contractum, nec posse Ecclesiam in nonnullis illorum dispensare aut constituere, ut plures impediant et dirimant, anathema sit.*" (Denzinger-Bannwart, n. 973).

century.   Consequently, she had the right to establish such impediments.

a) The major premise of this syllogism belongs to Apologetics or Fundamental Theology. The minor must be proved from history.

The Council of Elvira, A. D. 300, regarded the defect of Baptism (*disparitas cultus*) as a diriment impediment.[4] The Council of Neo-Cæsarea, 314, mentions affinity among the diriment impediments.[5] St. Basil (+ 379) says no man can marry a woman with whose sister he has had illicit intercourse.[6] Pope St. Leo the Great (+ 461) ordained for the diocese of Rome that no deacon should marry, and that if a man espoused a slave, mistakenly thinking her to be free, the marriage should be null and void (*impedimentum conditionis*).[7] Gregory the Great (+ 604) forbade marriages between first cousins, which were permitted under the Roman law.[8] Spiritual relationship arising from Baptism was made a diriment im-

---

4 Can. 15 "*Propter copiam puellarum gentilibus minime in matrimonium dandae sunt virgines christianae, ne aetas in flore tumens in adulterio animae resolvatur.*" (Hardouin, *Concil.*, I, p. 252).

5 Can. 2: "*Femina si duobus fratribus [i. e. successive] nupserit, extrudatur usque ad mortem; sed in morte propter humanitatem, si dixerit quod ubi convaluerit, solvet matrimonium, habebit poenitentiam.*"

6 "*Si quis impuritatis vitio aliquando victus in illicitam duarum sororum coniunctionem inciderit, neque id matrimonium existimetur neque omnino in Ecclesiae coetum admittatur, priusquam a se invicem dirimantur.*" (*Ep. 160 ad Diodor.*, n. 2; Migne, P. G., XXXII, 623).

7 "*Ancillam a toro abiicere et uxo-rem certae ingenuitatis accipere, non duplicatio coniugii, sed profectus est honestatis.*" (*Ep. 67 ad Rustic. Episc. Narbon.*, c. 6).

8 In his instructions to St. Augustine of Canterbury (L. XII, ep. 31): "*Quaedam terrena lex in Romana Republica permittit, ut sive fratris sive sororis seu duorum fratrum germanorum vel duarum sororum filius et filia misceantur. Sed experimento didicimus, ex tali coniugio sobolem non posse succrescere, et sacra lex [i. e. Leviticus] prohibet cognationis turpitudinem revelare. Unde necesse est, ut iam tertia vel quarta generatio fidelium licenter sibi iungi debeat. Nam secunda, quam diximus, a se omni modo debet abstinere. Cum noverca autem misceri grave est facinus.*"

pediment by the Council in Trullo (692).[9]   A synod held
at Mayence, in 813, prohibited marriage in the fourth
degree of consanguinity and designated the spiritual relationship arising from Confirmation as a diriment impediment.[10]   Pope Zachary testified at the Roman Council of
743 that the archbishops and princes of Germany had
asked him for instructions with regard to marriage.[11]
Pope Nicholas I (+ 867), in confirming the diriment impediments of consanguinity and spiritual relationship,
cited "the sacred canons, and especially the decrees of
Pope Zachary." [12]

b) In order to understand how the Church can in-
validate the Sacrament of Matrimony without changing
its matter and form, we must consider that the validity
of the Sacrament is conditioned by the validity of the
matrimonial contract.[13]   By nullifying the contract, the
Church deprives the Sacrament of its basis.   The validity of the contract does not depend solely on the free
will of the contracting parties; it depends also on the will
of God, which may manifest itself in a threefold man-

9 Canon 53: "*Quoniam . . . in
nonnullis locis cognovimus quosdam,
qui ex sancto et salutari baptismate
infantes suscipiunt, postea quoque
cum matribus illorum viduis matrimonium contrahere, statuimus ut in
posterum nihil fiat eiusmodi. Si qui
autem post praesentem canonem hoc
facere deprehensi fuerint, ii quidem
primo ab hoc illicito matrimonio de-
sistant, deinde et fornicatorum poenis
subiiciantur.*"

10 Can. 54, 55: "*Contradicimus
quoque, ut in quarta generatione nullus amplius coniugio copuletur; ubi
autem post interdictum factum inventum fuerit, separetur. Nullus
igitur proprium filium vel filiam de
fonte baptismatis suscipiat, nec filio-
lam nec commatrem ducat uxorem,*

*nec illam cuius filium aut filiam ad
confirmationem duxerit: ubi autem
factum fuerit, separentur.*" (Hardouin, *Concil.*, IV, p. 1016).

11 "*. . . petentes apostolica prae-
cepta, qualiter liceat eis coniugia copulare et quomodo debeant obser-
vare.*"

12 *Resp. ad Consult. Bulgaror.*, c.
39: "*Sacri vero canones et praecipue Zachariae summi praesulis decreta quid hinc promulgent, episcopo
vestro vobis explorandum relinqui-
mus.*"   On the very ancient *impedimentum voti*, see *infra*, Sect. 2.   On
the historic development of these impediments in general cfr.   Palmieri,
De Matr. Christ., thes. 29.

13 *V*. Ch. I, Sect. 1.   Thesis II.

ner: through the law of nature, through a positive law, or through an ecclesiastical precept.

Hence there are three distinct classes of diriment impediments:

(1) Impediments flowing from the law of nature (*e. g.* impotency, error, violence) ;

(2) Impediments set up by a positive ·divine law (*e. g.* the bond of an existing marriage) ;

(3) Impediments established by ecclesiastical law (*e. g.* clandestinity, difference of religion, affinity).

No matrimonial contract is valid if the contracting parties are incapacitated for marriage by the law of nature, by a positive divine law, or by the law of the Church.

Persons thus incapacitated are technically known as *inhabiles.* A marriage entered into with such a person is null and void because there can be no true and binding consent between *inhabiles.* These considerations explain why the Church can establish diriment impediments without altering the matter and form of the Sacrament. Both matter and form of Matrimony consist in the valid consent of the contracting parties. Where there is no valid consent, there can be no valid marriage, and hence no Sacrament.[14] Conversely, the Church can, by establishing impediments, render a marriage unlawful, but she cannot prevent it from being sacramental if the underlying contract is valid.

3. TWO FUNCTIONS OF ECCLESIASTICAL AU-
THORITY.—As the Church has the power to regulate Christian marriage, she must also have the
power of dispensing from diriment as well as for-

14 *V.* Ch. I, Sect. 1.

bidding impediments (*potestas dispensandi*) and of haling matrimonial causes before her judgment seat (*potestas iudicialis*).

The *potestas dispensandi* is exercised both *in foro externo* and *in foro interno,* and extends to all impediments, except where the natural or a positive divine law form an insuperable obstacle; it may also validate an invalid marriage *in radice.*

The *potestas iudicialis* is the power to pass definitive judgment on all matters pertaining to the essence of Matrimony, *e. g.* the dissolubility or indissolubility of the bond,[15] matrimonial engagements (*sponsalia*), separation from bed and board, etc. In regard to the latter, the Tridentine Council declares: "If anyone saith that the Church errs in declaring that, for many causes, a separation may take place between husband and wife in regard of bed or cohabitation, for a determinate or for an indeterminate period, let him be anathema." [16] As matrimonial laws bind the universal Church, the Pope is the only competent authority for the definitive adjudication of marriage cases and the granting of dispensations, and no bishop can do anything without his consent.

A dispensation is a special exemption granted from the

---

15 *V.* Ch. II, Sect. 2 and 3.

16 Sess. XXIV, can. 8: "*Si quis dixerit, Ecclesiam errare, quum ob multas causas separationem inter coniuges quoad torum seu quoad cohabitationem ad certum incertumve tempus fieri posse decernit, anathema sit.*"

requirements of a law or rule.[17] What is the extent of the papal power of dispensing from diriment impediments to Matrimony?

All the diriment impediments to marriage but one are enumerated in the following hexameters:

> *Error, conditio, votum, cognatio, crimen,*
> *Cultus disparitas, vis, ordo, ligamen, honestas,*
> *Aetas, affinis, si clandestinus et impos,*
> *Raptave sit mulier, parti nec reddita tutae:*
> *Haec socianda vetant connubia, facta retractant.*

Of these fifteen impediments, five are based partly on the natural and partly on positive divine law. They are: (1) *ligamen, i. e.* the impediment of existing marriage; (2) *error, i. e.* a mistake as to the person married, either before or at the time of the marriage; (3) *vis* or *metus gravis, i. e.* grave fear, unjustly caused, for the purpose of extorting matrimonial consent; (4) *consanguinitas, i. e.* blood relationship within certain degrees; (5) *impotentia, i. e.* an antecedent incapacity to perform the functions of the married state. From these impediments not even the Pope can dispense. With regard to the *impedimentum ligaminis,* note that the dissolution of the marriage bond in certain cases [18] is not, properly speaking, effected by a dispensation but either by divine law or in virtue of the loosing power exercised by the Supreme Pontiff in the name of Christ.

The *impedimentum voti* arises from the solemn vow of chastity taken by religious. Being based upon a promise made directly to God, rather than to the Pope or the Church, this impediment is of divine right, but as it is self-imposed and a matter of free choice, there is no contradiction involved when the Pope, for weighty reasons, after

---

[17] *Dispensatio est relaxatio legis in aliquo casu particulari.* [18] *V. supra,* Ch. II, Sect. 3.

lifting the *solemnitas voti,* which is of purely ecclesiastical institution, dispenses from the simple vow of chastity just as he can and does dispense from a promissory vow (*iuramentum promissorium*).

Under the Code of Canon Law *relationship by adoption* in regions where this is an impediment under the civil law, has been added to the fifteen *impedimenta dirimentia* mentioned above. This, like the others not based on the natural or divine law, is of purely ecclesiastical institution, and it needs no argument to prove that the Church can dispense from laws of her own making.

The only difficulty arises in connection with the dispensation technically known as *sanatio in radice,* by which a marriage invalid from the beginning is made valid just as if there had been no ecclesiastical impediment.[19] How can the Church do this? Are we to assume that the Pope is able to undo past deeds or that his power is retroactive?[20] Nothing of the kind. The *sanatio in radice* is simply a *fictio iuris,* by which an invalid marriage, besides being made valid by a dispensation (*ex nunc*), is juridically regarded as if it had been valid from the beginning (*ex tunc*). The principal effect of this measure is to legitimize children begotten before the revalidation.[21]

---

19 *C. I. C.,* can. 1138–41.

20 "*Ad praeteritum nulla datur potentia,*" says an ancient proverb.

21 Also in other respects this papal favor is of far-reaching consequence, especially in questions of succession and inheritance arising in royal families. The theologians commonly teach that it behooves Christian princes to respect such papal acts, not only in their spiritual, but also in regard to their civil effects, (Cfr. Sanchez, *De Matrimonio,* l. VIII, disp. 7), though it would be difficult to show that they have a strict obligation to do so, especially ruling monarchs in questions pertaining to succession.— On the subject of this subdivision cfr. Palmieri, *De Matrimonio Christiano,* thes. 35.

SECTION 2

THE CHURCH'S CONTROL OVER CHRISTIAN MARRIAGE IS OF DIVINE RIGHT AND INDEPENDENT OF THE STATE

1. HERETICAL ERRORS VS. THE DOGMATIC TEACHING OF THE CHURCH.—Antonio de Dominis was the first to maintain that the Church derives her power over matrimonial causes from the State.[1] He was followed by Launoy[2] and the court theologians of Austria, France, and Italy. In 1786, the Jansenist Council of Pistoia put this teaching into practice by formally requesting the Archduke Leopold II of Tuscany, a brother of Emperor Joseph II, to abolish the two matrimonial impediments of spiritual relationship and public propriety and to limit consanguinity and affinity to the second degree. This impudent act led Pope Pius VI to condemn the principle espoused by the court theologians as heretical.[3] His decision merely confirmed and

1 *De Republ. Christ.*, l. V, c. 11, London 1618.

2 *De Regia in Matrimonium Potestate*, Paris 1673.

3 Bull " *Auctorem fidei*," 1794; cfr. *Prop. Syn. Pistor. damnat.*, prop. 59: " *Doctrina synodi asserens,* ' ad supremam civilem potestatem dumtaxat originarie spectare, contractui matrimonii apponere impedimenta eius generis quae ipsum nullum reddunt dicunturque dirimentia,' quod ius originarium praeterea dicitur ' cum iure dispensandi essentialiter

emphasized the teaching of the Tridentine Council.

Launoy's interpretation of the Council was arbitrary. We will give but one example. The Council declares: "If anyone saith that the Church could not establish impediments dissolving marriage, or that she has erred in establishing them, let him be anathema." Launoy claims that "Church" here means the *Ecclesia discens,* or community of the faithful as represented by the State, to which the *Ecclesia docens* owes whatever powers she enjoys in matrimonial affairs. Launoy further maintained that the Tridentine canons possess no dogmatic authority, but are purely disciplinary, and therefore revocable. As a matter of fact the Council expressly meant to define that the Church has the power to establish diriment impediments, and that she is infallible in exercising this power. No such infallibility resides in, or has ever been claimed by, secular rulers. Besides, the Tridentine Council had in view mainly the heresy of Luther, who denied jurisdiction in matrimonial matters to the Holy See, not to the State. The Council proved its independence of the secular power by establishing a new impediment (clandestinity), by limiting the scope of certain traditional impediments, and by refusing the urgent request of the King of France and other monarchs to declare the marriage of children without parental consent invalid.[4]

connexum' subiungens ' supposito assensu vel conniventia principum potuisse Ecclesiam iuste constituere impedimenta dirimentia ipsum contractum matrimonii,— quasi Ecclesia non semper potuerit ac possit in Christianorum matrimoniis iure proprio impedimenta constituere, quae matrimonium non solum impediant, sed et nullum reddant quoad vinculum, . . . in eisdem dispensare — : canonum 3, 4, 9, 12 Sess. XXIV. Concilii Tridentini eversiva, haeretica." (Denzinger-Bannwart, n. 1559).

4 Cfr. Palmieri, *De Matrimonio Christ.,* thes. 28.

2. PROOF OF THE DOGMA.—a) To refute the court theologians it is sufficient to point out that their teaching is contrary to dogma. No Catholic is permitted to doubt that the Church has the God-given right to control the administration of all the Sacraments, including Matrimony.[5] Now the control of the matter and form of this Sacrament, which consist in the matrimonial consent of the contracting parties,[6] is merely a function of the legitimate administration of Matrimony. Moreover the establishment of diriment impediments involves actual control over matter and form, and hence the Church has the right to establish such impediments and to condition upon them the validity of the matrimonial consent, which is inseparable from the Sacrament. This fundamental right comprises the power of granting dispensations and other acts of jurisdiction. It follows that the Church has received her prerogatives and rights, not from any monarch, nor from the secular power as such, but directly from Jesus Christ.

b) A sufficient argument from Tradition is furnished by the demonstration that the contrary thesis has no foundation in history.

a) When did the State confer upon the Church the power to regulate matrimonial causes? This cannot, in the nature of things, have happened during the era of

5 *V. Supra*, Ch. I, Sect. 1.　　　　6 *V. Supra*, Ch. I, Sect. 2.

the persecutions, which ended with the edict of Milan, 313. Did it perhaps occur after the reign of Constantine, at the beginning of what we are wont to call the Middle Ages? Impossible. The court theologians themselves emphasize, with no small degree of satisfaction, that the secular princes who ruled during this epoch (Theodosius, Justinian, *et al.*), far from relinquishing their alleged rights in favor of the Church, set up and abolished diriment impediments without her consent, nay contrary to her will.[7] The Middle Ages witnessed many sharp conflicts between the papacy and the rulers of the Holy Roman Empire, and the Church was often compelled to defend her rights against usurping princes. Nor does modern history furnish a single fact or document to prove that the Church derives her matrimonial jurisdiction from the State. Hence the assertion of the court theologians is groundless.

β) We can go a step farther and show that, in establishing certain impediments, the Church either had no precedent on the part of the State, or paid scant attention to existing civil laws. Take *e. g.* the *impedimentum voti.* This is one of the most ancient ecclesiastical impediments of which we know. As early as the third century St. Cyprian (+ 258) declared that young women who married after taking the vow of chastity excommunicated themselves.[8] When the Church was recovering from the terrible persecutions of the first three centuries, a Spanish council held at Elvira (A. D. 300) refused to admit such women to the Sacraments except on condition

7 Cfr. F. H. Vering, *Geschichte der Pandekten des römischen und heutigen gemeinen Privatrechtes*, 4th ed., pp. 556 sqq., Mayence 1875. — On certain objections drawn from the writings of Athenagoras, St. Ambrose, and St. Augustine see Palmieri, *De Matrimonio Christ.*, pp. 258 sqq.

8 *Ep. 4 (al. 62):* " *Quodsi obstinatae perseverant nec se ab invicem separant, sciant se cum hac sua impudica obstinatione nunquam a nobis admitti in Ecclesiam posse.*"

that they abstained from conjugal intercourse.[9]   St. Basil (+ 379) testifies that marriages of this kind were regarded as invalid in the Eastern Church.[10]   Pope Innocent I (+ 407) distinguishes two classes of virgins, veiled and unveiled, and says that the former cannot be absolved until after the death of their guilty partners.[11]   St. Jerome (+ 420) declares that virgins who marry after taking a solemn vow of chastity are " guilty of incest rather than adultery." [12]   Gelasius I (+ 496) brands as sacrilegious the attempted marriage of virgins who had dedicated themselves to God by a solemn vow of chastity.[13]

The Church proceeded with similar independence in determining the forbidden degrees of consanguinity and affinity,[14] in recognizing the diriment impediment of *disparitas cultus* (defect of Baptism), which was not generally enforced until after 1000,[15] in establishing the *impedimentum criminis,* for which civil legislation offered no precedent, and so forth.   To these and other canonical laws Christian rulers bowed in obedience without ever claiming that their own rights were being usurped.[16]

---

9 Can. 13: ". . . *ut abstineant se a coitu.*"

10 " *Canonicarum fornicationes pro matrimonio non reputentur, sed earum coniunctio omnino divellatur.*" (*Ep. 1 ad Amphil.,* can. 6).

11 *Ep. ad Victric. Episc. Rotomag.*

12 *Adv. Iovin.,* I, 7: " *Virgines quae post consecrationem nupserint, non tam adulterae sunt quam incestae.*"

13 The Council of Tours (567) cites in support of the nullity of such marriages the code of Emperor Theodosius the Great (+ 395), which punishes the forcible abduction of consecrated virgins for the purpose of marriage with death; but aside from the fact that the secular law is narrower in scope, the Council gives as a reason for the diriment effect of the vow of chastity (can. 20, *apud* Palmieri, p. 350): " *quod vel Apostolus Paulus vel Papa Innocentius statuit.*"— For fuller information see Palmieri, *De Matrimonio Christ.,* pp. 237 sqq.

14 V. *supra,* Sect. 1.

15 Cfr. Bellarmine, *De Matrimonio,* I, 23.

16 Cfr. Palmieri, *De Matr. Christ.,* thes. 30 and 33.— On the subject of marriage impediments from the standpoint of Moral Theology see Thos. Slater, S.J., *A Manual of Moral Theology,* Vol. II, pp. 285 sqq., New York 1908; from the canonical point of view, De Smet-Dobell, *Betrothment and Marriage,* Vol. II, Bruges 1913.

SECTION 3

THE CHURCH'S EXCLUSIVE RIGHT TO ESTAB-
LISH DIRIMENT IMPEDIMENTS

1. THE TEACHING OF THE CHURCH.—Abstractly speaking there is nothing contradictory in the assumption that the State, too, has the right to establish diriment impediments to marriage. In matter of fact there have been some theologians who held this to be the case. Prominent among them were Peter Soto, Ambrose Catharinus, Tournely, Collet, and Carrière. "Kings and secular princes," says *e. g.* Tournely, "possess the innate right to establish impediments which render marriage forbidden or invalid."[1] Gregory of Valentia, Gonet, Henno, and especially Th. Sanchez[2] thought it prudent to modify this thesis. They said the State originally did possess the right to set up marriage impediments, but it was taken away by the Church in the legitimate exercise of her *potestas indirecta in temporalia.* To-day it is *doctrina certa* that the State has no jurisdiction over matri-

[1] *" Reges et principes saeculares iure sibi proprio ac innato constituere possunt impedimenta matrimonium irritantia et dirimentia."* (*De Matrimonio*, qu. 7, art. 2).

[2] *De Matrimonio*, l. VII, disp. 3.

monial causes so far as they (directly or indirectly) relate to the Sacrament. The Tridentine Council declares: "If anyone saith that matrimonial causes do not belong to ecclesiastical judges, let him be anathema." [3] Pope Pius VI authentically interpreted this synodal canon as meaning that "all matrimonial causes belong solely to ecclesiastical judges." [4]

The correctness of this interpretation is evident. The proposition condemned as heretical by the Council, *viz.*: " Matrimonial causes do not belong to ecclesiastical judges," must mean either that " not all matrimonial causes belong to ecclesiastical judges," or that " all matrimonial causes do not belong to ecclesiastical judges." The contradictory of the first proposition would be: " All matrimonial causes belong to ecclesiastical judges; " and of the second, " Some matrimonial causes do not belong to ecclesiastical judges." But to assert this would afford no guidance to Catholics. Hence the Council can only have meant what Pius VI says it meant, or, to employ the Pontiff's own words, " The terms in which the canon is clothed are so general that they comprehend and contain all [matrimonial] causes." [5] If we further consider that the reason why matrimonial causes belong to the ecclesiastical jurisdiction is that Matrimony among Christians is a Sacrament, it follows that they be-

---

3 Sess. XXIV, can. 12: " *Si quis dixerit, causas matrimoniales non spectare ad iudices ecclesiasticos, anathema sit.*" (Denzinger-Bannwart, n. 982).

4 " *Omnes causae matrimoniales*

spectant ad solos iudices ecclesiasticos." (*Ep. ad Episc. Motulens. d. 16 Sept. 1788*).

5 " *Verba canonis ita generalia sunt, omnes ut causas comprehendant et complectantur.*" (*Ibid.*)

long solely to the jurisdiction of the Church.[6] Were we to grant for argument's sake that some matrimonial causes belong to the State, we should be at once confronted with the question: Do they belong to the State independently of the Church or dependently? To say that they belong to the State independently of the Church would be to deny the Tridentine teaching that "all matrimonial causes belong to ecclesiastical judges." To say that they belong to the State dependently of the Church would be to admit her exclusive jurisdiction in principle.

For the rest, the Council of Trent acted in perfect accord with the above-quoted interpretation of its twelfth canon when it declared clandestine marriages to be truly sacramental so long as the Church does not expressly declare them null and void. Hence it is *doctrina certa* that all matrimonial causes belong exclusively to the Church.[7]

2. PROOF.—A legitimately established diriment impediment produces two distinct effects: (1) remotely, it renders certain persons incapable of contracting a valid marriage (*inhabilitas personarum*); (2) proximately, it nullifies any attempted marital consent on the part of such persons (*inefficacitas consensûs*). The State cannot do either of these things. For if it were empowered to declare baptized persons incapable of contracting marriage, it would possess the right

---

6 " *Sicut haec sacramenti ratio communis est omnibus causis matrimonialibus, ita omnes hae causae spectare unice debent ad iudices ec-* *clesiasticos, quum eadem ratio sit in omnibus.*" (*Ibid.*)

7 Cfr. Palmieri, *De Matrimonio Christ.*, pp. 267 sq.

to regulate the administration of the Sacraments; but this belongs exclusively to the Church. If the State could render the matrimonial consent null and void, it would necessarily also possess the right to determine the matter and form of the Sacrament, which is equally inadmissible. Consequently, the State cannot establish or grant dispensations from diriment impediments, nor can it claim jurisdiction over matrimonial causes.

This argument derives strength from the philosophical consideration that no two tribunals can exercise independent and supreme jurisdiction over the same class of cases. If the State had equal jurisdiction in matrimonial matters with the Church, it might happen that the Church, by virtue of her divine prerogatives, would establish a diriment impediment which the State refused to recognize, or *vice versa*. In that case a marriage might be valid and invalid, licit and illicit, legal and illegal at one and the same time, and there would be no end of trouble between the two powers, while the faithful subjects of both would be sorely embarrassed; — all this not because of some human weakness or imperfection, but in consequence of a positive divine ordinance. Since it cannot be the will of God to bring about such an intolerable state of affairs, we must conclude that the control of Christian marriage belongs either to the Church or to the State. Matrimony being a Sacrament, its control belongs to the Church, and hence the State has no jurisdiction whatever over matrimonial causes.

In claiming jurisdiction over all matrimonial causes among Christians, the Church is not actuated by an immoderate desire for power, or by jealousy, but purely and solely by obedience to the commands of her Divine Founder. "Due weight must be attached to the sacramental dignity," says Leo XIII, "by the addition of which the marriages of Christians have become far the noblest of all matrimonial unions. To make laws and regulations with regard to the Sacraments is, by the will of Christ, so much the privilege and duty of the Church, that it would be plainly absurd to maintain that even the smallest part of such power has been transferred to the civil rulers."[8] This principle underlies the constant practice of the Church.

3. RIGHTS OF THE STATE.—It would be wrong to deny, however, that the State has some rights with regard to marriage. A wide field is open to civil jurisdiction in regulating the marriages of unbelievers and exercising a certain control over the civil effects of the marriages of Christians.

a) Some modern theologians assert that the State has no jurisdiction over the non-sacramental marriages of the unbaptized. These writers (Perrone, Martin, Feije, Zigliara, Chr. Pesch, and others) argue as follows:

(1) The so-called marriage of nature was originally intended to symbolize Christ's mystic union with His Church and thereby withdrawn from all purely human jurisdiction.[9]

---

8 " *Consideranda sacramenti dignitas est, cuius accessione matrimonia Christianorum evasere longe nobilissima. De sacramentis autem statuere et praecipere ita ex voluntate Christi ola potest et debet Ecclesia, ut ab-* sonum sit plane potestatis eius vel minimam partem ad gubernatores rei civilis velle esse translatam." (Encycl. "Arcanum divinae," Feb. 10, 1880).

9 Cfr. St. Leo the Great, *Ep. 2 ad*

(2) Marriage is older than civil society. The State found it in existence and incorporated it into its own organism. This explains why even to-day marriage is regarded primarily as a natural and only secondarily as a civil contract.[10]

Nevertheless the great majority of Catholic divines adhere to the traditional opinion that the secular rulers of non-baptized subjects undoubtedly possess the right to uphold and enforce the diriment impediments flowing from the natural law, and to establish new impediments of a purely civil character.

This power is, however, subject to two limitations. (a) The State cannot arbitrarily dissolve validly contracted marriages between unbaptized persons, and (b) a non-Christian, and *a fortiori* a Christian ruler cannot make purely civil impediments binding upon his baptized subjects. For the marriages of Christians are in no way subject to the jurisdiction of the State.

To prevent misunderstanding it may be well to note that the power of the State over the marriages of its non-Christian subjects is preëminently a religious prerogative, which owes its existence to the fact that in the purely natural order the secular ruler is the supreme representative of religion and unites within himself both political and religious jurisdiction.[11]

b) With regard to baptized persons, the State

Rustic. Narbon., 4: " Societas nuptiarum ab initio ita fuit constituta, ut praeter sexuum coniunctionem haberet in se Christi et Ecclesiae sacramentum." (Migne, P. L., LIV, 1204).

10 Cfr. Pius VI, Ep. ad Episc. Agriens., July 11, 1789: " Matrimonium non est contractus mere civilis, sed et contractus naturalis divino iure ante omnem societatem constitutus et firmatus."

11 On the rights of the State in the matrimonial causes of unbaptized persons cfr. A. Resemans, De Competentia Civili in Vinculum Coniugale Infidelium, Rome 1887.

must confine itself to the regulation of the so-called civil consequences (*effectus civiles*) of marriage.

Christian marriage is a Sacrament, and whatever concerns it as a Sacrament, *e. g.* the validity of the contract, the indissolubility of the bond, separation from bed and board, betrothment and the public celebration of marriage, the legitimacy of children, etc., belongs exclusively to the jurisdiction of the Church. The civil effects or consequences over which the State has control are such non-essential matters as property, dowery, and inheritance.

By virtue of her right to enforce the effects of marriage *in foro externo* the Church has established certain external consequences analogous to the *effectus civiles,* such as the incapacity of bigamists to receive Holy Orders.[12]

c) A word about civil marriage. Civil marriage (*matrimonium civile*), in the sense of a true marriage between baptized persons, under State control and without regard to the laws of the Church, is contrary to the divine law. Under the influence of the Lutheran view that marriage is "a worldly thing," and of the French Revolution, civil marriage was introduced by Napoleon I in France, whence it made its way into nearly all countries of Europe and North America and into some of the South American republics.[13] It has been repeatedly condemned, by Pius VII, Pius IX,[14] and Leo XIII.

12 Cfr. Palmieri, *De Matrimonio Christ.,* thes. 31.

13 Cfr. J. A. Ryan in the *Catholic Encyclopedia,* Vol. IX, p. 698.

14 See the Syllabus, prop. 65-75.

When civil marriage cannot be regarded as an ecclesiastically valid clandestine marriage, it is neither a true marriage nor a Sacrament, nay, according to a decision of the Holy Office of March 13, 1879, it is not even equivalent to a valid betrothal.

In some countries civil marriage is essential to the validity of the conjugal union before the civil law (*matrimonium civile obligatorium*). In others, *e. g.* the United States, it is merely one of several ways in which marriage may be contracted (*matrimonium civile facultativum*). In still others it is provided for cases in which a marriage for some reason, *e. g.* the lack of a dispensation from an ecclesiastical impediment, cannot take place in church.

Where the State conditions the civil effects of marriage upon the fact of its being contracted before a civil magistrate, or where it refuses to recognize as legitimate children born of a purely ecclesiastical marriage, Catholics have no choice but to submit, nay they are in duty bound to do so, since civil marriage in such cases is nothing but a legal form.[15]

READINGS:—A. Roscovány, *Matrimonium in Ecclesia Catholica Potestati Ecclesiasticae Subiectum,* 2 vols., Neutra 1871.—J. Schneemann, S.J., *Die Irrtümer über die Ehe,* Freiburg 1866.— Heuser, *De Potestate Statuendi Impedimenta Dirimentia Ecclesiae Propria,* 1859.—J. Becamel, *Tract. de Matrimonio et Dispensationibus Matrimonii,* Paris 1889.—De Becker, *De Sponsalibus et Matrimonio,* Bruxelles 1896.—J. Pompen, *Tract. de Dispensationibus et de Revalidatione Matrimonii,* Amsterdam 1894.—F. X. Feije, *De Impedimentis et Dispensationibus Matrimonialibus,* Louvain 1890.—F. Huszár, *De Potestate Ecclesiae circa Matrimonium,* Rome 1900.—J. Hollweck, *Das Zivileherecht des bürgerlichen Gesetzbuches im Lichte des kanonischen Rechtes,* Mayence 1900.

15 Cfr. Benedict XIV, *De Syn. Dioeces.,* l. IV, c. 7; A. Visek, *Die Zivilehe vor dem Forum des Rechtes und des Gewissens,* Prague 1884.

Schnitzer, *Katholisches Eherecht,* Freiburg 1898.—F. Heiner, *Grundriss des katholischen Eherechtes,* Münster 1900.—M. Leitner, *Lehrbuch des katholischen Eherechtes,* Paderborn 1902.— * F. X. Wernz, S.J., *Ius Decretalium,* Vol. IV, 2nd ed., *Ius Matrimoniale Ecclesiae Catholicae,* Rome 1911.—De Smet, *Betrothment and Marriage. A Canonical and Theological Treatise with Notices on History and Civil Law,* tr. by W. Dobell, new ed., 2 vols., Bruges 1923.—F. M. Cappello, S.J., *Tractatus Canonico-Moralis de Matrimonio,* Turin 1923.

B. J. Otten, S.J., *A Manual of the History of Dogmas,* Vol. I, St. Louis 1917, pp. 25, 43 sq., 96, 164, 179, 197, 207, 347, 355, 475; Vol. II (1918), pp. 393 sqq.

APPENDIX I

THE "DECRETUM PRO ARMENIS" IN THE LIGHT OF RECENT RESEARCH

(See page 66)

Cardinal Van Rossum [1] has since demonstrated with absolute certainty that Eugene IV in his famous Decree positively intended to exclude the imposition of hands as an essential element of ordination and to place the essence of the Sacrament of Orders solely in the delivery of the instruments, as taught by St. Thomas. Hence it is plain that the Decree no longer binds under the present changed discipline.

That the *Decretum pro Armenis* was not an *ex cathedra* definition, and that its author did not intend it to be such, is further evidenced, according to Cardinal Van Rossum, by two facts. The first is that for at least a hundred years the Decree had fallen into complete desuetude in the Latin Church, until Ruardus Tapper (+ 1559) exhumed it. The second fact is that later popes, *e. g.,* Clement VIII [2] and Leo XIII,[3] have issued decisions that contravene both the words and the spirit of the *Decretum*. Add to this the common teaching of theologians since St. Bonaventure, which has never been questioned by the authorities of the Church, and the conclusion is inevitable that the *Decretum pro Armenis* was no irreformable ruling, but its teaching may, with all due respect, be set aside.

---

[1] *De Essentia Sacramenti Ordinis,* Freiburg 1914, pp. 155 sqq.

[2] In his decision concerning the holy oils; see *supra,* p. 19, note 11.

[3] In his decision against the validity of Anglican Orders, 1896 (*supra,* pp. 70 sq.).

APPENDIX II

ALL THREE IMPOSITIONS NOT ESSENTIAL TO THE
VALIDITY OF THE SACRAMENT OF ORDERS

(See page 70)

The opinion that all three of the impositions at present
employed in the Latin Church constitute one moral act
and, therefore, with their accompanying prayers (as partial forms) are essential to the validity of the Sacrament
of Orders, is inconsistent for the following reasons.
Either the first (or the second) imposition confers the sacramental grace of Holy Orders together with the sacerdotal character, or it does not. If it does, the third imposition can be no more than a solemn exemplification of
the sacred character already received. If it does not, how
can it be essential, since the sacerdotal character (in spite
of its varied functions) is in itself simple and indivisible?
This conclusion applies with still greater force to the different combinations of the ceremony of the *traditio instrumentorum* (paten and host, chalice containing wine)
with any one of the three (or two) impositions.

APPENDIX III

THE BLESSING OF DEACONESSES

(See page 127)

John of Faenza (+ 1190), Peter of Poitiers (+ 1205), and a few other medieval theologians regarded the blessing bestowed upon deaconesses (and virgins who dedicated their lives to God) as a true Sacrament. Others protested against this view. Thus Huguccio (+ 1210) declared the blessing of deaconesses to be no true ordination, but merely a ceremony authorizing them to perform certain services, for instance, to read the Gospel during choir. Nevertheless some medieval canonists erroneously taught that women who were " ordained " by the imposition of hands received the Sacrament of Holy Orders.[1] In view of these differences of opinion it is premature to conclude, as Morinus [2] did, and as K. H. Schäfer [3] does, that the blessing of deaconesses was formerly one of the minor orders, or to hold with A. Ludwig [4] that it was reckoned among the major orders.

1 Gillmann, " *Weibliche Kleriker nach dem Urteil der Frühscholastik,*" in the *Archiv für kath. Kirchenrecht,* 1913, pp. 239 sqq.

2 *Comment. de Sacris Eccles. Ordinat.,* Antwerp 1695, pp. 143 sqq.

3 *Kanonissenstifter im deutschen Mittelalter,* Stuttgart 1907; IDEM,

" *Kanonissen und Diakonissen,*" in the *Römische Quartalschrift,* 1910, II, pp. 49 sqq.

4 " *Weibliche Kleriker in der altchrist. und frühmittelalt. Kirche,*" in the *Theol.-prakt. Monatsschrift,* 1911, pp. 141 sqq.

INDEX

A

Abbesses, 127.
Abbots, 122 sqq.
Acts of the Apostles, 100 sqq.
Agde, Council of (506), 115.
Adam and Eve, 150, 176, 186, 219.
Adultery, 190 sqq.
Aërius of Sebaste, 80, 85, 87.
Aix-la-Chapelle, Council of (836), 11.
Albertus Magnus, 20, 22, 88, 111.
Albigenses, 147.
Alexander III, 199, 204 sq.
Alexander of Hales, 88.
Alphonsus, St., 107, 111.
Amalarius of Treves, 112.
Ambrose, St., 60, 118, 143, 155, 181.
Anabaptists, 174.
Ancyra, Council of (314), 133, 181.
Anglican Orders, 70 sq.
Antioch, Council of (341), 123.
Antoninus, St., 114.
Antonio de Dominis, 158, 229.
Apostolic Constitutions, 104, 119, 126, 133.
Archangelsky, 17.
Arcudius, 46.
Armenians, 11, 65, 66, 152.
Athanasius, St., 86.
Athenagoras, 181.
Atzberger, 49, 107, 124, 163.
Augustine of Canterbury, St., 119.
Augustine, St., 60, 74, 90, 97, 120, 135, 144, 153 sqq., 181, 205, 220.
Aureolus, 122.

B

Ballerini, 211.

Baltimore, Third Plenary Council of, 212.
Baptism, 12, 28, 44, 48, 60, 75, 90, 92, 126, 127 sq., 162, 171, 208, 223, 233.
Bardenhewer, 83.
Barlow, William, 71.
Barnabas, 81 sq.
Basil, St., 182, 223, 233.
Becanus, 22.
Bellarmine, Card., 9, 32, 41, 66, 88, 90, 103, 110, 111, 132, 162, 166, 170 sq., 187, 195, 206.
Benedict XIV, 23, 46, 66, 97, 107, 120, 128, 132, 180, 207, 212.
Benevento, Council of (1091), 108.
Berlage, 202, 215.
Bernard of Pavia, 152.
Berti, 9, 10, 66.
Bickell, 132.
Biel, Gabriel, 88.
Billot, Card., 66, 111.
Billuart, 36, 66, 111, 207.
Blessings of marriage, 143 sqq.
Bonaventure, St., 7, 9, 26, 36, 62, 88, 111, 187.
Boniface VIII, 207.
Boniface IX, 124.
Bonum fidei, 143 sq., 178.
Bonum prolis, 143 sq., 173, 178.
Bonum sacramenti, 143 sq.
Bosco, 76.
Boudinhon, 40.
Braga, Council of (563), 61.
Brancatius, 211.
Braun, 212.

C

Caesarius of Arles, St., 14 sq.
Cajetan, Card., 88, 103, 107, 111, 163, 190, 202.

247

Calvin, 5, 47, 54, 150, 174, 177.
Cano, Melchior, 158, 159, 163, 164.
Cantor, Peter, 109.
Capreolus, 65, 162.
Caramuel, 124.
Carrière, 234.
Carthage, Fourth Council of, 112.
Casus Apostoli, See Pauline privilege.
Catacombs 152 sq.
Cathari, 5, 179.
Catharinus, Ambrosius, 9, 190, 234.
Celestine I, 76.
Celibacy, Clerical, 130 sqq.
Chalcedon, Council of (451), 61, 127.
Châlons, Council of (813), 11.
Character, See Sacramental Character.
Charismata, 9 sq., 57.
Χειροθεσία, 69 sq. (See also Imposition of hands).
Χειροτονία, 69 sq. (See also Imposition of hands).
Chorepiscopi, 122 sq.
Chrisma, 14, 17, 40.
Chrysostom, St., 12 sq., 39, 57, 59, 85, 89, 97, 103, 135, 197 sq.
Civil effects of marriage, 240.
Civil marriage, 240 sq.
Clandestine marriages, 164 sq., 215, 230.
Clement IV, 179 sq.
Clement VIII, 124.
Clement of Alexandria, 102, 133, 176, 181, 196 sq.
Clement of Rome, St., 101.
Clericatus, 41.
Collet, 202, 234.
Colluthos, 86.
Collyridians, 126.
Concubine, 177.
Confirmation, 75, 92, 120.
Coninck, 76.
Consecration, Rite of, 68, 119 sq.
Constantine, 232.

Constantinople, Council of (1672), 10.
Copts, 48, 152.
Cornelius, Pope, 111 sq.
Cyprian, St., 83, 96, 112, 232.
Cyril of Alexandria, 156.

D

Deaconesses, 126 sq., 245.
Deacons, 56, 99 sqq., 223.
De Augustinis, 23, 111, 112, 207.
Decentius of Eugubium, 39 sq.
Decretum Gratiani, 41, 108.
Decretum pro Armenis, 16, 21, 24, 25, 32, 44, 65 sq., 72, 113 sq., 116, 120, 191, 243.
De Lugo, 64, 66.
Denzinger, 104.
Diaconate, 99 sqq., 123 sq.
Digami, 179 sqq.
Dionysius of Alexandria, 118.
Diriment impediments, 227 sq., 234 sqq.
Discipline of the secret, 11.
Dispensing from marriage impediments, The Church's power of, 225 sqq.
Divorce, 189 sq.
Divorce, Mosaic bill of, 185 sqq.
Döllinger, 66, 195.
Donatists, 60, 90.
Drouin, 202, 206.
Durandus, 22, 26, 88, 103, 107, 111, 128.

E

Edilthryda, 205.
Egbert of York, 27.
Edwardine Ordinal, 71.
Egger, 111.
Elvira, Council of (about 300), 130 sq., 223, 232.
Encratites, 147.
Epiphanius, St., 85, 127, 134.
Episcopate, 80 sqq.
Episcopus, 81 sq., 95 sq.
'Επίσκοπος, See *Episcopus*.
Estius, 41, 65, 111, 158, 187.

Eugene IV, 21, 65 sq., 113 sq.,
  120, 124, 180, 191.
Eustathius, 85.
Extreme Unction: Name 1
  sqq.; Definition, 3; A true
  Sacrament, 4 sqq.; Divine institution, 5 sqq.; Matter and
  form, 16 sqq.; Sacramental
  effects, 24 sqq.; Necessity, 35
  sqq.; Minister, 38 sqq.; Recipient, 44 sqq.

F

Fabian, Pope, 108.
Fabius of Antioch, 111.
Feije, 238.
Florence, Council of (1439),
  151, 159 sq.
Formula of administering Ex-
  treme Unction, 21 sqq., 49 sq.
Fornication, 192 sqq.
Franzelin, Card., 62, 64, 81.
"Free love," 189.
Funk, 132.

G

Gasparri, Card., 124.
Gaufridus, 152.
Gelasius I, 121, 152, 233.
Glossner, 111.
Goar, 46, 62.
Gonet, 65, 111, 234.
Gotti, 36, 66, 111.
Gratia curationum, 5, 8, 9 sq.,
  33, 39.
Gregory of Nazianzus, St., 197.
Gregory of Nyssa, St., 59, 97.
Gregory of Valentia, 65, 132,
  234.
Gregory the Great, 11, 104, 119,
  120, 131, 223.
Gregory VII, 130.
Gregory XIII, 206.
Gutberlet, 48, 64, 66.

H

Habert, 206.

Hallier, 66.
Health, Restoration of, as a
  conditional effect of Extreme
  Unction, 32 sqq.
Hefele, 132.
Hegesippus, 83.
Henno, 234.
Henriquez, 162.
Henry of Ostia, 152.
Heraclas, 118.
Hermas, Shepherd of, 196.
Hillel, 188.
Holtzclau, 158.
Holy Office, 18, 21, 241.
Holy Orders: Definition, 52
  sq.; A true Sacrament, 54
  sqq.; Divine institution, 54
  sqq.; Matter and form, 62
  sqq.; Sacramental effects, 72
  sqq.; Division of Orders, 78
  sqq.; The episcopate, 80 sqq.;
  The priesthood, 94 sqq.; The
  diaconate, 99 sqq.; The subdi-
  aconate, 106 sqq.; Four minor
  Orders, 110 sqq.; The minis-
  ter, 116 sqq.; The recipient,
  125 sqq.
Hugh of St. Victor, St., 7, 107,
  111.
Huguccio, 123.
Hurter, 163, 212.
Hypodiaconate, 109, 110, 113.

I

Ignatius of Antioch, St., 82 sq.,
  95, 97, 101 sq., 156.
Impediments, 217, 221 sqq., 234
  sqq.
Imposition of hands, 55 sq., 62
  sqq., 105, 244.
"Increase and multiply," 219 sq.
Indissolubility of Christian
  marriage, 183 sqq.
Inefficacitas consensus, 236 sq.
Infants, Can they be validly or-
  dained? 128 sq.
Inhabilitas personarum, 225, 236.
Innocent I, 13 sq., 18, 39, 40, 233.
Innocent III, 109, 178, 204, 215.

Innocent V, 26.
Innocent VIII, 124.
Instruments, Delivery of 62 sqq., 105.
Interpellatio, 211.
Irenaeus, St., 83.
Ischyras, 86.
Isidore of Sevilla, 216.

J

James, Epistle of St., 5 sqq., 11, 12, 13, 15, 16, 19, 22, 24, 29, 31 sq., 33 sq., 36 sq., 38, 39, 41 sq., 44, 45.
Jansenism, 27.
Jerome, St., 59 sq., 86 sq., 97, 118, 134, 181, 233.
John X, 182.
John Chrysostom, St., See Chrysostom.
John Mandukani, 14.
John of Jerusalem, 86.
Justinian I, 131, 232.
Justin Martyr, St., 196.

K

Kern, Jos. (S.J.), 23, 26 sqq., 32, 48, 49.

L

Lamech, 177.
Laodicea, Council of, 181.
Lateran, Second Council of the (1139), 130.
Launoy, 40, 41, 158, 190, 229, 230.
"Lay Sacrament," The, 215.
Lea, H. C., 137, 139.
Ledesma, 66.
Lehmkuhl, 206.
Leopold II of Tuscany, 229.
Leo the Great, St., 67, 122, 131, 223.
Leo XIII, 70, 161, 202, 238, 240.
Lessius, 206.
Libellus repudii, See Divorce.
Luther, 5, 54, 147, 150, 153, 174, 222.

Lyons, Council of (1274), 173.

M

Mahaffy, 136 sq.
Maldonatus, 9, 66, 187.
Maltzew, 45 sq.
Manichæans, 147.
Mark, Extreme Unction insinuated in the Gospel of St., 9 sq.
Marriage, 134 sq., 140 sqq.
Marsilius of Padua, 80.
Martène, 62, 76, 104.
Martin V, 202.
Martin, 238.
Mary, B. V., 126, 142.
Mastrius, 162.
Matrimony: Definition, 140 sqq.; Blessings of, 143 sqq.; Division, 145 sq.; A true Sacrament, 147 sqq.; Matter and form, 164 sqq.; Sacramental effects, 168 sqq.; Properties, 172 sqq.; Unity, 172 sqq.; Indissolubility, 183 sqq.; Minister, 214 sqq.; Recipient, 217 sqq.; the Church's control over Christian marriage, 221 sqq.; The Church's right to establish diriment impediments, 234 sqq.
Matth. V, 35 and Matth. XIX, 9 explained, 192 sqq.
Matrimonium legitimum, ratum, consummatum, 184 sqq.
Mayence, Council of (813), 224; (847), 11.
Melanchthon, 54, 174.
Mesolaras, 46.
Metrophanes Kritopulos, 17.
Michael Palaeologus, 10 sq., 173, 180.
Minor Orders, 110 sqq., 120 sqq.
Minucius Felix, 176.
Monogamy, 172 sqq.
Montanists, 126.
Morinus, 22, 62, 107, 111, 113, 122.
Mormonism, 174.

Mystery, Matrimony a great, 149 sqq., 159.

N

Napoleon I, 240.
Natalis Alexander, 132.
Navarrus, 88, 166.
Neocaesarea, Council of (314), 181, 223.
Nestorians, 11, 17, 42, 152.
Netter, Thomas, 40.
Nicaea, First Council of, 128, 133, 179.
Nicaea, Second Council of, 61, 121.
Nicholas I, Pope, 176, 215, 224.
Nicholas I of Constantinople, 182.
Nuptiae, 216.
Nuptial blessing, 216.
Nuytz, J. N., 158, 161.

O

Olive oil, 16 sq.
Optatus, St., 102.
Origen, 12, 39, 102, 156, 197.
Orleans, Council of (533), 61.
Oswald, 32, 33, 45, 62.

P

Pallavicini, 191.
Palmieri, 163, 207.
Paludanus, 22, 76, 88, 111.
Panhölzel, 124.
Paphnutius, St., 133.
Parker, Matthew, 71.
Patrizi, 195.
Pauline privilege, 198, 201, 208 sqq.
Paul, St., 56 sqq., 73, 81, 88 sqq., 117, 125 sq., 127, 133, 135, 148 sqq., 159, 169, 174, 180, 185, 208 sqq., 219.
Paul V, 18.
Paul VI, 71.
Pelagius II, 131.
Penance, 1, 32, 48, 49, 50, 166.

Perrone, 62, 163, 207, 211, 212, 238.
Pesch, Chr. (S.J.), 62, 163, 238.
Peter Lombard, 7, 36, 74, 88, 107, 111, 187.
Petzek, J. A., 158.
Philip of Hesse, 174.
Phillips, 132.
Photius, 11.
Pistoia, Council of, 229.
Pius V, 124.
Pius VI, 160, 229, 235.
Pius VII, 240.
Pius IX, 160 sq., 188, 240.
Polyandry, 172 sq.
Polycarp, St., 102.
Polygamy, 172 sqq.
Pope, The, Can dissolve an unconsummated marriage, 201 sqq.
Prayer-Unction, 8 sq.
Πρεσβύτερος, 82 sq., 95 sq.
Priest's part in the marriage ceremony, 215 sq.
Priesthood, 94 sqq., 122 sq.
Priscillianists, 147.
Probst, 132.
Profession, Solemn religious, Dissolves the bond of an unconsummated marriage, 203 sqq.
Propaganda, S. C. of, 50.
Protestants: Their view of Extreme Unction, 5 sq.; 26 sq., 39; Of Holy Orders, 54; Of Matrimony, 147 sq., 151, 190, 192, 194, 222.
Puller, 51.

Q

Quasi-character of Matrimony, 170 sq.

R

Reordination, 74, 128.
Remarriage, 179 sq.
Repetition of Extreme Unction, 47 sq.
Rhallis, 46.

Roman Catechism, 23, 30.
Roman Ritual, 22, 23, 65, 99.
Rusticus of Narbonne, 122.

S

Sacramental Character of Holy Orders, 72 sqq., 98; Quasi-character of Matrimony, 170 sq.
Sacramentum exeuntium, 45.
Sanatio in radice, 228.
Sanchez, 162, 163, 166, 170 sq., 207, 218, 234.
Sainte-Beuve, 9, 32, 46.
Sardagna, 206.
Sasse, 111.
Schell, 37, 41, 76.
Schmid, Fr., 48.
Schwetz, 62.
Scotus and the Scotists, 9, 22, 31, 47, 48, 88, 111, 123, 166.
Second marriage, 179 sqq.
Separation from bed and board, 191 sqq., 226.
Serapion of Thmuis, 11.
Shammai, 188.
Simeon of Thessalonica, 17.
Simmonet, 162.
Sin and its remains, 29 sqq.
Siricius, Pope, 131.
Society of Jesus, 206.
Socrates, 133.
Soto, Dominicus, 65, 88, 163, 187.
Soto, Peter, 36, 62, 88, 234.
Sozomen, 133.
State, Rights of the regarding Matrimony, 145, 199, 218, 229 sqq., 238 sqq.
Stephen, St., 100, 103, 104, 108.
Suarez, 9, 27, 36, 49, 73, 166 sqq., 206.
Subdiaconate, 106 sqq., 121 sq., 131.
Successive marriages, 179 sq.
Sylvester II, 60.
Sylvester Maurus, 76.
Sylvius, 158, 187.

T

Tabaraud, M. M., 158.
Tametsi, 164 sq.
Tanner, 162, 163.
Tapper, Ruardus, 26, 202.
Tepe, 32, 62, 163, 206.
Tertullian, 97, 102, 111, 156, 176, 181.
Thecla, St., 205.
Theiner, J. A., 137, 158.
Theodosius the Great, 232, 233.
Theophilus of Antioch, 175 sq.
Thomas, St.: On Extreme Unction, 9, 20, 26, 33, 36; On Holy Orders, 65, 67, 71, 74, 88, 89, 108, 115, 123, 128, 152, 159, 189 sq., 202, 206.
Thomassin, 76.
Thomists, 22, 162.
Thurston, Herbert (S.J.), 126, 137.
Tillemont, 132.
Timothy, 56 sqq., 73, 82, 88 sq., 117.
Titus, 82.
Toledo, Council of (653), 61.
Toner, 20.
Tonsure, 114 sq.
Tournely, 22, 32, 36, 62, 128, 132, 158, 202, 207, 234.
Traditio instrumentorum, See Instruments, Delivery of.
Trent, Council of, 6 sq., 10, 17, 18, 24, 25, 29, 31, 32 sq., 36 sq., 38, 44 sq., 47, 48, 54 sq., 64, 72, 73, 78 sq., 80 sq., 84, 90 sq., 93, 94, 97, 98, 99 sq., 105, 110, 114, 115, 116, 118, 121, 130, 134 sq., 145 sq., 147 sq., 151, 160, 163, 164 sq., 168, 169, 174, 185, 190 sq., 204, 215, 222, 226, 230, 235 sq.
Trullo, Council in (692), 132, 224.

U

Unity of marriage, 172 sqq.

Urban II, 108, 109, 131.
Urban VIII, 213.

V

Vasquez, 66, 75, 103, 107, 111, 119, 132, 162, 165 sq.
Vigilantius, 134.
Virginity, 134 sqq.
Vows, 227 sq., 232 sq.

W

Waldenses, 5.

Wedding ring, 216.
Wiclifites, 5.
William of Auxerre, 88.
Women, 125 sq., 232 sq.
Worms, Council of (868), 11.

Z

Zaccaria, 132.
Zachary, Pope, 224.
Ziegler, Th., 158.
Zigliara, Card., 238.
Zosimus, Pope, 76.